A SON OF A GUN

A SON OF A GUN

An Immigrant's Story

P. Sigmund Roseth

iUniverse, Inc.
New York Lincoln Shanghai

A Son of A Gun

An Immigrant's Story

iUniverse books may be ordered through booksellers or by contacting:

iUniverse
2021 Pine Lake Road, Suite 100
Lincoln, NE 68512
www.iuniverse.com
1-800-Authors (1-800-288-4677)

ISBN: 978-0-595-42554-9 (pbk)
ISBN: 978-0-595-86883-4 (ebk)

Printed in the United States of America

A Son of a Gun

Stories from a singular life

Son of a Gun
… *a rascal.* Of nautical origin,
referring to a child born onboard ship …
Cassels's Dictionary of English Idioms (1999).

Contents

PART III

Introduction

This is a story about an immigrant's life. It is ordinary and unordinary, common and uncommon, about success and about failure. It is about my life as an immigrant, but not necessarily about immigration. It ranges widely from sea to prairie, from the west to the east, from labourer to industrial management, and to entrepreneurship.

I grew up in the "backwoods" of western Norway, after the War, when Norway was rather poor and prostrated after five years of German occupation. At fifteen, I signed on as training-cadet on a four-masted schooner; at sixteen came an eighteen-month stint as an ordinary seaman on a Norwegian tanker in the Middle and Far East. It was a rough, intemperate life—a sailor's life.

I immigrated to Canada in 1960, and spent my first two years in Regina, Saskatchewan.

After two years there, I left Saskatchewan, and moved to Ontario, where I also went back to school, and progressed to various management positions in several firms over a period of fifteen years. I also got an education, graduating from York University with a degree in Economics.

In 1985 I became an entrepreneur, operating my own firm, A and S Roseth Inc., a moving and storage company, and international forwarder. Following a checkered career in industrial management, I became a small business owner—almost by default. After fifteen years of fixing other peoples problems, I thought working for myself would be better. I was wrong. As too often in my life, I choose impetuously. I picked a business without much preplanning or forethought, and for which I was singularly unsuited and came to detest. However, once you are committed to pushing up a rope, it is hard to stop, lest it all come crashing down.

You cannot just leave, as you quit a job. You are committed for the "long haul." You sink or swim. I swam, but the waters were often stormy and I almost drowned. I took on too much, and I worked too hard. Like Don Quixote, I fought too many windmills, and like for him, *my* Dulcenia was also a delusion. In my drive to succeed, I left much potential happiness and joy in my wake. It seems that I had only one speed: full ahead and damn the torpedoes—come what may! The final chapter has not been lived yet. It is still a story in the making. Perhaps people like me must reach our twilight years before we can relax and smell the roses. Whatever may come, good and bad, I hope I can face it with courage and wisdom. Especially wisdom. Of courage I still have some. Wisdom is a work in progress. This, then, is my story.

PART I

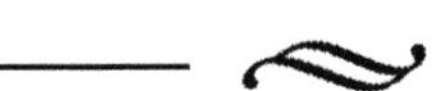

CHAPTER 1

Growing up in Norway

I should not talk so much about myself if there were any body else that I knew as well. Unfortunately, I am confined to this theme by the narrowness of my experience.

—Henry David Thoreau: *Walden.*

Western Norway is rugged country, with deep fjords, high mountains and rocky shores. Warmed by the Gulf Stream, its climate is better than justified by its latitude. Since before history, this rugged land provided the basics needs of its inhabitants: fish from the waters, meat and produce from the ground, and water transportation along its coast and fjords. There, the people built their homes on the windblown and rocky outcrops and lived off the ocean's largesse. Along the littoral coast, and in the fjords, they precariously practiced husbandry on tiny plots of land clinging precipitously to the steep mountainsides, and caught fish in the deep fjords below.

The people were as rugged as the land. They eked out a living, farming the thin layer of earth covering the rocky ground. They planted hardy fruit trees that thrived on the sunny side of the mountain, grew potatoes and vegetables for their table, and grass for the cows, goats and sheep, which gave them milk, meat and clothing. Fish was abundant, and the diet was an eclectic mix of sea and land—of seafood and agricultural products.

They were largely self-sufficient in foods, except grains, which were difficult to grow in the mountainous terrain. Fish and meat were salted and smoked for preservation, wheat was milled in the community with water-powered millstones, flatbread baked and kept for the long winter. Some food was quite peculiar to the region, like *Lutefisk* (lye-fish), salted and dried cod thawed and soaked in lye to break up the fibers and jellify the flesh, making it easy to chew. It is still eaten at Christmas and on special occasions.

The sheep provided wool for clothing, and the wool was carded and spun by the farmwomen and knitted into garments for everyone. They churned butter and made cheese from cow's and goat's milk. Potatoes, turnip and carrots were harvested and buried below ground for storage over the winter; plums, pears, cherries, gooseberries and currants preserved and made into jams, and hardy locally grown apples kept for most of the winter.

In the summer, the cows were taken to a summer pasture on the mountain, called a *Seter*, or *Støl.* There, local maidens (*budeier*) lived in small cabins that combined a barn for the milk cows and living quarters for the milkmaids either beside or above the barn. On Sundays, the people would visit, and often have a dance outside, with accordions and fiddles providing the music. Many a marriage was initiated at one of these remote mountain cow pastures. It was mostly hard, sometimes quaint and always a simple life. The mountains, valleys and forests provided fodder for the folk tales of trolls and fairies related at night by the fire, to entertain the adults and frighten the children.

Fishing provided employment for many landless sons, as did the merchant marine. The Norse have, since before the Vikings, been a seafaring people, both as fishermen and traders. These occupations provided outlets and opportunities in the days when Norway could not provide for all its people.

Eventually, the population outgrew the meager ground. Land-hungry farmer sons and daughters emigrated to the North-American prairies in large numbers during the nineteenth century and the beginning of the twentieth—half the population left for the new land and the promise of a homestead on the prairies. Letters home, from those already there, extolled the virtues of a land where you could plow and plant without fertilizing and not worry about hitting solid rock; where the fertile ground stretched to the horizon, without a mountain blocking the view or impeding the work. These glowing stories created further emigration waves of land hungry Norwegians.

Thus it was that the mountain dwellers of western Norway became prairie farmers in the American and Canadian west.

The second largest fjord is Nordfjord, stretching about thirteen kilometres inland from the coast, more than a kilometre deep in some places. Inland rivers dilute the salty ocean water. Roads, where there were any, clung to the mountain-sides, wound themselves in and out of the bays and inlets, up and down rugged mountain passes, and hung precipitously at the edge of the sheared cliffs, large rocks and steep hillsides. Occasionally, the road would end suddenly at the water's edge, along the fjord, at a ferry dock. A little ferry would scuttle back and forth across the fjord, to the other side, where the road picked up its thread, until it ended at the next ferry harbour, only to repeat the pattern. Traveling was slow and cumbersome, whether by road or by water.

Once a week, the postal steamboat arrived with mail and passengers. From my family's mountain farm, they could see it arrive, and hear the steam whistle blowing from far away, the steam rising some time before a sound was heard. It was a hoarse, deep kind of sound, starting low and then increasing in pitch and volume until it ended abruptly, with only the white steam cloud lingering above and behind the vessel. The pier at the waters edge would erupt in a beehive of activity.

The farmers brought cattle and sheep that they were shipping to the city for slaughter, while others just came to watch, or wait for the mail. The ship's crew put a sling underneath the animal's bellies and then hoisted them high in the air. The sheep bleated and the cows mooed plaintively as they were swung above the deck and were lowered into the hold of the ship, where they would munch happily on hay en route to the slaughterhouse.

The steamboat stopped at other small hamlets along the way and repeated the same routine. It took three full days to travel to Bergen by the slow steamer, with one night of sleeping onboard. Today, it takes eight hours by catamaran, and about the same time traveling by car or bus.

In the hamlet of my birth, there was no road connection with the mainland, and though there was a small general store by the dockside, for anything more—including baptism, marriage and burial—you had to cross the fjord by boat.

In the deep fjords and in the mountain valleys, the sun is absent for a good part of the winter; the exact time depends on whether you are on the sunny side of the mountain, or the shady side. Daylight is limited to about five hours a day in mid-winter, but by March, on clear days, the sun begins to creep slowly down the valley. Each day the light lingers a little longer and the sun shines a little further down the hillside, its bright, golden light sparkling on the slowly melting snow, until the sun stays up all day, and the snow is gone. In turn, the brooks get noisier; you can hear them purl and gurgle below the snow cover, until the ice breaks. As the snow melts, the brooks get bigger and stronger and show off their power by flooding the low areas. Once the snow is gone, the brooks calm down and resume their old journey; the days get longer and longer, until midsummer solstice in June, when night never comes.

The people resembled the country: dour, humorless and pious, slow to anger and slower to forgive. In days gone by, theirs was a dark and joyless life, with few smiles and many frowns, hard work and little rest. The few respites from the tedium were weddings, baptism and funerals. In the countryside, weddings lasted a whole week, with huge amounts of food and homemade brew consumed; fighting, therefore, was not unusual. In the very olden days, it was said; a woman would bring funeral cloth to a wedding feast, in which to wrap a corpse, in case her husband should come to an unfortunate end in a drunken brawl.

In the old days, the denizens of these dark mountains followed religiously the dictum that children should be seen but not heard, and that attitude lingered into my parent's day. Today, however, the children rule the Norwegian society, and this child-centeredness is apparent everywhere: ferries and passenger boats have TV areas where children can watch their favorite program, play areas and even babysitters. In one generation, there has been a complete turnaround in attitude and behaviour as far as child rearing is concerned.

In other areas too, the change has been profound: social security takes care of you, "cradle to grave", and everyone, including homemakers and farmers, has six weeks vacation ordained by law. There are government-paid "farm-sitters" who come to do your farm chores while you vacation on the Spanish Riviera! Government-subsidies to farmers and fishermen are substantial, and this is one reason Norway opted out of the European Union membership. I am sure my grandparents, in their wildest dreams, could not have envisioned the coming changes or would recognize the country today.

Today, there is little commercial fishing going on in the fjords, but the shorelines are dotted with fish farms—the new-age Norwegian fishermen. Fast catamaran passenger boats now ply the fjords, and many of the old roads are gone, replaced with modern highways that are wide and straight, and where this was not possible, bored through the hard rock of the mountain, some places for several kilometres. It is efficient, fast and safe, but hardly scenic. The mountainsides along the fjords now look a lot like Swiss cheese, the round tunnel openings is all that shows of the highway system hidden inside, made possible by the prosperity of the North Sea oil revenue flowing like a river of gold into the government's coffers.

The Viking spirit, if there ever were such a thing, is long gone. It lingered on in the last century with such intrepid explorers as Roald Amundsen (South Pole), Fritjof Nansen (Greenland; Northwest Passage) and Thor Heyerdal (Kon Tiki), and was last seen alive in World War II, among the patriotic young men that fought the Germans at home and abroad. Today, Norwegians are more concerned with vacation days, sick days and their pension benefits. They are mostly a complacent lot, deferential to authority, self-satisfied and narcissistic. The citizens are quite happy to let the government decide what is best for them, though they reserve the right to grumble and complain, especially about the amount of "oil money" the government is willing to lavish on them. In that matter, the government wisely keeps the purse string fairly tight. The ferocious Vikings of yore are now the peacemakers (e.g. the Oslo accord), and in this, they are joined by Canada, another nation of navel gazing peaceniks.

This might be a profitable strategy for a small nation, as long as Big Brother, U.S.A., is willing to shoulder the load of defending the peace.

My parents both came from mountain farms: my mother, Margaret, from Hardangerfjord; my father, Jorek, from Nordfjord. Today, these are idyllic and popular tourist destinations. But, during their childhood, life was less tranquil. Norway was a poor country then, and life was hard on the farm. Half of my paternal grandparent's twelve siblings went to America and Canada, mainly Saskatchewan and North Dakota, as did several of the ten siblings of my maternal grandparents.

My father's father was the eldest of ten children, and therefore, he inherited the family farm. All of his siblings, but one brother and two sisters, went to America, leaving him and his wife to raise their children on the rocky mountain farm.

Two of their children died of tuberculosis at the ages of twenty-one; the eldest, Christian, was an aspiring poet, and had published poetry and short stories. One poem, his "Song of Nordfjord", was set to music and is still being sung and performed locally. His death at twenty-one extinguished a promising light.

Life was rough in that age; children were not much more than unpaid workers. My grandparents were stern disciplinarians who showed limited compassion and paid little attention to their brood. The oldest had the responsibility of supervising and more or less raising the younger children, after the first toddler years.

My father was the second eldest, living son, so his elder brother, Gudmund, got the farm. He also got the education. Gudmund was in college when the father died, but he quit and took over the farm. I think my father had hoped he could get the farm, if his elder brother got the education, but it was not to be. The eldest son got both. Such were the rules of primogeniture.

My mother's family was also large, but less formal, though theirs was also a rather joyless upbringing. When the parents began farming the mountain, there was barely enough soil to grow grass for cattle. My grandfather would carry soil from one place to the next, where he would cover the barren rock and seed grass. Grandmother was just seventeen when she married and they had eight children in the next fifteen years.

My parents never talked about it much, but they were both farmers at heart, and they missed the farm life. Reality was different, but I think they, and in particular my mother, imagined a life that had never existed. This sublimation was also present in most of her siblings, and only toward the end of her life did she admit that her childhood had been somewhat less than ideal.

Nostalgia about our childhood is common, even if we have had a difficult one. One of my uncles, who became a very successful businessman, wrote stories and plays extolling the country life with the protagonist lamenting the loss of his farm. In reality, it was a miserable life, and my uncle fared much better in business than had he been a farmer. Farming and fishing seems to leave an indelible imprint on the sons of farmers and fishermen, who—for one reason or another—could not continue their father's vocation.

My father leased a small farm at one time, which he and mother tried to operate in addition to my dad's full-time work. It was pure folly; they almost killed themselves in the process.

It nearly killed my mother. She was pregnant with my youngest sister at the time. It was summer, and they had the milk cow tethered to a pole in the field. My mother went to move the pole to an area with fresh grass, when something startled the animal. The cow took off down the field and onto the gravel road, trailing the rope behind. However, my mother's foot got caught in the rope, and the stupid critter dragged her by her leg down the graveled road. Fortunately, my younger brother who was at home, just happened to see it, and he ran after the runaway ruminant, grabbing the rope, and managed to stop the frantic beast. My mother was bruised and sore, but otherwise all right, and so, fortunately, was my unborn sister.

The first few years after the war were difficult. Norway imports more than a third of its food products, so there was food rationing until the end of 1954. The whole Norwegian merchant marine was sunk during the war, carrying war materials from America to Britain and to Murmansk in Russia. My father did not drink alcohol, so he would exchange his liquor ration cards for coffee and sugar. The coffee was usually mixed with chicory to extend it, except for special occasions when "pure" coffee was served. One day in late 1954, we heard that the local merchant had chocolate in the store, and my mother took us there to buy some. It was a special occasion for my mother, and I think she was a little disappointed when I didn't like it. We also got bananas and oranges and grapes, which I liked right away. However, one fruit was very disappointing: coconuts. There was a song by Merv Griffith (translated to Norwegian) called the *Coconut Song* ("I have a lovely bunch of coconuts ...").My parents had tried to explain what a coconut was, so I was filled with anticipation when we finally got to buy one. This coconut was a disappointment.

My father managed, with limited education, to become a public schoolteacher, but he had to take jobs in small, isolated areas for many years, until he gained the experience to teach in more "civilized" communities. Consequently, ours was an unsettled existence.

The first teaching job he had as a teacher was on a desolate coastal outcrop at the mouth of the fjord, called Krakhella. We rented a house on an island nearby, in a place called Bøvågen. There was only one other family there on the island, running a small, self-contained farm where the owners made most of their own food—they even made their own cheese. We would buy milk from them, carrying it home in a tin can, but for other goods, we had to go by boat about forty-five minutes to the small general store on the mainland, where the schoolhouse also stood. My father had a small, open boat with a single-stroke, one-cylinder diesel engine that had to be started by first heating a metal rod, then turning a flywheel until it got going. In this contraption, he would travel to the school each day. We could hear him returning in the late afternoon, the engine making a very distinct sound. Then the boat would round the point to the bay and my brother and I would run down to the water to welcome him home. The boat was tethered to a pole on the rocky shore in the bay, and kept away from the rock by a weighted line at the rear. When we had to go onboard, we would walk down some steps cut into the rock, pull the boat in, and jump onboard.

I remember once going with my father to the store in the open boat, in fairly bad weather. I was sitting at the bow, and the waves were huge, the size of houses, pounding at the bow where I sat. The little boat crested the swells with little trouble, but I was scared. Dad told me to come aft, and sitting there in the stern beside him made me much braver—I actually enjoyed the ups and downs. It was probably an omen of my future. My dad didn't walk on water, but I can understand how the apostles felt in the storm on the Sea of Galilee.

On the island, we had a cow and a couple of sheep and a few chickens. Once, dad had bought a ram from a farmer on the mainland, and he brought it home in the evening. He must have been proud of it, for he brought it right into our bedroom to show it off.

Some farmer friends on the mainland gave us a rooster, and we called him Goliath. The name turned out to be very apt, because the darn fowl became quite belligerent, and attacked my brother and me whenever he got a chance. I don't know what it was that made the bird so vicious, but whenever he saw my brother or me, he would run after us, jump on our head and peck away. One day I ventured outside, and the rooster was watching me from the garden. My father was standing in the doorway of the barn, and told me to run towards him. I did, with rooster chasing after me.

MY BROTHER KJELL & ME, SUMMER 1946

SAME GUY, SAME ROCK, JUNE, 2005

As I dived inside the door, with the rooster right behind, my dad kicked him so he went flying in an arc back into the garden. The crazy bird left us alone after that, but it was too late for him. A couple of weeks after, the head with the beautiful red comb was lying behind the barn, together with some of his hen-harem's heads. He made a very good stew.

If you had to travel any distance, you advised the boat agent on the mainland, and the steamer actually stopped in the fjord to let you onboard, and drop you off when you returned. I remember going with my father in the little boat to pick up my mother who was returning from the city. A small metal door opened on the side of the steamer, and my mother stepped out into the open boat.

My first sister was born on the island. The midwife came with a large chest where she kept all the instruments of her trade, and since we had been told that the midwife was bringing our sister, my brother and I opened the lid to look for the baby. We were quite disappointed to find the chest empty, but reasoned that the baby was all ready delivered. And so she was.

Our neighbour's son was about my age, and I quite envied their outhouse. It had a small seat for the children to sit on (I had to climb up on the adult height seat in the barn where our toilet was located). I complained about this state of affairs to my mother, and she told me that for my birthday, my dad would make a small toilet seat beside the large adult one in the barn for my brother and me. And he did. I remember how happy we were, my brother and I, having our own downsized toilet, where we could sit side by side and do our stuff. It is quaint to remember, in my striving and accumulating of later years, and watching today's children and grandchildren, with their expensive, fancy toys, that I was so very happy having my own little hole in which to shit.

It is a strange thing, envy. It was a Norwegian-American economist in Minnesota, Torstein Veblen, who first coined the phrase "conspicuous consumption". If our neighbour has a better outhouse than us, we must have one like it. If our neighbour has a better car or home, we covet it. Sometimes, if he has a better wife, we covet her too. We are never satisfied. We are always comparing ourselves to our peers, looking back to see if someone is gaining on us—what social scientists call "reference anxiety." In the working world, if our fellow worker gets paid more than us, we are envious. This is the reason for the excessive salaries of top executives. It measures "success" in the corporate world. Not that they need it for sustenance; they need it to show that they are worthy and successful, and earning power is social power and often their only goal and measure of achievements. Envy and greed are the twin cylinders of our economic engine. Driving a Hummer in city traffic is vanity run amok.

Today, we have so much more. We have conquered smallpox and polio, but we are not happy. We have warm houses and nice cars, physically easy and reasonably secure jobs; medical benefits and pensions, and we don't have to send our sons to war. But, we are not satisfied. We see the richer people, the beautiful people, the stars, on the television, and we are dissatisfied with our lives, for we don't have and can't have what they have. There is always someone who has more, and in our interconnected and instant world, we can see these people as we can see our neighbours, and we are envious. We forget what we have. As the sociologist Abraham Maslow said "a satisfied need is not a motivator any longer." People like me, we can remember what it was like to not have much, and we can compare our present life to what was, and just maybe we can feel content. But, young people today have only known plenty, and have not known war, so they can only compare themselves and their lives to the other people who also have only known the "good life". Thus, they begrudge their neighbours for what they have, hate their own lives and envy those who have more, or seem happier.

There was still little food in Norway right after the war, and I recall mother mashing boiled potatoes with a fork and putting melted margarine substitute made from whale fat on it for us to eat for dinner. Porridge was also a staple. With what we fished in the fjord, grew in the garden and raised on the farm, we had enough to sustain us.

Norway of old was not a stranger to food shortage. During the Napoleonic wars, the British sacked Copenhagen and blockaded the North Sea, making it difficult for the Norwegians to import food, mainly grain which the country cannot grow in enough volume to sustain the population. A famous poem was written about this: Terje Viken, about a fisherman who ran the English blockade to get food for his starving family. It is strange how time and politics change. The former enemy—England—was our ally during the last war, and the Germans used this poem as anti-English propaganda.

Poetry and stories have a long history, and before general literacy, stories and fairy tales were the main entertainment for the common people of Norway. Many had a moral message; some were just entertaining. Food, of course, was a popular subject. One story tells of a gypsy (Tartar) who came by the farm begging for food, but the housewife told him no. Then he told her that he knew how to make a nice stew with just a nail, and this kindled the old lady's curiosity, so she asked him into the house to show her the trick. First, of course, he needed a kettle, and some water, and he just happened to have a rusty nail. He mentioned that he usually added a bit of meat to the brew, and some peas. The stew was simmering along pretty good, and began to smell quite nice. The beggar then mentioned that potatoes also added to the flavour, as did carrots and turnips and even some smoked ham the woman had in her cupboard. Finally, the stew was ready, and the woman praised the gypsy for the delicious stew he had made from just one nail!

The Norwegian men were rather chauvinistic, as were most men in the old societies, but the women were often getting the better of them. The first Norwegian women's liberation group must have made up one old tale. It tells of a farm couple that always quarreled about who was the more important. One day, the woman told the man that she could do his job, but he could not do hers. They agreed to switch roles for a day, and the next day, the woman grabbed a sickle and went out to the field. While she was gone, the man set about the chores. Farm houses in those days had birch bark roofs, with sod on top, and grass growing in the sod. This made a pretty good roof, except that you had to cut the grass once in a while. The man thought he had a better and easier way to do it. He put the goat on the roof, and just so it would not get away, he put a rope around its neck and dropped the rope through the chimney, and tied it around his waist while he was going around sweeping the floors, and getting ready to cook the evening meal.

The woman cut the grass and tilled the soil all day. In the early evening she came home, looking forward to a fine meal from her husband. However, when she got back, she found the goat grazing in the front yard. It had fallen off the roof, and pulled the man up the chimney, where he had been for most of the day. She cut him down and made dinner, and since that day, the man never argued about who had the hardest job.

During the war, farmers had a quota for food to be shipped to Germany, and a ship loaded full with potatoes was strafed by a British warplane, and ran aground on the coast at the mouth of the fjord. The local farmers were quite busy for a while, repatriating their potatoes. The ship stayed there even after the war, rusting away, half above and half below the water.

The Germans had mined the mouth of the fjords, and long after the war ended, we would get mine warnings on the radio; the mines would break loose from their cables and pop up on the water, making navigation dangerous until the minesweeper came and blew it up.

The place we rented belonged to a lady by the name of Dagfried Evensen, who was a communist member of the Bergen city government. Her husband, Schrøder Leonard Evensen, had been in the resistance during the war. He was betrayed, and the Gestapo was after him, so he hid out in a cave on the island. One day, the Gestapo suddenly appeared, while he was at home with his daughter, Cesilie, who was about five years old at the time. On the way to Bergen by boat, handcuffed, he jumped overboard and ingested seawater, drowning himself before they could retrieve him. In so doing, he probably saved many of his compatriots, for the Nazis were quite expert at extracting confessions under torture.

When we moved to the mountain valleys, skiing became an important part of a young boy's life. I was about eight years old, and learning to ski on my mother's skis, but they were about twice as long as me, and very hard for me to handle. In time I got fairly good at it, and used the skis for cross-country and downhill, as well as going to school. The skis had lost their camber, and the tips were almost straight, instead of curving upwards, so in loose snow, they burrowed into the snow. It was a nuisance, and a bit embarrassing, since most of the other boys had proper skis, so I began importuning my mother for a pair of skies.

My father finally relented and purchased a pair of skis for my brother and me. We were thrilled, but the joy didn't last too long, I soon broke a ski. The trouble was that the skis were made of pine, which was cheap but not strong, being softwood. I reverted to using my mother's skis, and used them until I was an adult.

I have wondered whether my father was just cheap, or really didn't have enough money to buy proper skis. The other families in the village were not rich either. Most were small-time farmers with limited incomes, and my father was a public school teacher. Though not earning a large salary, at least he was paid in cash.

It was the same situation with skates. Most of the boys had proper skates with shoes, but I had old hand-me-down, strap-on skates. It was hard to compete with proper speed skates, and I never did learn to skate well, a definite handicap in Norway. Those two things, good skis and skates were the only things I did not have and other boys had, but I don't remember being resentful or complaining a lot. Not that it would have done me any good anyhow.

I liked to ski jump, and when I was about nine or ten, we lived in a valley where there was a lot of snow in the winter. The school would have outings with the whole class on skis, competing in "cross-country" skiing. The boys would build a ski-jump and compete with each other. Those were fun times. We lived upstairs in the schoolhouse, which was built into a hill. I built a ski-jump above the road, and jumped across the road, landing on the hill below. I managed to jump about thirty meters. At the age of ten, that was not bad, considering I was using my mother's adult-size skis. Usually, there were no other boys to act as spectators, so I made my mother watch from the living room window. She spent many an hour watching me jump.

The gypsy life of moving every year was especially hard on my mother. Dad had his work, but mom was stuck at home in a strange community. Each year we had to become familiar with a new village, and make new friends. This was not always easy. In most of the places, families were intermarried or related to some extent, and we were outsiders. If I got in trouble with one boy, I had to fight all of them. I was quite gregarious and did not have too much trouble making friends (or enemies), but my brother was quiet and had a harder time adapting, though on the plus side, he also got into less trouble with other boys.

Only once did my brother get into real trouble. It was April 1st, April Fools Day, and in Norway, this was taken seriously. In those days, there were very few telephones, and when a telephone call came in for someone in the village, the operator would fetch one of the young children and pay them a coin for bringing the message to the individual, who then would come to the station and speak to the calling party in the telephone booth at the station.

There was this old lady living in a house almost at the top of the mountain, about a fifteen minute walk for a young person, probably a half hour for her. My brother went to her house and told her that there was a 'phone call for her, and she went all the way to the telephone station where a few of the boys were waiting to yell "April Fool!" It was the only spanking my brother got by himself, without me joining him. I remember feeling just a bit smug, being innocent this time.

Smoking was something that exuded a grown-up aura for young boys. A couple of us boys decided we had to try this mature habit. We managed to steal some matches and collect some toilet paper and some dry moss. We hid ourselves behind a large rock at the back of our house, and set about firing up a moss stogie, but we did not reckon on the smoke rising above the rock, and in no time my father was upon us! It was a do as I say, not as I do situation, for my father was a smoker also.

Sometimes a bad example can have a positive impact. Despite my early experiments, I did not acquire that habit. Over the years, my father tried to quit smoking on numerous occasions. He would switch to snuff or chewing tobacco, but my mother hated that even more than the smoke, so invariably, she relented and let him go back to smoking, as the lesser of two evils. Dad was a sucker for the various smoke-quitting schemes, and he bought books on how to do it. Alas, it never lasted, after a few weeks he was "off the wagon". Then, the tobacco prices would increase, and he would be on another "cure." "I am not going to let tobacco run my life," he would say, but it did. He was never able to quit, until he had his second heart attack and was too sick to smoke. He did not touch alcohol, but he could not stop smoking. He died of heart disease at sixty-six; no doubt his smoking had much to do with it. He would have done better if he had had the occasional drink, and left the smoking to the chimneys.

It is a terrible habit, smoking. My brother died of heart disease at the age of fifty-one. He lived for ten years after his first heart attack and triple bypass, but could not quit smoking. His doctor told him he would not be responsible for him if he con-

tinued to smoke, but he persisted, right up to about a year before he died—when he too was too sick to smoke anymore. B.F. Skinner, the Behaviourist, wrote that deterrence is inversely related to the distance in time of the deterrent. This is very true for smokers. Death from smoking is usually not imminent, so they keep going, using every rationalization to avoid facing facts. Whenever I told my brother that he must quit, he would answer that he was just as likely to die in a car accident, or some such silly rationalization, though he was an intelligent man.

I am angry with my brother for dying. He was my only brother, and I miss him.

In the London Tower, there is a copy of the History of England, written by Sir Walther Ralegh while he was imprisoned there, before they chopped off his head. James I, who had incarcerated him, was probably the first anti-smoking advocate in history, for he had insisted on writing a prologue, attacking smoking as a filthy and unhealthy habit. Ralegh, of course, had introduced tobacco from the New World, but that was not the reason he lost his head—though perhaps it should have been. King James had some strange habits, and was not the greatest King England ever had, but he had it right about smoking. In his preface to Ralegh's Histor of England, he said that the burning weed was "loathsome to the eye, hateful to the nose, harmful to the brain and dangerous to the lungs". In that, the king was a man ahead of his time.

I was seven when I began school. There were no such things as kindergarten or pre-school then, we jumped right into the first grade. I got a ride on the back of my father's bicycle that first day, which probably made the day a bit easier. I was a little nervous, but also excited. I knew I was going to learn to read. I used to pretend to read my dad's newspaper, and I could not wait to learn the real thing. Right away, the first day, we had our first lesson. I had a book, and the first page had a capital E, with the picture of an apple (*epple* in Norwegian). We had to learn the alphabet first; then, we would spell the word and sound it out. It was not long before we could read slowly and haltingly

I think I noticed girls for the first time that fall. The boys would play ball in the yard, and the girls would play other games, because the boys played too rough. I caught myself watching the girls play, and had this feeling that it would be fun to play the same game, with them. Of course, as a boy you would never admit that, or even be caught looking at a girl! But I did sneak a furtive glance at the girls when I could get away with it.

That year we lived in a farmhouse not too far from the school where my father taught. In fall and spring, I would bike to school on an adult bike, standing on the pedals, as I was too short to reach the seat. Most of the boys used adult bikes; very few parents could afford to buy a child's bike. I preferred my mother's bike, as it did not have the bar on it. The bar got in the way, and you had to pedal bent around the bar, looking like a bracket, with it rubbing against your side, while slanting the bike to your right in order to stay balanced. In the winter, we would ski to school.

That winter, we got a scare that stayed with my brother and me for a very long time. A young man from the village had arranged to pick up some food items for my mother, as he was going to the small general store in the next town. It was morning, and I was in bed with a cold. My brother had not begun school yet, so he was also at home. The man came into the kitchen, a pleasant and quiet young fellow. Mother was writing up a list for him, when he suddenly stiffened, stuck out his tongue and with a loud, long yell, fell straight to the floor, stiff as a log. My mother was frantic. She ran out in the hall and rang the 'phone, getting the local operator on the line. My brother and I ran outside, barefooted in the snow, where we screamed our lungs out. The operator told my mother not to worry; the guy had epilepsy and had these falling down periods once in a while. My mother fetched us in, and we discovered the man sitting up with his hands around his knees, looking as if nothing had happened. My mother finished the list with shaking hands, and he was soon on his way.

That our neighbours had not bothered to tell us about the fellow's illness now seems incredible, but I think the country bumpkins were so used to him that they did not give it any thought. Following this incident, I got very sick with the influenza. I don't know if standing naked in the snow for a few minutes contributed to it, but it surely did not help.

The telephone central was also the local post office. After picking up their mail, the townspeople would gather in the lobby and talk about the weather and other things uppermost on their minds. One day I was at the post office to fetch the mail, this man and his father was also there. The father was speaking with another man, when his son had an incident. He stiffened up and made a growling sound. As he fell, his father stretched out his arm, caught him and lowered him to the floor, where he left him until he recovered, not missing a beat in his animated conversation with the neighbour.

That fall, one of the boys at school had gotten a new watch for his birthday, and lost it. As he was probably afraid of getting a beating if his father found out that he had lost the watch, he told his father that I had stolen it from him. The father came to our house and berated my father, accusing me of the theft, and demanded that we pay for the missing watch. At first, I received a severe interrogation, but I could not confess to something I had not done. Eventually, I think my father believed me and decided to look for the watch where we boys usually played after school. Sure enough, he found the watch in the ditch. That is one of the very few times my father came to my defense. He went over to the fellow's house and gave him proper hell. I felt vindicated, but I also felt something else: a tremendous sorrow and anger, that my friend lied, and that my father at first believed him and not me.

My father was a rather humorless man, most of the time. One thing he did not abide was displays of affectation and of self-aggrandizement. Someone could have told him that this rule should not be applied too stringently to children who are just developing their personalities, and need positive reinforcement to become secure and confident grownups.

One day, I was practicing signing my name in a rather fanciful way, the way my father would sign his name. When I had written a whole page, I showed it proudly to my dad. "Do you think you are so great that you need to show off by writing your name all over?" was his comment. His admonition about not being too forward was well taken, but at the time, I was embarrassed and hurt.

Ever since, there have always been two people in my psyche, fighting for supremacy: one little boy jumping up and down, yelling "look at me, look at me!" and another, older and mature one saying "don't be so forward, don't think you are smart, don't be a showoff. You are embarrassing yourself—you are a nobody!" Over the years, the little boy, with much effort has managed to overcome the older one to a point, but never to his complete satisfaction.

* * * *

That year, my parents went to the city for a few days, I don't know why, but a local maiden was hired to mind my brother and me. Our younger sister went with them. The woman was a bit of a frump, and when she was washing the floors and steps, we noticed that she had a rather large hole in the rear of her bloomers. This, we thought, required further investigation, and we arranged to lie on the floor, just below the stairs, while she was working her mop on the upper stairs. This, we figured, should give us a better view of her bare bottom where the ripped bloomers exposed the flesh.

But the best of plans can be foiled, and ours were, when she looked down and realized what we were doing. A spanking ensued—she had a proxy from our parents—and though not too severe, our pride was definitely hurt, even damaged. We swore revenge, and spent some time thinking about what terrible vengeance we could visit upon her person. It came to us quite readily, springing forth from our evil little minds, and we spent some delicious time contemplating her horrid reaction. We found a shoebox and some wrapping paper and string. Then we went to the barn and scooped up some cow dung, which we wrapped and put in the shoebox. This we presented to her, asking her to open it later. She thought we were making a "peace offering", and thanked us profusely, probably feeling bad that she had disciplined us for our past transgression.

I am not sure when she opened the box; her reaction is somewhat fuzzy in my mind by now, but I do remember what she said to my father when they returned later that day.

"Have the boys been good?" My dad asked. "Being good" was a minimum standard of behaviour in my father's world. "No", she said, "I cannot say they have. I am too embarrassed to tell you what the two little trolls did, but it is the worst thing I have ever experienced from any children". Of course, she said it in Norwegian, in real provincial dialect, but you get the drift. I won't delve into what our dad did next, suffice it to say that he believed fervently in the good book's statement about sparing the rod and spoiling the child.

There might be something to that. I went to the store one day—I was about twelve years old then—and the local merchant was selling chewing gum, which was something new for us, and we greatly enjoyed chewing the sweet gum. I didn't have any money, and when the store clerk's back was turned, I scoffed a stick of chewing gum. When I got home, I split it with a friend. I also told him how I got it, and he told his mother, and she told my mother, and I was in real trouble. I think that stick of chewing gum was the dearest snack I ever had. I was in the "dog-house" for a long time. I never stole anything since.

Of course, I did not turn into an angel. The same boy and I decided to make wine. We got some red currant juice and some sugar and yeast, which he took from his mother's cupboard, and as we did not have a proper vessel for the wine, we put it in a large crock. It was winter and we knew we had to keep it warm, so we put it in an old, empty chest in the hall on the second floor above our kitchen, and forgot about it.

That was a pretty dumb thing to do. Eventually, the smell from the fermentation process would have alerted someone. However, before it got that far, one day I noticed some liquid running down along the wall in the kitchen. In a flash I realized what the problem was, and ran upstairs. The yeast had fermented and expanded, forcing the liquid up and over the edge of the container and into the chest, leaking through the kitchen ceiling. I carried the vessel outside and dumped it in the snow. Then I managed to wipe up the "wine" from the bottom of the chest. Later, while I was wiping the kitchen wall, my father came in and asked what I was doing. I don't recall exactly what I answered, but it satisfied his curiosity. I felt like a convict that just escaped the gallows.

It wasn't the stupidest thing I ever did, but it ranks right up there.

Some outposts by the coast were especially primitive, and so were the fishermen. They lived off the sea, but the majority could not swim, and when they did fall overboard, they often drowned. They would jump from the piers into their rowboats in their wooden clogs, landing perfectly with one foot on each side of the boat, the vessel barely moving in the water.

One fellow was fishing alone, setting nets, when he fell overboard. He managed to get hold of a line and held on for his life. The boat went around and around for a few hours before someone saw it and saved the poor wretch.

In one such locality, we lived in the schoolhouse, above the school where my dad taught. There were no roads at all, just trails, and no electricity. We used oil lamps and a primus lamp that you pumped up. It would give a reasonably good light, except it cast shadows. My mother caught rainwater in a wooden barrel and used it for washing clothes with a washing board. She cooked on a coal stove, but also used a "primus" that would hold one pot or pan at a time. We often got free fresh fish and seafood from the fishermen, and mother would cook up a big pot of crab. My brother and I would sit on the floor with pliers, cracking the shells and stuffing ourselves.

We got quite tired of cod, especially, since we had some version of cod several days a week. Wish I had some of that fresh cod now. In Canada, people ate fish once a week; we ate hamburger or meatballs once a week, on Sunday. The rest of the week was fish but Wednesday, which was potato-dumpling day.

Many of the fishermen were lushes and drank to excess when they had the time and money to make homebrew. I have seldom seen people stagger around like those guys did, totally out of it. However, a majority of the people were what they called *Pietists*, a very religious Protestant sect, similar to the Puritans, that believed that playing cards was sinful, as was dancing. It wasn't gambling—but the cards themselves were the devils tools! My dad would play cards with my brother and me, but if anyone came to visit, we would hide the cards quickly. Once, one of the school board members came by unexpectedly, and my mother came running to tell us to put away the cards. As the fellow came in, right behind my mother, dad slid them underneath the tablecloth, just in the nick of time!

These people were very superstitious, and believed in spirits and the supernatural. Many insisted that they had seen the devil in person. They could even describe him—usually he had a hoofed leg and a tail. One story told was of a local farmer who had some milk cows that got stolen by the devil. Apparently Lucifer had put empty barrels, tied together with rope, underneath the cows and ferried them across the bay, where they were found grazing the next day. Another time a local man complained of constant banging on walls at night, and things being moved about outside. There was some discussion about the cause: some thought, of course, that it was the devil again—this man was very pious and the devil was clearly out to get him for his faith. Others were not so sure. They thought maybe it was monkeys that had somehow hitched a ride on a ship and landed on their coast to harass them. There was much praying and commiserating about this conundrum. The puzzle was eventually solved, and it was neither the devil nor simians. It was the man's grown son who had gone mad, and rummaged around at night banging on walls and creating havoc.

The naiveté of these people was incredible. There were still people who believed in trolls, and the *huldra*—usually a beautiful girl with a cow's tail—had been seen by more than one local. The *huldra*, of course, is entrenched in Norse mythology. She would entice young men to marry her, but usually, she got caught at the last moment because of her cow's tail sticking out from underneath her skirt.

Usually, these Norwegians sowed their wild oats when young, and then spent the rest of their lives brooding about it and seeking forgiveness at weekly prayer meetings. In some villages, this took place in "prayer houses" (the Lutheran state church was not religious enough for them), but at one hamlet we lived—again above the school—they used the school premises for their meetings. Of course, my parents, since my dad was the teacher, would have to attend. My brother and I usually escaped—with a babysitter. One babysitter was a fourteen-year-old girl who played the zither and sang gospel tunes with an angelic, dulcet voice at the prayer meetings. One evening she was "babysitting" my brother and me, while a meeting was in progress downstairs. She got us into bed with herself, and tried to get us to take her clothes off (I was nine, my brother eight). It was progressing somewhat clumsily when my mother came in to check on us. Mom was no more religious than the average local, but her morals were impeccable. The poor girl got a severe "dressing down", but not the kind she had anticipated!

The hypocrisy of these bumpkins could not escape my young mind. There were itinerant preachers coming by regularly, and they had to be lodged with the village teacher. Some were really strange birds. One local preacher got caught playing around with underage girls. That was fairly easily forgiven this Godly emissary, but another guy really crossed the Rubicon. He was caught fornicating with a parishioner's wife. She got feeling guilty and confessed the whole mess at a prayer meeting. But this time it ended in real tragedy: the woman jumped into the farm well and drowned herself. The guy was expelled from the congregation, but he joined the Pentecostal assembly and continued preaching. It is an addiction.

Many of these people were coarse, uncultured and fanatic. Not all, but many. I loathed those isolated "backwoods". It must have been hell for my parents—especially my mother.

I went to my father's school the first four years of schooling, and did reasonably well; mainly because my father made sure his boys did their schoolwork. His expectation that I do well in school and behave myself was tough to live up to, especially for the rather irascible boy that I was becoming. If I got in trouble at school, I would get detention there, then when I got home, my mother would take a "a strip out of me." My father's professional and personal pride, as well as his own rigid upbringing, made him a strict disciplinarian. It was a "donkey's" life, and I was straining at the bit.

My father had a bout with stomach ulcer, and for six months we had a substitute teacher. And what a substitute she was. She was a retired schoolmarm—retired for about fifteen years, with poor eyesight and limited hearing. She assigned an essay subject, and I had difficulty deciding what to write. Then, I found a story in a reader, which fit the subject just fine, and I copied it, word for word. I handed it in, only half expecting to get away with it, but the old girl bought it. Not only that; she praised my writing, and then proceeded to read the story to the class. That was my downfall. One bright girl in class had also read the book, and she gleefully spilled the beans. Luckily for me, the old lady did not tell my dad. She probably should have, for I got my first taste of cheating, and it was too easy.

I guess my father got tired of my importuning, because he arranged for me to transfer to another teacher in another school. This meant that I had to bi-cycle in the summer and ski in the winter to the other school, about five kilometers away—something I did willingly to escape the tight "reins" of my father.

It was not a good move. I found out that I could get away with a lot there, and I think my father now thought I was his teacher friend's responsibility, so he stopped checking my homework, and I stopped doing most of it. I found my father's math answer book, and copied the answers for my math homework. This did nothing for my math skills, and I lost my head start in that subject. Fortunately, I liked languages and writing, so I did all right in grammar and essays.

I still love books and reading. I attribute my literary interests to my mother's reading to my brother and me every night when we went to bed, beginning in early childhood. I can still recall, at about age four, my mother sitting by our bedside reading aloud, and we asking her to read "just one more chapter" before going to sleep. As well as being the teacher, my father was usually the librarian, so I had easy access to books. I would go there in the evening and borrow books. My father did not pay much attention to what I read, but my mother, who had a deeply religious bent and a heap of old fashioned morals, caught me once in a while reading "inappropriate literature" such as the Norwegian translation of *Oliver Twist*, or *The Treasures of Sierra Madre*." I was also caught reading *Knut Hamsun*, a Norwegian writer, who had won the Nobel prize in literature, but was an outcast in Norway after the war, since he had been a Nazi sympathizer. Other books, such as *Gulliver's Travels* were "acceptable", and I read such adventure books as *A Thousand Leagues Under the Sea* and *Moby Dick*—in Norwegian, of course. Cowboys and Indians were also favourites, anything from *The Last of the Mohicans* to *Hopalong Cassidy* and *Tom Mix*. I even managed to read some of the better Norwegian writers.

I became very interested in stories of the war, and my new teacher let me borrow books that he was reading. I started spending whatever money I could save up on war-story books, but when my father caught on to what I was spending my money on, he put a stop to it. I think he could have channeled my love for reading into more of the classics and educational works, but though he was a teacher, he did not have that insight (in his defense, he was probably very sick of war, and did not want me to dwell on something that for him was too recent and disturbing—he had barely escaped being sent to the work camps). In fact, he became rather aloof as we got older, and paid minimal attention to our development. That job was left to my mother, who did the best she could with limited resources.

I was not the easiest of children to manage, and I am sure my parents reached their limit more than once. However, some of the things they did were not helpful.

In one town, there was a correctional school for boys who were juvenile delinquents. It was not a Dickensian kind of workhouse, but having read *Oliver Twist* and *David Copperfield*, my imagination ran wild, and when my parents threatened to send me there, I was terrified. But, rather than behaving, it made me angry, and I acted out even worse. My parents were not evil or bad, they just had a bad example from their own stern parents, and no one to show them otherwise. They meant well, I am sure, but as they say, "the road to hell is paved with good intentions".

My father's youngest brother, uncle Ivan, was a bird of a different feather. He was an "afterthought", quite a bit younger than the rest of the siblings, and had stayed at home on the farm while his mother was alive. When young, he had fallen and cracked open his knee. The knee was destroyed, so they cut his leg, shortening it so he could walk. He walked with a stiff, unbending leg, swinging it behind him as he walked. He could move quite fast, but with some difficulty. Probably as a result, he spent more time at home, so he took up music as a hobby. He became a very good accordion player, and also played the guitar well.

In those days, when very few people had records or record players, and the government-owned radio only played chamber and other classical music, he became in great local demand as a musician at wedding and local dances. When he visited us, the local girls would come out to hear him play. He would play his accordion and sing, sometimes yodel, and the young girls would swoon as if he was a local Mario Lanza (or a modern day Ricky Martin). Once when he was visiting us, my mother caught him in our living room, smooching with one of my father's grade eight students. She would have been about fourteen, my uncle about twenty-five. My mother was furious, and told him to pack his bags and get out. It is the first and only time I ever remember mother having the upper hand and my father not saying a word in his brother's defense. If he had, I think my mother would have thrown him out too. When it came to morals, there were no gray areas for my mother.

Our play was often rough, alternating between cowboys and Indians and Viking warriors, as the spirit moved us. A few such "games" stand out in my memory. When I was about eight or nine, we were visiting the farm in Nordfjord during summer vacation, and with our many cousins and the other local children there, we were a formidable gang of rowdy boys with overactive bodies and imaginations. There was an old abandoned grain mill on the farm, which provided a perfect location for an imaginary fort or a castle, depending on whether we were Indians or Vikings. It was a simple but practical contraption, with a small log house situated above a brook and two round grinding stones, one attached to a shaft which dropped though the middle of the floor to a baffled millwheel lying horizontally to the little waterfall below, providing direct power without any gears to the grinding stone above in the cabin. Our fertile minds, nurtured on books like *The Last of the Mohicans* and the *Viking sagas,* easily turned this log cabin into a pioneer fort. We chose one group to be the fort's defenders—the white settlers—and another group to be attacking Indians. We had a difficult time getting enough settlers, as most of the boys wanted to be the glorious and fearsome Indians. I got to be an Indian, but my younger brother had to "settle" for settler.

Soon, the battle began; the Indians attacked and the defenders defended. Some of us had homemade wooden "tomahawks" and swords (I am not sure how we got Indians with swords—some Viking intermingling there, I suppose); others had jerrybuilt bows and arrows. The fort, however, was quite impermeable (and impenetrable); the walls were made of hewn logs and the door of heavy planks. The two window openings were small and had wooden shutters. It would have been a fortress fit for the real new world settlers.

The brave defenders lowered buckets into the stream below and poured the content through the windows onto the attacking "Indians", who were getting frustrated and a bit weary, banging their "swords" and "tomahawks" on the heavy wooden door. Some brave "braves" tried to enter from below, but were repulsed with a torrent of water and loud shrieks from the defenders. We were just about to concede defeat when a stray arrow went through an open window and hit my brother in the head. It bounced off without doing any visible damage, but it scared him sufficiently that he ran home crying. The grownups came out to admonish us and the battle-weary group slunk home, humiliated and defeated.

This became the Battle at the Old Mill (or, in Norse, *Slaget på Kværnhuset*) in the "folklore" of the participants, and was properly embellished and refined into heraldic depiction of a glorious battle of heroic proportions.

Another time—I was about eleven or twelve—the local village boys decided we should have a secret society, and I was elected the chieftain. We would have preferred to be B*oy Scouts*, but the remote village where we lived was not large enough to have an organized activity such as the Scouts, so we decided to make our own group. We set about writing down rules, and decided we also needed some punishment for infractions. The gravest crime was, of course, tattling to grownups about any of our shenanigans. Such nefarious acts required the ultimate punishment, and after much debate we hit on the perfect penalty: *pseudo-electrocution*. We had read about the electric chair in America, and we had just the answer: the farmer's electric fence, used to keep the cows contained in the pasture. The fence consisted of a single wire, about two feet above ground, with regular twelve-volt shocks surging through the wires—just enough to sting the cows and convince them to stay on the inside. The culprit would have three shocks administered from the fence, through a wire attached to the fence and to a stick with an insulating cup at the other end. This "capital" punishment seemed to be a fair deterrent, for we did not have a serious breach of discipline until Alvin got caught while we were raiding the local pastor's apple orchard. Stealing apples were a regular pastime, and not too much effort was made to apprehend us, as long as we did not break any branches. Alvin, however, was quite fat, and when he attempted to climb up a tree to fetch a particular nice a bunch of red apples, the branch broke and poor Alvin and the branch came crashing down. Alvin went home crying and told everything to his parents, with the result that we all were given a dressing down from our own folks.

Now, this certainly was a serious breach of our secret code, and the transgressor had to be punished. Alvin was called before the whole membership and a "martial" court was convened. It was agreed that there were certain extenuating circumstances: Alvin was fat, and the branch weak, thus it was not his fault that he fell down. However, he did confess (although under duress); he was certainly guilty of tattling—he did not try to deny that. Therefore the "court" unanimously sentenced him to a reduced sentence of just one shock of the electric fence, considering the mitigating circumstances and the severe parental interrogation he had had to endure.

Alvin was taken to the fenced area, and he went along quite cheerfully. However, he was wearing leather-soled shoes, rather than rubber which insulates better, and his shock was probably greater than we had anticipated (we used to hold onto the wire and take shocks ourselves to see who could hold on the longest, counting each jolt of electricity). He yelled like a knifed pig and ran home, again spilling the beans, this time about our "secret society". Now we had real trouble, and our society was wound up in a hurry, by the order of the Supreme Court—our parents.

As you might have guessed by now, I had a penchant for getting into trouble. A neighbour's boy and I were playing "Vikings". We fashioned a couple of Viking axes, and were looking for something on which to test their efficacy. Now, the farmer, from whom we were renting the upstairs flat, had raised silver fox in the past (the silver fox market went flat after the war, as fashion changed) and the wire cages were still standing on posts above the ground. I don't remember what possessed us to attack these posts, but attack it we did, like a couple of Don Quixotes beating up on windmills, and managed to chop a couple down. This so weakened the structure that the whole set of fox cages came crashing down. I assume the noise had alerted the farmer, because he came to take a look, and we intrepid Vikings flew the scene. We went to my friend's home, with the farmer in hot pursuit. He told my friend's mother what we had done, but she told him it was no big deal, as the old cages were of no use to him any longer. The farmer went away, still angry, and set about telling my parents the same story. I had a faint hope that I might escape the parental wrath as my friend had done, but no such reprieve was in store for me. I was told to come in to face my punishment. I thought this patently unfair, considering my friend's exculpation. Consequently, I resolved to run away, and headed for the mountain. There I found an old hut where the farmer stored wooden stakes for drying hay. It was evening, but not dark (in Norway it does not get dark at night in the summer, due to the country's northern latitude), and I tried to make myself comfortable on top of the wooden stakes. I tried to sleep, but could not, as I were feeling cold. I realized that I needed to be someplace warmer—like in a barn. I dared not go home, knowing that unlawful flight was now added to my sentence, and the punishment would, accordingly, be more severe. These were the days of corporal punishment, and though I don't think it ever damaged my soul, it sure stung my bare rear when my mother applied it (it was, usually, my mother's job to spank us—my father was the judge, not the executioner). I calculated that if I could keep away long enough, my mother's anger might subside and the punishment mitigated somewhat, possibly reduced to spending time in my bedroom—with a book—or at worst, having to do the dishes. So I went off to the neighbouring farm and crawled into the hayloft, burying myself in the dry, warm hay.

I fell asleep, and was awoken by voices and the noise of men rummaging around the barn and trampling in the loose hay around me. It was now full daylight, and I burrowed down so as to not be seen. Now I had really overdone it! I had gotten the whole village out looking for me—a turn of events I had not bargained for. I did not know what to do, but the need for a decision was eliminated when one of the searchers trod on my head and I yelled and jumped up from the hay. "Here he is—I've got him!" hollered the man. He then grabbed me and carried me outside. I could not escape the man's firm grip. When I got outside, my mother was there, crying, and I realized that I was not getting a spanking this time. I began to feel much better. I was starving, and my mother made a fine breakfast for me, fussing around like I was the prodigal son returning home. It was a good feeling—being appreciated and fussed over—although I had deserved punishment. It was also a strange feeling, this dichotomy between feeling guilty and feeling righteous. However, I resolved not to try it again—I'd rather face the music right away than spend another night in a barn. The perfect solution would, of course, be not to do wrong in the first place, but the logic of that sensibility escaped me at the time.

I guess we were no worse than today's children—but the environment was different, and we had less resources. There were no Boy Scout Clubs where we lived, no sports arenas—in fact, no organized sports whatsoever. We were left to our own devices—relying on our own imaginations and inventiveness. Sometimes it got us in trouble, but we learned to play together, giving and taking, and to use our imagination in games; including making our own toys from the woods and the trees around us—making our own toy ships of wood and sailing them on the many ponds dotted about the countryside.

I was about twelve when we got a dog. It was a grownup dog and the owner wanted a good home for her. I went to the bus stop to pick her up, and opened the shipping crate and attached a leash around her neck. She seemed happy to see me, so I made the mistake of letting go the leash. The dog must have suddenly realized that she did not know me, for she took off and ran back up the road and disappeared into the forested mountainside.

I was heartbroken. All day I looked for her, but could not find her. It was winter and I looked for tracks in the new snow, but to no avail.

The next day, Sunday, I was up early and went looking again. It had snowed, and I thought I might see her tracks in the new snow. I passed a farmhouse, and heard their dog baying. He was barking towards the mountain, but I could not hear any other dog. However, I thought I would walk up the mountainside, just in case. Halfway up, I found dog tracks underneath the pine trees, but they disappeared where new snow had fallen, so they had to be from the day before or earlier.

I walked in the direction of the tracks and again came to a clump of trees, where I picked up the tracks again. Soon, I could hear faint baying. Then I saw her; she had wound herself around a fence post so her head was tight against the pole. There were no tracks leading up to her, so I knew she had been there all night in the snow and cold. I untied her and picked her up, carrying her all the way home.

That dog and I became inseparable. Later, she would follow me to the ferry in the morning, and meet me at the ferry dock when I came back from school in the afternoon. I am sure she knew I had saved her life.

Generally, I was healthy, but I had a problem with tonsils and adenoids. Every winter, I would get a cold, and they would swell up and give me a high fever, and I would be sick in bed for about two weeks. Once when I awoke, I could not breathe at all. Today, you would call an ambulance and go to the hospital emergency, but not then. My dad didn't know what to do, but my mother got the kettle going, then put a blanket over my head with the kettle inside, and after a while I could breathe quite well. It scared me, though; it is a wild feeling to not be able to breathe.

Then, when I was thirteen years old, my teacher told my father that I should have the tonsils and adenoids taken out, because I was losing too much time from school. Dad agreed, and I went to the hospital. However, for some strange reason, the surgeon decided to operate on me with just local anesthetics. It was probably cheaper, though Norway had social medicine even then, so it does not seem too likely a reason.

I was put in a chair and the doctor gave me several needles down my throat. Then he used a tool that looked like a pair of scissors, with a metal wire loop at the end, which he used to snare the tonsil and adenoid with. I had a metal bucket under my chin, in which he dumped the bloody things. He even held up a tonsil to show me before dropping it into the bucket. I think he got his training with the Marquis de Sade. Each time he pulled, my head exploded—four times. Afterwards, I walked to the gurney and they rolled me back to the ward.

That night, I was feeling pretty lonely and ill. I could not swallow food, my throat was on fire, and my head was pretty hot too.

Then an angel came to sit beside my bed and read to me. She was a volunteer, a middle aged lady in a white smock. She stroked my head and promised that I would feel better in the morning.

Norway has a peculiar people called "Tartars"(Tater), who are a kind of gypsy, but are Norwegian citizens who live in cities during the winter when the children have to be in school. They are pretty well settled down nowadays, but then they traveled around the countryside in the summer, living in tents and farmer's barns—wherever they could find shelter. They made kitchen utensils and trinkets, which they sold to the locals. They were outcasts and disliked by the townsfolk, but tolerated. We were told not to play with their children, as they were lousy and were known to use knives for other things than tools. They were also suspected of stealing, whenever they had the chance.

When they came around begging for food, or asking to sleep in a farmer's barn, the farmer was caught in a bind. If he refused, he was afraid they would do damage to his property or steal something, so he usually played it safe and chose the lesser of two evils: letting them stay in the barn, and hoping they would not burn it down accidentally.

In olden days, the farmers would just set their dogs on them, and even now, the Tartars were very apprehensive about dogs. The farmers kept dogs in part to keep away the Tartars.

We were not Tartars; my dad had a job and a standing in the community, but we were always strangers, and our constant moving had some elements of the Tartar life, but without the benefits of a familial, supportive community.

When I was about eleven, my father bought a "cottage" on an island called Sotra, on the coast not far from Bergen. There was no bridge to the mainland at that time; we had to use a ferry or private boats to reach there. Most of the people were fishermen, usually living on small farms, keeping a few cattle and sheep to supplement their income from fishing. They would be considered poor by today's standards. The house, or cottage we bought was very small, but it had two bedrooms, which meant that my brother and I had our own bedroom. My sister shared my parent's bedroom. There was a separate kitchen, and a living room, and for the summer, an additional sun room that was not insulated. It was heaven for us, and especially since it was the only home we ever had that we owned—not rented. We would go there for the summer vacation and the Christmas holidays, and for a couple of years we felt like we had a real home. We had a cat and a dog—the dog would go with us for the winter, but the cat stayed and was feed by the neighbor, welcoming us home when we arrive during the holidays. The two animals had a strange relationship: when my brother and I went to the neighbors to buy milk, the dog and the cat would follow along, the dog first and behind it the cat, tail straight in the air. Sometimes, the dog would see a strange cat, and as dogs will do, he chased the strange cat, while our cat sat waiting for him to return. When he did, they continued their journey with us, following behind us on the way.

Up on the mountain there was a small lake, and the local boys would go there to swim. It was a rather deep lake, with a muddy, dark bottom, and no beach, so we would swim by jumping directly into the lake. However, this was a problem when you don't know how to swim. I had just learned to swim—barely, and not wanting to seem a sissy, I dived right into the lake from the steep berg alongside. I went down and down, realizing I did not know how to get back up. Somehow, I instinctively knew that I would eventually come back up, if I could just keep the air in my lungs, and I held on, slowly coming to the end of my decent and then beginning to ascend towards the surface. I could see the light above, but my lungs were busting and I thought I would run out of air.

Finally, I broke the surface, and there was my brother and some of the other boys looking down on me. I was next to the rock, and climbed ashore without difficulty, but with some relief. I knew it had been a close call! Years after, my brother would relate the story—he thought it was the end of me.

The next year, my father sold the cottage. He needed the money, I guess, but it was a sad day for my brother and me. It was the only "real" home we ever had, and where we felt we really belonged.

I think my mother always felt guilty, somehow, that I had wanted to leave and to stay in a foreign country, though I visited her as often as I could, especially during her latter years. She blamed our gypsy life for my wanderlust.

Once, I lamented to my brother that we had no real place we could say we were from—we had not lived long enough anywhere to set down roots, and every year brought a new home. My brother had an philosophical way of looking at it: "We could have been just like one of those country bumpkins" he said. "Instead we got around, seeing new places and learning different ways of life, expanding our horizon". It was perhaps an elitist statement, but when I thought about it, I realized that he could be right. Though for me, two louts are alike, so changing locations did little to enrich our lives, and added little to our cultural enlightenment. Yet, who is to say that those yokels were not living their lives as happy or happier than we? Looking back, am I more satisfied than they? Perhaps their families are intact, their children and grandchildren gathered around on the holidays, singing their praise. Perhaps. Then again, happiness is in the eye of the beholder, we can be happy or unhappy anywhere.

Happy families are all alike, every unhappy family is unhappy in its own way.

Leo Tolstoy: Anna Karina

Too much moving about can engender insecurities—even identity crisis—in children. I do wish there was a place I could remember as my childhood home. A whole country is too large a focus. Many great men of history came from small communities and became world-wise and sophisticated, but their strength and character was formed in the crucible of a small town and in the security of the stable community where they lived as children. Like a willow swaying in the storm, when anchored by strong roots, the winds of life can bend the trunk and break a limb, but it cannot wreck the tree.

Life is a journey, not a destination. There is no way to happiness; happiness is the way …

* * * *

When I was about fifteen, I got a summer job at a tourist hotel at Strandebarm, in the Hardanger Fjord. As I had picked up some English in school, I was given the job of guiding English tourists to the local glacier. The trip was by boat along the fjord, then a one-hour walk up the mountainside to the foot of the glacier. Halfway there was an inn that existed mainly to serve the English their tea. Without their afternoon tea, I don't think the elderly English ladies could have made the trip.

The Germans have now overtaken the English as the largest tourist group in Norway. How ironic—sixty-some years ago they invaded with guns, now they are using cameras.

It was the summer of 1957 and the movie "The Vikings" was being filmed there. The production had constructed a "Viking village" on an island, and built a huge fence to block out the few homes there.

The main actors, Kirk Douglas, Tony Curtis and Ernst Borgnine (and later, Janet Leigh, Tony Curtis' wife) stayed at the hotel, and I spent some time taking them on sightseeing trips and once to a local dance. At the dance hall I tried to get "dates" for them and managed to find one for Curtis but none for Borgnine, he was too old and not very good looking.

They befriended the captain of a navy destroyer that had been assigned to the production to make artificial fog. He, Curtis, Borgnine, and a "stand-in" for Douglas, were real "party-animals"—at least before Janet Leigh showed up (she was filming in France and arrived some two weeks later). One night the room buzzer went off at around midnight—I had the late shift in the reception—it was from the Curtis room. When I got there, the whole gang was whooping it up with a couple of local bunnies; they demanded I bring them a bottle of wine. I didn't have the keys to the bar (booze in Norway was guarded better than the gold in Fort Knox. It was illegal to sell drinks to the locals, as the whole area was "dry". Only guests could drink at the hotel, but even for them, there was no room service of alcohol available), so I went and knocked on the owner's door at his house next to the hotel. He got very angry with me, telling me to get lost, and I had to report back to the guests that Norwegian liquor laws trumped any hand they had—rich *or* famous.

Generally, the group, except Douglas, acted in a very worldly and friendly manner and attracted little attention. Kirk Douglas kept mostly to himself and appeared a bit haughty. He once called me to his room to pick up dry-cleaning for him, and I was amazed at the number of ties he had. Funny what can impress a fifteen-year-old. I can't say anything else impressed me about him. He was quite short and when they filmed one fight between him and his adversary, they had to do it on a slope so he would appear taller.

One day Kirk went for a walk and met a local girl he liked. He gave her a forgettable role as an extra. Her film career began and ended there, and it did nothing for her local reputation.

I don't think the townsfolk paid much attention to them, nor seemed to care. Only once did a couple of local girls come in and ask me if they could get an autograph of Curtis. He happened to walk by and they got his signature, said thank you and left. As an afterthought, I had him write a note in my diary book, which I still have. That is the only autograph I have of that gang—it never occurred to me to ask the others, though I saw them almost every day. Another memory I have about them is how incredibly cheap they were with tips, considering they must have been quite wealthy. While the American dollar did go far in those days (seven kroners to a dollar), they probably overestimated its value, or perhaps when they paid in local currency, they thought the krone would go as far there as a dollar did in the U.S.A. Americans then, as now, were not known for their sensitivity to other cultures and mores, and often were thought arrogant and haughty.

The group ate in a separate wing of the dining room; there were about twenty of them and a couple of children, boys about ten years old. The talk of the kitchen staff was how bad their eating habits were: uneaten food left on the plates and on the floor, a no-no in a country that had recently escaped five years of war and German occupation with food shortages and rations. The children were particularly bad mannered, spilling drinks and leaving the table in a real mess.

Kirk Douglas got his name in the paper in a rather unexpected way. The extras wanted more money, since they were made to jump into the rather cold fjord. Douglas made the comment that they were not much like Vikings, since they were afraid of water. That got a few "Hagars" horribly (pardon the pun) angry, and they built a replica Viking ship and sailed it to New York City. I don't think Kirk was there to greet them. Much later, after I had immigrated to Canada, I did see the movie, and my impression of it was that it was pretty silly.

CHAPTER 2

Apprentice Sailor

Since the time of the Viking marauders, Norway has had a tradition as a seafaring nation, and depended on its native sons to man their merchant fleet. It was, at the time I joined, the third largest merchant marine in the world, even though its population was less than four million people. For young men not inclined to get a higher education, going to sea was a shortcut to the working world and to a fair income, as well as feeding into the adventurous spirit of the young men who "would rather go sailing".

Nowadays, the country is oil-rich, thanks to large oil and hydrocarbon deposits in the North Sea, and is, therefore, less dependent on the merchant marine. Fishing is still being done, but is much less important to the economy, and has taken a backseat to *fish farming*, which was pioneered by Norwegians. Another, formerly large industry, shipbuilding, has given way to the construction of huge oil exploration platforms and drilling rigs; its ships are now built in Japan, Korea and Finland. The merchant marine (and the large cruise ship fleet) now utilizes foreign workers such as Filipinos and Chinese, with only the officers being Norwegian nationals. Many ship-owners use "flags of convenience" countries, such a Liberia, Panama, Costa Rica and a multitude of others who just collect the registration fee without taxes or much regulation or control. Not so in 1958. In those days, anyone sailing under these flags would be "blacklisted" from Norwegian ships. The Norwegians took pride in their ships, making sure they were freshly painted and no rust was visible anywhere; in contrast to, for example, ships owned by Greek shipping tycoons Nicharos and Aristotle Onassis (later famously married to Jacqueline Kennedy).

Onassis purchased the old Liberty ships from the Americans, very cheaply. These ships, assembly-built during the war, and expected to make one or two trips across the Atlantic, were still sailing in the 1960's and well into the seventies. Norwegian sailors would look derisively at these rusting hulks, sometimes with pigs and chickens running around on deck, providing fresh food for the crew. Of course, Onassis & Co. made fortunes with these old wrecks.

I was an irascible fifteen-year-old when I decided I wanted to be a sailor. I had a tenuous relationship with school and a tempestuous one with my parents, so it was probably not without some relief they agreed to let me attend the sailors apprentice training course on the Norwegian sailing ship "Statsraad Lehmkul", a large, four-masted square-rigger built in the beginning of the twentieth century, and used by the merchant navy to train sailors. They might also have figured that the three months of cadet life would disabuse me of the romantic notion of a sailor's life.

There were about 150 boys in this course, between the ages of fifteen and twenty-five. Life on the sailing ship was nothing like I had expected. Discipline was strict, the work was hard, and the food was heinous, even for a poor country boy like me. For breakfast we got some watery gruel that was made from grain and tasted like dishwater. I think this must have been the kind of food they served POW's in the camps during the war. I do remember being often hungry, but not starving. Dinner was usually adequate though simple. The cooking and bread baking was done on board by young cadets, but supervised by an experienced cook.

One day the cook had lost his wedding ring in the bread dough and asked us to keep an eye (or should I say tooth) out for it. Another time the busboy fell into the flour bin. He climbed out, looking like a snowman. The flour was still used for baking bread.

My uncle, Hans, the oldest of my mother's brothers, was a VP of administration with Norway's largest meat packing plant, *Vestlandske Salslag*, where he had worked himself up from office boy upon leaving school. He also belonged to the *Salvation Army*, where he and his wife, Ovidia, played in their music corps. The Steward (the officer in charge of food services) on the ship was a friend of his, and also a *Salvationist.* One day this Steward came by and told me that uncle Hans had asked him to look out for me. He then brought me into the storeroom and sliced a piece of bologna and gave it to me. I took it and said thank you very much, realizing that the guy was, by this minimal gesture, acquitting himself of the responsibility undertaken on my uncle's behest, and my uncle could assure my mother that he had "looked after me."

We had to "stand watch" for four hours during the night, then work four hours during the daytime. Staying awake on the "dog watch" from midnight to four a.m. was pure hell for a fifteen-year old. All the deck-hand apprentices, of whom I was one, had to take their turn. I was one of the youngest of the cadets and found this task especially difficult. I was so tired that I would try to find a place to sleep during the day, whenever I could, but if caught, it meant no shore leave that week, a fate almost worse than dying from lack of sleep.

Upon returning from shore leave, you had to check in with the duty officer, and if you were late by as little as one minute, you got a detention. We all had assigned numbers, mine was twenty-one, and these numbers were used exclusively instead of names—even when addressing each other. An officer would circle your number in red if you were late.

The one bright spot was shore leave. We pressed our uniforms and polished our shoes before mustering for inspection and were rowed ashore. There, the young teenage girls, or "chocolate bunnies" as we called them, were waiting for us. There is something about a uniform that makes young girls hearts flutter, but I have never figured out what it is. I can hardly imagine a less desirable mate than a poor sailor boy.

It might have a historical base. Arthur Herman *in his book* To Rule The Waves *quotes a ditty, sung by girls in seaports in mid-nineteen century England:*

Sailors, they get all the money,
Soldiers they get none but brass,
I do love a jolly sailor,
Soldiers they may kiss my arse.

At night, we all lined up below deck, with an officer doing the roll call to ensure everyone was there. We had to stand at attention with our hammocks slung over our right shoulder while the inspection was performed. Then we hooked our hammocks into the ceiling hooks, grabbed the overhead beam and pulled ourselves into the hammock. You had to sleep on your back, since the hammock had a substantial curve, or slack, to it. The curve remained, no matter how much you tried to tighten the hammock. If you had to go to the bathroom during the night, you had to lower yourself to the ground, then maneuver through the sea of hammocks with sleeping boys, to the bathroom and back again.

During the day work-hours we learned such archaic things as splicing rope and wire cable, and hoisting the sails, even though we were stationary in the Bergen Bay for this particular short course. We scrubbed the wooden deck planks, scraped rust and painted; polished the abundant brass railing in the officer's quarters; swiped food from the quartermaster's stores and passed our free time arguing or beating each other up.

Life onboard was mostly tedious and boring, so fights were a break and a bit of excitement. I don't remember anyone getting seriously hurt, though I got a couple of black eyes. Being among the youngest and of only medium size, I would get the worse of it, but usually I had the good sense to throw in the towel before I got *really* hurt. Except once: I had words with this other boy, and must have gotten to him, for after we got to bed in our hammocks, he cut the rope on mine. Fortunately it was at the foot end, but I fell to the deck rather hard. It was dark, so I could not see who did it, and I repaired the rope and got back into bed. He came back, but this time I was ready. I felt some fumbling with the bottom of the hammock, and I jumped out onto the deck and struck out as hard as I could, landing a blow right on his nose. He yelled like a knifed pig, and ran to the washroom, with me following behind him. I now saw who it was, and gave him a stern "lecture". I felt tremendously proud of myself for having beaten up a bigger and stronger boy. We later became fairly good friends—it's amazing what a little physical force does for the primitive mind of a teenager. I learned that even if you are not very strong, you could often bluff your way, as long as you didn't cross the line and actually have to fight the other guy—he then realizing that you were just full of hot air.

What wasted efforts. I learned to splice rope, but never had a need to use that training. On modern ships, you seldom spliced rope, and never cable, they hardly ever broke, and if they did, you would just clamp them together, or get another one.

Following my exposure to the sailor's life, I had some misgivings and thought I would explore some alternatives to sailing that did not require high-school education. I answered an ad from one of the major hotels in Bergen, the *Hotel Bristol.* They were looking for a waiter's apprentice. Believe it or not, in Norway those days, there was an apprenticeship for waiters. I did not know at the time that this apprenticeship mainly consisted of setting and clearing tables and doing the waiters bidding.

I got a cheap room in a seedy part of Bergen, on a seedy street called Hollendergaten (Holland Street), in Old Bergen. I shared an upstairs room with a middle-aged drunk who worked sporadically on the docks, whenever he was not too busy drinking. I worked from seven in the morning to eleven, and then I was free until seven p.m., when I again worked until twelve. After midnight I walked home across the harbour district, passing the drunks hanging out at the public toilet area, fending off beggars and drunks on the way to my shared room.

I had a hell of a time waking up in the morning. Since I had to be at work at seven, I got up at six. The wind-up alarm clock would ring, and I'd sit up in my bed, then fall asleep again, sitting up. After a few late starts, I was warned by my boss, and decided I had to figure a way to ensure I awoke in time. I devised a rater elaborate scheme: I put a tin ashtray on top of a water glass, then, in the ashtray I put the alarm clock. The clock would ring and vibrate around until it got to the edge of the tray and the whole shebang fell down on the table, making an unholy racket.

My feet hurt from being on them all day, I think the shoes were part of the problem, and I was constantly tired. After a few months I decided that being a sailor was better than being a waiter's slave, so I quit and went to the sailor's hiring office.

It is ironic to think back and remember those days, fifteen years old, walking home through the dock area, and my parents not having any concerns. Years later, as a thirty-five year old man, when I was visiting my mother, I was at a restaurant with some childhood friends. About midnight, I called my mother and told her that I was leaving the restaurant and walking across town to the train station and taking the last train home. She insisted that I take a taxi to the station, as walking through the dock area was too dangerous. I could have told her that I knew those streets well; I used to walk them at midnight when I was just fifteen!

CHAPTER 3

Deckhand

... heavy drinkers, coarse frolickers in moral sties ... heavy fighters, reckless fellows, ... foul-witted, profane, prodigal of their money, bankrupt at the end of the trip ...

—Mark Twain: Life on the Mississippi

In days of yore, it was common for restless young men in Norway, to go to sea. Norway had the world's third largest merchant navy, most of it charted by other countries, and operating in foreign trade outside Norwegian waters. The men (for it was mostly men) that provided the crew, were a rough lot, mostly uneducated and unrestrained, fond of strong drink and weak women, rootless and unattached; they roamed the world on trampers, hardly ever going home. They were truly international, signing off and on ships in foreign ports, a community of floating gypsies, crude and classless. The ship was their world and their family, the Captain was their King, and for minor offences, the Justice and the Law. Short of murder, there was little they could do that drew real punishment, the *cat—o'—nine tails* lash having been abolished for some time. The norm was monetary fines, for there was no jail on the ship, and no police. The ultimate punishment was to be sent home in disgrace, there to be dealt with by the Norwegian courts. The merchant navy provided an escape and employment for many of the social outcasts and misfits of Norwegian society.

Going to sea was also a way for young men, not inclined to further education, to see the world and still earn some money. Many made just one trip, and settled down at shore. The ones who went back, usually "got it in the blood" as they said, and often spent most of their lives away from their country.

The young and inexperienced, and the weaker, learned to avoid conflicts with the strong, or did so at their own peril. This "society" had its own rules of fairness and behaviour—its own pecking order—and disapproval of the group was a deterrent from extreme and aberrant behaviour. The system of apprenticeship, with its classifications and hiearchy—ordinary seaman, able-bodied seaman, etc.—provided a ready made social structure which made it easier for newcomers to fit in. This was especially important when a ship had to be refitted in dry-dock and with the exception of a few officers and a "skeleton" crew, had to be totally re-manned before it could sail.

The more intelligent and motivated worked themselves up in the ranks, and then took schooling at shore in seamanship: navigation if on deck, diesel mechanics if in the engine room, or food science if aspiring to be cook and perhaps steward. There were also some specialist trades such as electrician and the telegraph operator, or "spark" as he was called. These were subalterns, not officers, but not part of the crew.

It was a tenuous road to walk, on a ship, between being accepted by the group, yet not becoming caught up in a culture of drinking and carousing each time the ship was in port. For young, impressionable men, it was a rough and perilous life.

This was the world I entered when at the age of sixteen I went to sea in September of 1958. For the next fifteen months, I would need all my mental and emotional resources to survive. I packed more experience into these few months than most "landlubbers" get in half a lifetime. If you can maintain your own standards and not become inured with the life of the lowest denominator, the experience will make you stronger. I always felt I was an observer—a spectator to the histrionics—yet I was also part of the play.

I grew up fast, and though I am happy I did not make the sea my vocation—I never "crossed the Rubicon"—I am glad I had the experience.

Amsterdam

The ship I had signed on to was in dry-dock in Amsterdam, where she had undergone major refitting and was getting almost a totally new crew. This crew, of which I was part, left together, on a passenger boat to Amsterdam. My parents and my brother followed me to the departure pier in Bergen to say goodbye. My brother, acting the clown, took out his handkerchief, wiped his eyes, then he waved it goodbye, as the ship slowly backed away from the pier.

It took a day and a half to reach Amsterdam, and by the time we got to there, we had gotten to know each other fairly well. The first evening we had dinner at large tables in the dining room, and I was sitting right across from another first-time sailor, Nels. I was accustom to the sea, having lived near water and boats most of my life, but Nels was from inland somewhere. As we got into the North Sea, it became a bit rough. This old hulk did not have stabilizers, and rolled around quite a bit. The tables had ten-centimeter high edges so the dishes would not end up on the floor as the ship rocked and rolled. Nels's face was getting a bit red, and suddenly, he threw up, right across the table, most of it landing in my lap!

It was not a very auspicious beginning to our relationship.

Gilda

Our ship, *Gilda,* was owned by a Bergen-based firm by the name of *Leif Erickson Rederi.* She was a 17,000-ton deadweight tanker, small even for that time, and aging. She was built in 1942 in Sweden during the war, and had no air conditioning, even though she spent most of her time in the tropical zones. She was a "tramper", which meant she did not have a set route, but would take crude oil from the Persian Gulf area to various countries in the Middle and Far East. She had a crew of thirty-two, including eight officers. The crew was mainly Norwegian, but there were four Dutchmen, (and the one Dutchwoman), a Dane, a Swede, one Englishman and one Israeli Jew.

There were two women aboard working as stewardesses, in the officer's mess. One was an older woman from Norway who was sailing with her husband—an officer in the engine room. The other was a former prostitute from Amsterdam, hoping to snare a Norwegian officer for a husband. She was rather plain, nearly homely, with a large nose and Clairol blonde hair, which after a few weeks at sea, began to turn black at the bottom—the black portion getting longer and longer as time went on. She clearly had run out of hair coloring materials. She would come aft to the kitchen to get the officers food, and the men would tease her mercilessly, singing "Rudolph the Red Nosed Reindeer" and making comments about her hair (later, she complained to the first mate—her "mate" and protector—about our incessant teasing, with the result that *we* had to *deliver* the officer's food amidships. The first mate was an older "gentleman" who, carnally speaking, had greater needs than taste).

The officers were quartered mid-ships, the crew aft. There was a strict social and physical separation between officers and crew, the officers had their own dining room and mess room mid-ships. It was a rather motley crew, since a tramper, especially in the Far East, was at the bottom of the list of desired ships on which to sail.

The ship's captain decided whether alcohol could be served onboard. In our case, the ship was "dry", probably for good reason, for several of the men were alcoholics, or at least, binge drinkers. Norwegian sailors have never been known for their temperance, alcohol or otherwise, and this "crew" was a glaring example.

Onboard Gilda in the Pacific.

There was a dockworker's strike in Amsterdam at the time, so dry-dock cranes were not operating. We had to carry fifty-pound pails of paint and other provisions up a steep gangplank and across the deck of a neighbouring ship in the dry dock. Fortunately, the strike ended after a couple of days. The ship was manned and ready after about a week, which was fortunate, since Amsterdam was a place where bored Norwegian sailors could get in trouble aplenty. There were hundreds of pubs and beer was ten cents a glass. In the red light district around Kanalstrate (Canal Street) hordes of prostitutes carried on their trade. There was a kind of hierarchy amongst the whores: the poorest ones walked the streets; the better off ones had a street-level apartment with a window to the street. Curtains up meant open for business.

We negotiated a group rate, but at least for me, the experience was less than stellar. Incredibly, they had a certificate or license on the wall testifying to a monthly medical checkup for venereal decease. I remember watching a middle-aged gentleman with a walking cane and hat walking into one of the apartments. After about twenty minutes he came back out and walked away, as if he had just paid a visit to a store or a coffee shop. He was probably going home for dinner with the wife and kids!

I was sitting in a pub one evening, with a few of the ships crew and a variety of Dutch denizens, when a woman in a Salvation Army uniform came in collecting money. Every single patron upped up some cash, some quite a bit, showing her a lot of respect. That this motley group displayed such generosity was surprising. I asked one of the veteran sailors why this was so. He told me that the Army had a shelter nearby, and everyone knew that someday they could be in need of the Salvation Army's assistance (or just "salvation")—something like "there but for the Grace of God go I."

The easy access to alcohol of all kinds was quite a contrast to Norway, where alcohol sales were highly regulated, and the alcohol outlets were government monopolies and were actually named "Monopoly" (Monopolet). I must hasten to state that I think the Dutch's approach to alcohol was a healthier one than the Norwegian. In Norway, alcoholic spirits (and beer) were very expensive and restricted, leading to home stills and homebrews, and over-imbibing when alcohol was available. The Dutch, and other sensible drinking societies, learn to drink moderately when growing up, and binge drinking is less prevalent.

Having a "dry" ship was no help when in port. There was much bacchanalia and carousing among the crew. Some of the men spent every cent they had on booze, and then borrowed from the crewmates to buy more.

I meet Kaare for the first time in Amsterdam. He was lying in his upper bunk in the cabin he shared with another imbiber, also named Kaare (we called them Little Kaare and Big Kaare, they were drinkers and brawlers, constantly in trouble, of which more later).He had gotten into a fight with some dockworkers in Amsterdam and got a severe beating. Worse, he must have had his tongue out when he got a punch in his jaw, for he bit it right off! They took him to the hospital where it was stitched back on. His tongue had swollen up and filled his whole mouth, but he pointed to a bottle of whiskey on the desk, and I gave it to him. He nodded a thank you and poured the content straight down his throat, making a sound like water sucked down a drainpipe. This would not be the last time he shocked me. This guy would have been right at home in the American Wild West.

To sea

We were leaving Amsterdam, and I sent a letter off to my parents, knowing we would be at sea for over a month. Our destination was *Ras at Tannura* (Saudi Arabia), in the Persian Gulf. It was fascinating to see our ship moving through the locks from Amsterdam to the ocean, a climb of some ten metre.

The first day in open sea, I was told to come to the bridge for steering lessons. There was a small wheel, about two feet in diameter and a gyrocompass clicking off the degrees. I think this was some kind of indoctrination for a new deck hand, for when I was finished and returned to the crew mess, the guys were laughing and pointing to the wake I had left—a zigzag pattern stretching back as far as the eye could see.

As we proceeded down the Mediterranean, the weather got warmer and warmer. One evening while I was sitting aft (the rear of the ship), pensively staring at the ships wake, it suddenly struck me: I was far away from home, heading further and further away, with no chance of return for eighteen months. I was momentarily panicked, but the anxiety was temporary and passed quickly. I never again got homesick.

One Sunday, one of the Hollanders—a guy about six foot five we called "Big Dutch", set himself up as barber, cutting the crew's hair (you could call it "crew cuts"), with more or less success. I decided I had to cut my hair too. Though I was proud of my Elvis Presley-style hair, it was getting too warm for long hair.

Big mistake. The guy gave me a brush cut, right to the skin, and the whole gang had a hearty laugh on my account. I looked like a plucked chicken for a while, to the continuing amusement of the men, and to my consternation. It was a rough world I had entered, but there was little point in complaining. This was just lesson number one in *Sailor 101,* and I intended to pass the "examination."

As we got further down the Mediterranean, the heat began to get to us. It was hard to sleep at night in our cabins, and a few of us camped out on the lifeboat deck. One fellow had brought a battery-operated record player that played the new 45 RPM single records, and he had a few of the latest American rock and roll tunes. One tune stuck in my head: Billy Vaughan's "Wonderland By Night" blared out into the empty ocean, nothing around us but the vast blanket of water and the dark, star studded sky. The large funnel hummed above us, a regular, low vibrating din, as the ship plowed through the night, this little Norway all by itself in a huge ocean.

We chatted about everything and nothing, and bonded and related as only a group of young men alone and away from home can do. It was a new world for some of us, and it seemed both romantic and a little melancholy, being so far from home.

Oftentimes, while at sea, I would go outside at night and lean over the railing, watching the sea slip by and look at the open sky, thinking about what a speck we were in the order of things, chugging along in the emptiness. Sometimes, another ship would pass, a few lights blinking in the distance; then it was gone. Once in a while, a passenger ship would cross our path, lighted up like a Christmas tree; it could be seen for miles, until it disappeared under the horizon. When the moon was full, the ships superstructure and the huge funnel would cast an eerie, fleeting shadow over the ocean. I would scare myself by thinking about what it would be like to fall overboard, with no one knowing and no chance of being found, hopelessly swimming and trashing until I could no more and the huge expanse of water mercifully swallowed me up.

Suez Canal

We arrived in *Port Said*, *Suez* and anchored in the blazing sun of that desert kingdom. The temperature was over 50 degrees, and one of the crew fried an egg on the steel deck, just to prove it could be done. We tried swimming in the canal, but the water was too hot to cool us down, and the sand burned the soles of our feet when we ventured onto it. When sleeping in the cabin I shared with the other deck hand, I would put the forced air-jet blasting directly on me, but it was just warm air, and I still perspired so much I made an outline of sweat on the bedding.

Our ship was invaded by a horde of Arabs setting up shops on deck and hawking anything from soup to nuts. They were extremely pushy and aggressive, tending not to take no for an answer. I bought a pair of shoes after much haggling, a transaction I was later to regret. The shoes got wet and just disintegrated—they were made of impregnated paper! I did buy one item that I still have: a bone-inlaid wood cigarette box that plays "The Blue Danube".

I awoke in my cabin the next morning to find fellow rifling through my clothes, putting one item in his bag, and then placing one of his "souvenirs" on the table in "trade". Before I knew it, I had "purchased" several toy camels and other junk. I had little choice, but managed to get rid of him before he took my whole wardrobe.

The Arab workers all stopped work at the same time in the late afternoon, got down on their knees facing east (towards Mecca) and prayed. Perhaps they needed to, after all the junk they foisted on us.

I observed one man wearing a heavy, European style wool overcoat in the sweltering fifty-degree heat. I asked how he could possibly stand it, and was told that in this heat, wool actually absorbed the perspiration and helped him keep cool.

One of the Dutchmen had a vial of some yellowish liquid he had bought from an Arab, purported to be "Spanish Fly". This was a chemical that was supposed to act as an aphrodisiac. He put it in a mug of coffee and offered it to the Dutch stewardess. We all watched intently to see if she would turn into a nymphomaniac, but we were disappointed. It was probably just coloured water they had sold him.

It seemed to take forever to reach *Ras at Tannura*, a desolated oil port in the Gulf, on the edge of the Saudi Arabian desert. There were no women, and as the Saudis did not allow alcohol, our thirsty crew had to drink Coca-Cola and watch American movies in the American compound. After a couple of days of filling crude, we departed for Manila in the Philippines.

Philiphines

By the time we anchored in *Manila Bay*, we had been onboard (we didn't count Ras at Tanura as land) ship for over a month and the guys were just about bonkers, hating the sight of each other. As soon as we arrived, we were surrounded by little boats selling "Manila Rum", a potent 160 proof rum, for which we traded cigarettes (cigarettes were tax free for us and we paid just one dollar a carton), one carton to a one liter bottle. By the time we were cleared to come into dock, there were not enough crewmembers sober enough to handle the wheel and the ropes. Even the boatswain had passed out in his cabin, and I watched "Big Dutch", slowly sliding along the wall until he fell flat onto the deck and stayed there. The captain came out on the bridge and looked down onto the carnage, lamenting the sight of "his *Norwegian* sailors", scattered prostrate around the decks in various degrees of drunken stupor. He had no choice but to stay at anchor until the flower of this seafaring nation sobered up.

The pubs and the whorehouses in Manila did a brisk job while we were there, and I must say, I did not see much of the city. It was monsoon time and the streets were huge water puddles. We spent most of our free time in the many pubs, where the women servers doubled as prostitutes, with rooms upstairs for their use, just like in an American western movie. They encouraged the patrons to buy them drinks, but this largesse abruptly stopped when one of our guys tasted the drink he had bought for his woman and found it to be coloured water. He broadcasted his find, and the rest of our gang got busy tasting their mate's drinks—every one being coloured water! I am surprised there was no riot, but the guys were probably too preoccupied with their drinking and the women.

Our next stop was Zebu. We tied up at the pier of American Standard Oil in Opon, a small town across the bay from Zebu. I was determined that I should see more than the inside of bars there, and walked downtown by myself. The locals were very friendly and all seemed to speak English—better than me. One experience showed me how small differences in culture can lead to misunderstanding: While walking down a street in Opon, I noticed that the shop owners standing in front of their small shops appeared to be waving me away. They would move their open hands, palms down, in a downward sweep, a "go away" movement to me, but the smiles on their faces indicated otherwise. Later, I asked them why they were waving me away, and they said, no, it meant "come here", which in my culture is indicated by an upwards and inwards movement of the hand. They were, on the contrary, inviting me to enter their shops. One shop owner had a young daughter—her name was Dominga Espinoza—who seemed to take a liking to me. Her father intimated that I might want to stay there. I politely declined, but I did correspond with her for some time afterwards.

We were getting ready to leave Zebu. Little Kaare had spent all his money on booze, and wanted some money to go back on shore for a few more drinks. When he could not convince anyone to lend him money, he hit on the idea of setting up a bet. He said he would jump from the ship into the sea and swim to shore if we would give him a certain amount each. I should explain that the ship was now empty and rode very high above the water—about twelve meters. The swim to shore would have been about thirty or forty meters. After collecting the money for the bet, the crazy guy jumped overboard. Somehow, he managed to hit the water straight, head first, and after a long pause, he appeared on the water, swimming ashore.

Later that day, the ship was getting ready to sail, but Kaare was missing. We sent a party to look for him. Fortunately, Opon was not a large town, and we found him sitting in a pub, his wet money drying on the table, still drinking beer. We dragged him back to the ship, where the captain was hopping mad—he had delayed the sailing by a couple of hours.

By the time we left Zebu, the drunks among the crew had sobered up, having long ago spent all of their money. One guy, we called him Clark Gable, for he bore a very strong resemblance to that movie star, mustache and all, was going around collecting *Aqua Velva* shaving lotion from the others. At first, I refused to give him mine, but his persistent supplications wore me down, and I gave him the bottle, lest "he should die!" Shaking the greenish liquid into a cup, he told me that I "had saved his life".

"Clark Gable" had been a member of Captain Linge's commando group in the war, made up mainly of Norwegian expatriates making commando raids on the Germans along the coast of occupied Norway. The long, boring waiting in port, interspersed with intensely stressful and dangerous missions, made alcoholics of many of these young men.

Clark had a very strong and deep voice, and when he got drunk, he would sit on the deck and sing old war songs, both in Norwegian and English, his voice booming across the whole ship. It was a sad and pitiful sight, this former brave warrior now a common drunkard.

Working at sea

In open sea like the Pacific, the ship would be on autopilot during the days, with just one officer on the bridge or in the map plotting room behind the wheelhouse. We would do four-hour shifts; four hours on, four hours off, so we worked twelve hours in a twenty-four hour period, seven days a week, or an eighty-four hour week. Accumulated overtime would usually be taken as shore leave, or paid upon the completion of the contract. During the day, the deck hands would scrape rust and paint. Painting is a constant, ongoing job on a ship, where salt water quickly corrodes anything metal not properly coated with paint. We would also clean cabins and scrub decks.

At night, two men took turns steering and being lookouts, one hour at the wheel and one hour at the bow keeping an eye out for other vessels. You could tell if they were on a collision course because you would see both the green starboard and the red port lights. You would then signal the wheelman by ringing the ships bell three times if the ship was straight ahead, one ring for a ship on starboard and two rings for port side.

The name starboard *has a Viking origin; it comes from the Norse "styrebord", or steering board; essentially an oar tied to the aft right side of the boa and used to steer with..* Port *is a later expression, meaning the port or loading side of the ship. Originally, it was called "larboard", also meaning the* loading side.

In large oceans such as the Pacific you seldom saw any other vessels, and the job was very boring. In the moonlight, I watched the flying fish jump, glittering as they left the water and sailed along, landing on the metal deck with a thump. They were not truly flying; their little, thin wings could not carry them far, but they jumped high enough and glided far enough to land on our ship. They were not edible, so we would just scoop them up and throw them overboard before they started smelling.

One night I was on the lookout when a small bird alighted on my arm. We were far from any shore, so there must have been a small island somewhere. The poor bird was totally exhausted and huffed and puffed while perched on my arm, seemingly having lost all fear. I took him aft to the mess hall to try to feed him some bread, but he would not eat anything. I let him sit on the deck railing, and after a while he up and flew away. I am sure if he could talk, he would have said "thank you".

Later, I realized from where that bird had come.

The following night, I had a scare that still sends a chill down my spine. The moonlit sky was starry and clear. We were somewhere in the Indian Ocean and I was at the wheel. Presently, I thought I saw something dark in the far distance, straight ahead. It was just a faint, shadowlike spot in the horizon. At first I thought I must be mistaken, for there was not supposed to be any island in this area, and I had not heard a bell from the lookout. I tried to check the radar, but I was unfamiliar with its use. There was a blip on the dark screen, but I was unsure of what it meant. But the shadow ahead would not go away; it was not moving, but we were, and it kept growing larger. I rang the bell, hoping to get the lookout's attention. No luck. I realized he had fallen asleep, not unusual in these warm, quiet nights. The third mate was in the map plotting room right behind me, but he was a terrible grouch and I was afraid of being called a fool for bothering him with a mirage. I let go the wheel and fetched the mate's binoculars. It was no imagination; there was an island all right, I could make out the dark silhouette of trees against the moonlit, sparkling ocean surface. The third mate had clearly made a plotting error, and we were headed for disaster! I let go the wheel again and peeked through the door to the plotting room. He was sitting at the table, looking at a map in front of him. "Do you want me to steer around the island in front of us?" I asked smartly. He grunted and came out to take a look. "Hva faen!" (What the devil!), he swore, and hollered "hard port". I twirled the wheel counter clockwise several turns, and the ship slowly responded, leaning over to starboard as we slowly veered to port, and then straightening out as it responded to my frantic turning of the little wheel in front of me. The island passed on the starboard side, still a couple of hundred yards away.

The engine room duty officer called the bridge and asked what was going on. The third mate gave him some story about having to yield for an oncoming ship, and, of course, blaming the other ship for getting too close. There would have been no possibility of reversing the engines to stop in time. The ship, even though relatively small by today's standards, would have taken more than a mile to come to a dead stop. Had we hit the island at full speed, there would likely have been an explosion and fire, with serious consequences for the ship and for us. The third mate would have suffered more than an embarrassment!

No one but the engine room noticed the maneuver and I am proud to say I contained my urge to tell everyone what an idiot we had for a third mate. He never mentioned the subject again, but he was very friendly to me after that and I accepted it as his way of saying thanks.

I wondered if that little bird had tried to tell me something. If so, I now know what it was.

Life at sea was mostly boring routine, but fortunately, the ship had a fair library of which I took good advantage. Another deckhand, Ron, also liked to read, and we got on reading books by the English humorist P.G. Wodehouse, translated into Norwegian. The translation must have been a good one, because when I later read him in English (after having immigrated to Canada and learned rudimentary English) I did not find him half as funny in the original language. However, Ron and I read every one of his books in the ship's library, and had much enjoyment from it. I recall the two of us on a scaffold along shipside, painting, and quoting some hilarious line from one of Wodehouse's books, while laughing so hard we almost fell overboard. These are the small pleasures in life that one remembers fondly, while other memories fade.

I get in trouble—twice

Big Dutch and I did not get along well. I had not forgiven him for shaving my head, but as he was much bigger and stronger, I could not do much, other than verbally picking on him, using sarcasm when I could get away with it. One thing that really got to him was my critical remarks about his drinking ability—he was the one I watched falling flat on his face on deck in a drunken stupor in Manila Bay, and I didn't let him forget it. He was not a bad guy—if he was he would have flattened me long ago, but his inability to hold liquor was an embarrassment in the macho culture of a Norwegian merchant ship. One day in port, he challenged me to a drinking contest, and I, big mouth, accepted!

This was the fight at the O.K. Coral in a nautical setting. We congregated in the boatswain's cabin, about a dozen men, with two guys as "umpires," one representing me, the other Big Dutch. They poured a glass of cheap whiskey for each of us and kept score of the number downed by each. Well, after I don't know how many drinks, Big Dutch did his falling down routine and I was declared the winner! I staggered upstairs, sick as a dog, heading for my cabin on the other side of the ship. I did not make it—I fell down into a large coil of rope, where I slept it off, no one the wiser. I was a bit of a hero for a short time, to the consternation and embarrassment of Big Dutch. I had stupidly made an enemy of him for no good reason, and was to find out later just how dangerous it could be to make enemies far from home on a ship in the middle of the Pacific.

It was a starry night … well, it was a hot, clear night anyhow, and I was trying to catch a breeze, leaning over the railing aft, watching the ships wake, and smoking a Chesterfield cigarette. I heard someone behind me, and before I could react, there was Big Dutch, grabbing me by the neck and leg and lifting me up, holding me over the railing with the oozing, foaming dark water of the Pacific ten meters below. I did not even yell, knowing it would be useless. I was frozen in fear, dangling above the foaming brine, fully expecting to be dropped into the dark waters. However, when he did not drop me immediately, I realized I had a reprieve, and after a minute or so he pulled me back in and sat me down. "You zee," he said in his broken English, "I could dropped you in the zee and nobody know nothing." I nodded, and thanked him for not doing so. I told him that murder was a bit severe as payback for a bit of sarcasm. I think he was trying to make a point, and I got it just fine. I determined not ever to tease him again, and we maintained an uneasy truce after that.

It was not to be the last time my big mouth got me in hot water. My next altercation was with Big Kaare, the brawler and former boxer. I sure knew how to pick my enemies.

I cannot remember exactly what it was that got me in trouble with Kaare, probably a bit of my verbal sparring got the better of him. Verbal dexterity doesn't cut much ice with a boxer. But I think the one thing that really pissed him off was my refusal to lend him money, after he had spent all of his own on women, wine and song. For good measure, I told him how foolish was such behaviour.

One night, in harbour, I think it was Singapore; I was on duty on the bridge. Kaare had been on shore leave, and suddenly showed up in the semi-dark in front of me. I hadn't heard him coming. "Hello", he said, and hit me square on the jaw. I awoke some time later, on my back on the bridge deck, looking straight up at the twinkling stars. I soon realized what had happened, but resolved not to tell the Captain. If reported, it was a serious offense since he had attacked me whilst on duty. It would have meant, in the least, a severe financial penalty for Kaare, the guy who never had any money in the first place. So, I said nothing to the Captain, but the next morning at breakfast I gave him proper hell. At first he thought I had reported him, but I told him I had not and would not, as it was no use, but that if he ever did anything like that again, I would see that he was sent home—with no money. He started to laugh, partly from relief, but also because he probably found my anger amusing—reminiscent of a Chihuahua barking at a Great Dane. He thought I was a real trooper, or a "never-minder" (a devil may care guy) as he used to call me thereafter. Inadvertently, I had made a friend and gotten a protector; he became my unpaid bodyguard thereafter. God knows I needed one.

Persian Gulf

From Zebu, Philippines, we went back to Abadan in the Persian Gulf, to take on another load of crude oil. On the way, we went through the routine of cleaning out the inside of the tanks. Crude is more volatile than refined gasoline, as it contains nitro glycerin in its raw state. Thus, when empty, dangers of explosion are even higher than when under load, until the tanks have been blown and fumes cleared out. This was accomplished by hanging up a wind funnel made of sailcloth above each tank section, forcing the air into the tanks thus blowing out gases while en route. A small burning flame was later lowered into the tanks to ensure it was cleared of gases. Smoking was strictly forbidden, loaded or empty, except in your cabin or the very aft, behind the caboose (cook house).

We arrived in Abadan, a place not, even then, too friendly towards westerners. The British had left a few years before, and the refineries had been severely damaged in the prior conflict. The locals went around telling us that they had "beaten the English", but looking at them I got the impression that they were the ones at the losing end.

Iran was (and is) a Muslim country and we could not buy alcohol at shore. However, their religion apparently did not forbid them to sell "moonshine" or home made hooch, which was barely drinkable, even for our un-discriminating tastes. I remember one of them telling me that he was a Communist, but when I asked him to explain what being a Communist meant to him, he could not, and I don't think it was just our limited English that stumped him.

We were told to be very careful with the natives, because not so long before, crewmembers of another Norwegian ship had thrown one of the swill-sellers overboard and he sank like a stone and drowned because of all the bottles of moonshine he carried in his pockets. The guys that did it were, of course, arrested and got the death penalty, even though it was an accident—they did not mean to kill the poor wretch. The Norwegian government saved them by paying a large fine (bribe) to the Iranian government and a monetary settlement with the aggrieved family of the man.

Our lone Englishman, John, the other deckhand, Nels, and I decided to take a walk in downtown Abadan. It was not a wise decision. Somehow, we got talking to some young men outside a restaurant, and John told them he was English, which seemed to engender some hostility with the men. Suddenly, they started shouting at him, and one brandished a knife. Well, John took off like a jackrabbit, and we followed on his heels. I cut down a side street, and hailed the first cab I found. Nels was right behind me, and also jumped in the cab. When we got to the ship, John was nowhere in sight, and we were quite concerned. We were debating what to do—some thought we should go at shore and look for him, others said we should advise the captain. Then we saw him, running like hell toward the ship, but no one following him. He arrived onboard, wrung out with sweat and panting like a dog. He had outrun his pursuers. We didn't go downtown again.

Pakistan and India

We all breathed a sigh of relief when we left Abadan, heading for Karachi, Pakistan. We made four calls in all to Karachi, and one to Bombay, India, just "down the coast" in the Arabian Sea. I was becoming quite well acquainted with that part of the world. Karachi, at that time, had been plagued with cholera epidemics, so we all had to get vaccinated before entering port.

The city was then really two parts: the "native" section, the majority of the city, and the European, or British quarters, remnants of the colonial times. The English there did not seem aware that the sun had set on that part of their Empire. For example, when we went to the movie theatre, we had to stand while they played *God Save the Queen* before the movie began. The streets were reasonably clean and you could see the British nationals sitting on terraces and in tea parlors sipping their afternoon tea, right out of a Rudyard Kipling novel.

Not so in the "native" section. The streets were filthy and crowded, and I observed on several occasions the locals squatting down, reliving themselves right in the street gutters. Vendors were hawking their wares and selling something cooked in a pot resembling spaghetti, which the patrons then ate with their fingers directly from the pot. In the pubs, there was a hole in the floor, usually in a corner, where you could urinate or defecate at your pleasure, standing up. It was shielded by a half-wall without a door. One "pub" we visited had a large metal barrel with cold water in it, where the empty glassed were dumped, then picked out and dried with a towel before refilling. The "bartender" repeatedly spat into the barrel. I guess it is redundant to say that I did not buy any beer there. It must have been a parasite's paradise, a haven for viruses of all kinds.

Generally, we would patronize the hotels in the European part of the city, and when at the end of an evening of imbibing we staggered outside, there were half a dozen taxicabs racing toward us, intent on being first to pickup their rides. We usually preferred the services of the more leisurely (and less dangerous) horse-drawn taxis, but one experience got me so upset I stopped utilizing them. This taxi-driver had problems with his poor horse, and whipped him mercilessly until the horse had turned around inside his hitching. We yelled at him to stop, then paid our fare and left, but I had a hard time forgetting about the poor horse. This kind of cruelty, to a poor defenseless hard working horse, or any animal for that matter, is something I cannot abide, and it troubled me greatly.

One street had about three hundred prostitution houses. They were not really houses, but individual "rooms" with a bamboo curtain in front, and a flap what you could open to peak inside to view the commodity. Some had the bamboo curtain rolled up so you could see right in to their residence. Another deck hand, more of a "man of the world" than I, took me along one evening to view the goings on and possibly sample the wares. We stopped at a place where the bamboo curtain was open and a middle-aged man and woman were standing with two young girls, their daughters, between seventeen and twenty years of age and not ugly. The parents were prostituting their children, a rather common sight there. We paid the mother, and she put the money inside her brassiere. I lost my courage, but my buddy went ahead. Lucky for me, because a few days later he had gonorrhea, and had to suffer the indignity of having our sadistic captain give him a penicillin needle in the buttocks, in full view of the men.

This "public needling" became a tradition of sorts, with several men, usually the same group, having to be injected shortly after we left harbour. Some guys consider it an achievement, on par with the notches in the belt of a gunslinger. I asked one gonorrhea veteran what it was like to get this illness, and he said it was very painful when urinating, but after getting the needle, it went away after a day or so. They must have been a bunch of masochists!

Karachi had a quite nice Zoo, which I visited. It was probably the most enlightened thing I did while we were there. I regret the opportunities missed by not taking the time to see some of the cultural and historical aspects of the places we visited. It seemed all we did was pub-crawling. But, I was only sixteen and had not developed much of a cultural sense, though I think I had more than most, if not all of the crew.

I don't remember much about Bombay, except that a tattoo artist came onboard, and I got talked into getting a tattoo—a small one on my arm. Some of the guys had large tattoos all over. One poor fellow kept tattooing his girlfriend's name on his arm, except that he kept changing girlfriends, or they kept changing him, so consequently he had to cover up the old name and tattoo the new name below it. It made for a strange looking tattoo. I told him he better stop changing girlfriends or he would run out of arm space.

It was in Bombay that I first collected on the I.O.U. from Kaare. We were in a pub, and one of the older sailors had gotten pretty drunk. For some reason (I can only imagine!), he got angry with me and was getting ready to hit me when I saw Big Kaare across the room, and yelled to him for help. Kaare came over, took a chair and swung it over his head and right down on the unfortunate fellow's skull. Both the chair and the guy crashed to the floor. We were politely urged to leave, which we did. I never again had trouble with that man; in fact I had little trouble with anyone after that, though a few had the temerity to suggest I was propitiating Kaare for my protection. Indeed, I was. That's probably why I am alive today.

Singapore

Our next destination was *Singapore*. Singapore in those days (1959) was not like today—it was still relatively poor, and a "free harbour"; i.e. there were no duties or taxes, and goods were very cheap—especially electronic goods and toys, and such items as watches made in Japan (Japanese manufacturing was producing knock-off copies much like China is doing today). I bought a new suit made of some kind of silky material, and was wearing it on shore the next evening. When we returned to the ship, most of the men quite drunk and noisy, Kaare got into an altercation with one of the Singaporean guards at the harbour. He walked up to the man and said in English "salute when you see a Norwegian sailor". I don't know what the man answered, but it was not to Kaare's liking, for he hit the guy and knocked him down. Another guard managed to call for help, and the local police overran us. I stood on the pier and watched the proceedings, thinking I was safe since I had nothing to do with the fight, but someone clubbed me over the head and I ended up prostrate on the pier, in a puddle of oil and sawdust. When I came to, all was quiet; I didn't see anyone. I picked myself up and stumbled onboard without any further mishap. I had a bump on my head, and my new suit was a total write-off, with oil and sawdust all over it.

Kaare was brought onboard the next day, before we sailed; sober, with a black eye and a couple of bumps on his head that did not belong there. I guess the captain paid the fine for him, and he would be broke again for some time. I told him his fighting had cost me my new suit, but he didn't seem too sorry about that, he blamed the watchman for not showing enough respect!

"The outcasts"

Kaare was a study in self-destructive and borderline psychopathic personality. He was the son of a vice-president of a large insurance company in Bergen. He managed to get a high school education, which was a fair education in those days, but his unruliness kept getting him into trouble. He was an amateur boxer, and this made him even more dangerous when drunk and provoked. A regular Jeckyl and Hyde, he was pleasant and jocular when sober, but a hellish fighting machine when drunk. He was tall, muscular, and good looking, and could have been successful at shore if he really wanted; but something went wrong. He went to sea and ended up jumping ship in Australia, where he lived illegally for about two years. Then he got into trouble with the law and was sent home, after finishing a short stint in an Australian jail. Back home, he met a very beautiful blonde whom he married. His father got him a job at his insurance company, until one day he lost his temper and hit his father right there in his office. That was enough for the old man—he fired him. After that debacle, he left his wife at home and went to sea again, on the *Gilda.*

I never did find out much about Little Kaare, his buddy, but he was of the same ilk. He did not get as belligerent, and that was just as well, since he was quite a bit smaller of stature. However, he still managed to get into trouble. One day he came back from shore leave without his front teeth. He had gotten into a fight with the Karachi police and they knocked them out with a baton and threw him in jail overnight, from where they delivered him in the morning, collecting his fines from the captain.

Little Kaare had a peculiar habit. When he got drunk, he would bet someone that he could eat the glass from which he was drinking at the time, and then proceed to do so. He would chew it into small fragments, and then stick out his tongue to show the glass bits were all there, whereupon he would swallow the whole thing! One day he tried to bet with someone that he could eat the chair on which he was sitting. Having seen him eating a water glass, no one took him up on the bet! I don't know what use glass eating has in the evolutionary process; I think he was probably working on a dead end.

One late evening the two Kaares came back very drunk, as usual, and I walked in to their cabin to see something I could barely believe: the two of them were urinating into a bottle, and then drinking their own urine! I think they were trying to reuse the alcohol. It is the most unusual attempt at conservation I have ever seen.

They had a habit of selling their clothes at shore when running out of money, then buying new ones on credit from the ships store. One evening they were going to shore, it was rather chilly, and Little Kaare asked if he could borrow my jacket, as it fit him quite well. I reluctantly let him have it, after he promised me that he would not sell it, no matter what. Well, the next day at breakfast, he told me that he had sold my jacket, and that he was very sorry. The two of them were intently watching me to see how I reacted. I just told him I would not lend him any more clothes. He left the table and returned with my jacket. They had a good laugh on me, but I was just happy to have my jacket back. If anything, I was surprised that he had *not* sold it.

I think, somehow the two of them reveled in their reputation for reckless behaviour—a kind of cloak of courage covering a rather insecure ego. They were skilled sailors and not reckless at all when on duty, and quite pleasant and helpful in their daily routine, but when on shore and with a few drinks in them, they turned into madmen.

Mealtimes were a carnal feeding frenzy. At breakfast, if either of the Kaare's, or Big Dutch got hold of the plate of eggs first, they would just dump the dozen or so of fried eggs on their own plate and send the empty plate back to the kitchen for more. Meanwhile we chickens had to wait until the big boys were sated. Little Kaare once, on a lark, ate twenty boiled eggs for breakfast.

In the routine onboard a ship, mealtimes were mini-feasts and a break from the boredom. The food was plentiful and tasty. The cook had a special, exalted status on a ship, and he'd better be good at his job.

Fiji

From Singapore we sailed to *Suva*, the capital of Fiji. It was a beautiful place, with a colonial past, and quite English, though the citizens were mostly black. I remember there was a policeman directing traffic in a stall at a four-way intersection downtown. He had long white gloves, a white bandolier across his shoulder and chest, and a white English "bobby" type helmet. I was impressed. No one managed to get into trouble there, and the short visit was pleasant, almost serene, and rather uneventful.

The next stop in Fiji was an oil pumping station located about two kilometers from a small, Lilliputian town called *Ba.* The crew hired a horse-drawn rickshaw to take them to Ba, but I missed the departure, and decided to walk. I am glad I did. I walked past little farm huts and coconut groves, and watched the natives harvest the coconuts by clambering up the tall trees, toeing into pre-cut steps in the tree trunks, and chopping off the nuts with a swift blow of their machetes. I got talking with one man, in very halting English, and he invited me home to his hut. There he offered me homemade beer, which was quite good, as I recall. I gave them a little money and went on my way, arriving in Ba in the early evening, after about a one-hour walk.

The town of Ba had a small narrow-gauge railway that went right through the middle of town, and a little train with a Lilliputian steam engine huffing and puffing across the main street, unaided by any kind of crossing barriers or railway crossing signs. Locals would hitch a ride, jumping effortlessly on and off along the route. It was quite idyllic, the people seemed happy and I did not see any obvious poverty there.

Later, I met up with the gang from the ship, they had already downed a number of homemade brews, but we got through the evening without incident; not that they could find anyone to pick a fight with among those happy-go-lucky people. The whole place seemed to me like a bit of Paradise. I am sure it was not, but it was pretty. Amazingly, forty years later, in Toronto, I met someone from Suva who knew Ba well, the place was just the way I described it—so I know it was not a dream. Would that I could go back for a visit.

Australia the Beautiful

Next, we were off to *Australia*—first *Sidney* and then *Brisbane*. On the way, we celebrated Christmas and New Years in 48-degree temperatures. It was my first Christmas away from home, and for me a very unusual one.

The captain provided a few bottles of booze and some beer for the holidays, and the boozehounds traded goods for the allotment of the teetotalers and more moderate drinkers. Christmas Eve, after the traditional meal, the drinking began in earnest, and so did the arguing and fighting. Little Kaare and one of the Dutchmen got into an argument, which they decided to settle with a little pugilistic. Fortunately, they were too drunk to do much damage, so they mostly wrestled and clawed at each other. The last I remember of it was the two of them, like two cats, in an "embrace", rolling down the stairs to the hallway. That was enough for me. I went to bed.

The next day the mess hall was in a horrible condition (you could say the mess was a mess), and I got elected to help clean up. New Years came and went in the same fashion, except I don't remember much about it; I kept to my cabin to avoid any physical harm.

We arrived in Sydney in the morning, and I was totally awed at the beauty of the harbour. This was before the opera house was built, but the harbour was still spectacular. I stayed away from the bars and got to see a fair bit of the city, visiting Luna Park and other places of interest. I also visited the Norwegian Sailors Mission where I wrote letters home and read Norwegian newspapers.

The last evening there, on my return to the ship, I found a wild bacchanalia in progress. Someone had brought a couple of women onboard, unbeknownst to the captain, and the men were amusing themselves with these unfortunate females, who were totally inebriated and insensible. I told the boatswain, who for a change was sober, and he went there to tell the men to get the women ashore, because we were leaving. We weren't, but it worked, so the gang carried the two women—while singing old sea shanties—to the gatehouse where they dumped them on the sidewalk. I said to the gatekeeper "aren't these Norwegian sailors crazy?" He answered, and I quote him verbatim "yes, but the Greeks are worse, they bring onboard young boys!"

The next stop was Brisbane, in the Queensland Province. We had to go in dry dock there to have the annual compulsory seaworthy inspection of the ship's underside, and thus we had a whole week to spend there. As I recall, Brisbane was a bit of a cow town at the time, you could see horse saddles and other "cowboy" equipment for sale, except they didn't call them cowboys there. It was very hot, around forty every day—January is mid summer in Australia, and Queensland is close to the outback and semi-arid. Our intrepid crew was happy to discover that the Queensland Province had legalized prostitution, and the business was brisk. At least, no one got gonorrhea there. The only excitement we had was that one of the Dutch guys and the Jewish guy jumped ship. They had bought an old motorcycle on shore, which they used as their "getaway" vehicle. We received a letter from them a few months later; they had managed to get jobs, though I am not sure if they had obtained legal standing. In those days, Australia was actively seeking immigrants, especial white Europeans whom they would actually pay to emigrate. Immigration was a mere formality if you were white and came from the "right" part of the world, i.e. Northern Europe.

To partly replace them we got a Norwegian who had lived there since the war. He was an incredible grouch and a drunk, and it didn't take me long to get into an argument with him. However, he had seen better times, and was not very strong, so when he got drunk and belligerent, he just waved his arms and punched great holes in the air. Even verbal sparring was beyond him, as he became totally incoherent in both Norwegian and English—"bilingually incoherent"—I have known a few Canadians like him.

And so we left fair Australia heading back to the Persian Gulf for more of the black liquid gold. I was sorry to leave. I have never been a bigot, but I must say that seeing white people upon arrival in Australia was a breath of fresh air. And food! We could have milk again, and fresh vegetables. We had not been able to get milk in the far eastern and African countries, since milk too easily transmits decease, and all our vegetables were canned. Australia was like an oasis of western civilization.

Since then, I have often wondered how immigrants to Canada from Asian and African countries feel when they arrive in a strange country with such different culture, climate and language; at least in the "old" days, before the services and attention that today's immigrant gets. No wonder the immigrant communities stick together. They must feel a bit like I felt, engulfed in a "sea" of foreign culture and language.

The Persian Gulf—again.

We loaded in the port of Mena Al-Ahmadi, Kuwait. I noticed quite a difference in the people there. Kuwait was an oil-rich nation even then, and some of the largesse obviously drifted down to the plebeians, for it was the only place in the Gulf where the natives didn't try to sell us junk and trinkets, but purchased goods from us. The other thing I noticed was than they were well dressed, and many wore western style jeans and shirts.

I remember hearing a story that the Sultan there was so rich that he had twenty Cadillac's and when one got a flat tire, he just took another car. The workers were not driving Cadillac's, or any car, but they were well dressed.

Indonesia

After loading, we headed back through the Arabian Sea into the Indian Ocean, sailing through the strait of Malacca to *Palembang*, on the isle of *Sumatra*, *Indonesia*. The Dutch men onboard were a bit apprehensive, because the Indonesian war of independence from the Dutch had finished just a few years before, and the feelings against the Dutch were still fairly strong. However, our short stay in Palembang was uneventful. Palembang is up the river a ways from the coast, and before cleared to come in, we anchored in the middle of the river mouth in the jungle. The natives came out in their canoes, and would dive for anything we threw to them. Empty cans were in great demand; apparently they made kitchen utensils, pots and pans, from these empty tin cans. They did not try to barter—they had nothing to sell, but they put on quite a show of swimming around picking up the cans we threw on the water.

We left Palembang, and sailed down the coast to an oil pumping station called *Tandjung-uban*, just outside a little town called *Tandjung-bala*i. We anchored outside the port one evening. I was "on watch" when I saw a fire in the jungle and heard voices over the water. There must have been a small village there, but I could not see any houses or huts. Then I heard the most unusual thing: a record player playing one of the latest American hits of the time (1959), "The Story of My Life" (I think by *Neil Sedaka*). How quaint! Western popular culture had penetrated far into the jungles of Sumatra.

We tied up at Tandjung-uban and began pumping. As just a few people were needed for pumping, the rest of us got shore leave, and went off to town. I decided to go by myself, expecting trouble with the gang, as they were probably plenty "thirsty" by now. There was a banana plantation nearby, and I was intrigued to see bananas on a stalk—I had never seen how bananas grew before, banana trees being rather scarce in Norway. The main street of the town, the only street, had a few shops and restaurant/bars. The bar owners cranked up old gramophones and played rock and roll music, it blaring out to the street in competition for customers. I think the few tankers arriving to deliver oil to the small refinery was the only business they had, the banana farmers didn't spend much time or money there, I am sure. I ended up in a largely empty restaurant and was treated like a king. I spent the whole afternoon there, and most of my money.

I got friendly with the owner's dog. I love animals, and decided I wanted to buy one of the puppies she had. It was crazy, for we were not allowed to keep pets on the ship. The owner refused, so I left some money on the counter, grabbed a puppy and got into a rickshaw to go back to the ship. The owner came running after me, gave me back the money and grabbed the puppy. I went onboard without the dog, and upon sobering up, realized I was lucky he stopped me. Not many people would have such compassion for a mongrel pup that they would refuse money for it in order to keep it from a drunken sailor. That pub owner was a gem.

The next day, I found that Dutch and the two Kaare's had brought a puppy onboard. It was a black and white spotted dog, and they were hiding it in their cabin, feeding it canned sardines and condensed milk. After a couple of days, the boatswain got wind of it, and wanted to throw the dog overboard. There was uproar; the boys took up a petition and presented it to the captain, who avoided "mutiny" by giving in and letting us keep the dog. The sardines must have been powerful food because he grew very fast and became our mascot and entertainment. Later, someone brought a cat litter onboard, but the boatswain threw them overboard but one, which we got to keep after much serious negotiating. Next, it was a parrot, but after that the captain said, enough! So, our menagerie was now a dog, a cat and a parrot. I think the captain theorized that if we had animals to care for we would be better behaved. If so, I think he was mistaken.

There was a middle-aged sailor ("able-bodied seaman") whom I often spoke with. He did not drink, and managed somehow to steer clear of trouble with the others. I recall once I was visiting with him in his small cabin. He had a photo of his wife and children on his drawer top, and spoke softly about his family at home. He told me that he would like to quit the sea, but could not get work at shore that would pay anywhere near what he was making as an able-bodied seaman with his seniority. He also pointed out a real conundrum for seafarers: you get it in the blood, and while you long for home while at sea, you soon get tired of land life, and long to go back to the sea. Once you got the "bug", you are not happy anywhere. He told me to quit the sea while I could, get some education or training at shore, and stay put. It was good advice, which I eventually did take; or at least, I did leave the sailor life, but staying put I did not.

Djibouti—Hell on Earth

We returned to Abadan to refill our tanks, and headed to the city of *Aden*, in the *Gulf of Aden*. Aden was still a British protectorate at the time. There were English-speaking locals hiring themselves out as "shopping guides", and I hired one to help me buy a shirt. I purchased one, only to find out later that it was a ladies blouse. So much for "guides". Aden was reasonably clean for the area, and the locals seemed fairly content and not too poor.

Our next stop, Djibouti (then French Somaliland) was something else. Never before or since did I see such utter poverty and dereliction anywhere. The streets were just dirt, and young crippled children crawled around our table when in a "restaurant" or bar, trying to sell us junk or just begging, uttering over and over again "Bakshish! Bakshish!" (alms, mercy). Communication was very difficult, as the only language they spoke other than their local dialect was French. I was told that parents would not only prostitute their daughters, but would maim their children so they could make some money begging. Throngs of people followed us everywhere, hoping to get a handout, and it seemed that half the population was sleeping in the streets, the more fortunate having a cot and a blanket.

I went outside to relieve myself, as there was no toilet inside the pub, and leaned against the building corner in the dark, urinating into what I thought was an empty alley. Suddenly, I heard a holler, and a man got up with his cot under his arm, sounding quite perturbed, and shuffling further down the alley where he plunked his cot down and laid down on it again, paying me no further attention—nothing unusual there.

In the bar, Little Kaare had taken a liking to some kittens running about. He bought a can of condensed milk, put one of them on his table and poured the milk on the tabletop with the cat in the middle. This became a source of amusement for the crowd, including the locals there, which gathered around to watch the goings on and making "helpful" suggestions. Eventually, he stuffed his pockets full of kittens and went onboard with them. The poor kittens were doomed to a wet grave in the ocean.

It is strange that people like these guys, who really don't give a damn about much, including themselves, go totally "banana" over animals, especially cats and dogs. I guess there is some kindness deep down in their hearts, brought out by these small, cute and defenseless creatures. There is something good in everyone, if you can get past the flotsam and jetsam in their soul.

There were a bevy of assorted prostitutes trying to entice the men, and eventually, the guys drifted off with one or the other. The Ethiopian and Somaliland women are fine featured and many were pretty. In one pub, the owner's daughter was quite a beauty—a girl about eighteen, working at the bar. The owner was doing his best to sell me on one of his paramours, but I declined, telling him it was either his daughter or no one. I really didn't expect him to agree, but after a little hesitation he did acquiesce, and we went off in a taxi to the girl's home. We were driving through the countryside, not a light shone, the night was pitch dark and I could not see where we were going. I began to lose my nerve. Alone, with a girl in the middle of the east African desert! I regretted my foolhardy action, imagining being robbed and even killed. We finally arrived in a small village of huts. I asked the taxi driver to wait for me, and went nervously with the girl to her shack, a one-room hut, with a bed and a night table on a dirt floor and not much more. There was, of course, no electricity; she had an oil lamp on a table for light. When she undressed, I noticed in the lamplight some white spots on her belly and asked what it was. "Baby", she said. I did not understand, but panicked. I put my money on the night table and ran back to the waiting taxi, which took me back to our ship. I had to go onboard to borrow taxi fare, for I had given the girl all my cash.

The next day, I was telling the guys about the incident and the strange white spots I had seen on the girl's belly. The guys laughed heartily at my naiveté. "Those are stretch-marks, you idiot!" they said, "She's had a baby!"

The other deck hand set some kind of record, even for Djibouti. Soap was a favourite barter item, in high demand there. He managed to get laid for three bars of Lux soap! He was quite proud of his bargaining skills, and achieved some temporary notoriety for this achievement. I believe this record still stands!

Djibouti was a horrible place, and it has not gotten much better since. While Norway at that time was not the rich country it is today, I had never imagined this kind of poverty and lack of respect for the individual. The French Foreign Legionnaires were prancing around, and I could see that the locals were petrified of them. They were a rough bunch and proud of it. Even *our* wild Vikings were impressed.

I came to recognize over the time I sailed in the Far East, that in the remaining colonial areas, there was a huge difference in how the "colonials" were treated. In areas of American influence, such as Kuwait, but in particular Samoa, the native population were relatively well off. In areas of British influence, such as Aden and Fiji, they were poorer, but fairly clean, and the streets were relatively safe. Where the French were involved, if Djibouti was an example, there were utter chaos, destitution, and an appalling lack of concern for the plight of the native population. At least, that was my impression, and it was the consensus of the sailors with whom I discussed this observation. French Somaliland was a depressing experience. I was relieved to leave, and fortunately, I never returned.

Lifeboat adrift

Later, somewhere in the Indian Ocean we came upon a lifeboat adrift in the sea. The straits of Malacca and the South China Sea were then, as now, known for piracy, and for a while, we thought we had found the crew of a pirated ship. We hauled the boat onboard but found no one in it. It had a ships name one it: "Melika 1" of Monrovia (a "flag of convenience" country).

Shortly thereafter, one of the old sailors started acting strange. When we asked if he had been drinking (and more importantly, where he got the booze), he denied he had been drinking at all. He said, "you guys must drink to be happy, but I am happy without alcohol". He did not smell of booze, but his demanour became more and more lethargic. The boatswain searched his cabin, and found the answer. He had gotten into the lifeboat and found medicines, in particular morphine and needles, and was injecting himself with the drug. The stupid guy could have died!

Karachi again—and the end for our busboy

Our last trip to Karachi almost cost our busboy his life. He had been ashore, drinking quite heavily, and for some reason he came back alone. The doors from deck to the living quarters were made of steel, as was the outside structure, and the door jambs were about one and a half feet high so the seawater could not slosh into the hallways during heavy seas if the door is open. Thus, you have to step up quite high to enter, something not too difficult for a sober person, but a bit of a stretch for a drunk. And drunk he was. From what we could piece together afterwards, he had fallen down and hit his face on the top of the doorjamb, smashing his nose and probably cutting a large vessel. Bleeding profusely, he just went to bed and fell asleep. When the watch came to his cabin in the morning to wake him for duty, he didn't move, and there was coagulated blood everywhere. He was transferred to hospital in Karachi, and when they carried him out on a stretcher, he looked lifeless; his face was white and his eyes closed. He had lost more than half of his blood, and he barely survived. He spent several weeks in hospital in Karachi, having several blood transfusions before he was sent home. We got a letter from him several months later, telling us that he was slowly recovering. He was very, very lucky to be alive.

Our life continued in the same vein, with several trips back and forth from the Persian Gulf to various middle and far eastern countries, and not much unusual happened. Drinking, carousing, and whoring did not fall into the unusual category; it was like a broken record—the same singers, the same tune.

Then we got some great news! We received orders to go to Texas under ballast to load and then work South America for a while. Everyone was exited and happy. We were dreadfully tired of the Far East. Alas! It was not to be …

Collision in Suez

We were taking the short route through the Suez Canal into the Mediterranean to the Atlantic. Nowadays, tankers are too large for the Suez Canal, they go around the horn of Africa (Cape of Good Hope), but we could take the shorter route through the Canal. Thus, we arrived in Suez in the morning of Friday, February 27th, 1959. I had just had breakfast and was standing by the starboard railing having a cigarette. Our ship was backing slowly to turn around, and I noticed another tanker, an American, somewhat larger than ours, moving slowly forward at about four or five knots (five mph). Suddenly, I saw several men on the other ship running from the bow along the middle gangway. In a flash I realized we were colliding! Then I felt the ship slowly lift itself up at the bow, making no sound, and just as slowly settling itself back down. I started forward but was stopped before I got amidships by our guys running toward the stern. We did not know if the other tanker was under load or not. If it was, an explosion and fire could ensue, and in a crowded harbor like Suez it would have been a disaster. Fortunately, the American tanker was also empty, but the damage to our ship's bow area was incredible. The two-inch thick steel sides had curled up like an opened sardine can, almost to the capstan. The front bow had a long crack in it, to below deck. It looked a mess.

The next few days, we worked to repair the bow enough to make the ship seaworthy. With our carpenter's help, we built scaffolding and braced it with plywood, then poured cement in between to seal the crack where it extended below the orlop (main) deck. After a few days we were certified seaworthy and got the O.K. to proceed. We cleared the canal with no further incidents. As we headed into the Mediterranean we had some heavy seas and head winds; the ship chopping against the breaking waves, her flattened bow pushing against the wind and the sea.

Return to Europe

Steering a large ship is not easy in *good* weather. In a storm, it is much harder, especially when you bow has been rearranged like ours had been. We had a gale out of the northwest, and as we headed due west, the wind and waves would push us leeward, to port. The ships bow rose with the waves, and then slid down and to port in slow motion, the gyrocompass racing, clicking off the degrees faster and faster. I turned the wheel hard to starboard, spinning it as fast as I could. I had to be careful not to take it too far right, or we could end up going down the wrong side of the wave. Thus, it was a continuing whirl—starboard against the wave on the downslide, then, as the ship caught the uplift of another wave, quickly spinning it to port until the rudder was in the straight position again. If felt like the ship had a mind of its own, in collusion with the waves rolling and breaking before us; lifting us up before pushing us down sideways. Occasionally a rogue wave would break right against the bow—before the ship could follow it up, and the whole ship would shudder as it hit, spray engulfing the forward part of the ship and rushing like a raging river down the forward orlop deck until hitting the forecastle superstructure, making a huge splash, then sloshing out the sides and back from whence it came.

I was worried that the bow would just disappear into a huge wave, taking the whole ship with it down. I gave a few nervous glances to the first mate standing on the bridge. He was totally unperturbed, sucking on his pipe and paying me no mind. I felt assured.

The storm abated after a day or so, and we had clear sailing for the rest of the trip.

Our destination was now Liverpool, England, where we were to go in dry dock for repairs before continuing to Texas. Most of the men's contracts were up, as was mine. The captain offered promotions to anyone agreeing to stay on. A few did, but most of us signed off there.

Going home

In Liverpool Kaare had his last fling—he got into a fight with an Englishman in a pub and apparently really hurt the guy, for he was arrested and put in jail with a fairly serious charge of assault. Of course, he missed the train to Newcastle-on-Tyne and the ship from there to Bergen, Norway, where the rest of us were heading. It was a sad ending for Kaare. His wife had traveled to Stavanger, in the southwest of Norway (now a thriving oil-port) where the ship made a first call on its journey to Bergen. She arrived at the ship, a tall, stunning blonde, just to find out that her husband was in a Liverpool jail.

While disembarking in Bergen, I saw Little Kaare for the last time. He was checking through customs just ahead of me. It was early April and cold and rainy—a typical early spring day in Bergen. He was standing there in sandals, a shirt, no jacket, and with a small bag in his hand, containing all his earthly belongings—the result of fifteen months of sailing the Far East! I resolved there and then that never, ever, would I go to sea again.

I shall be telling this with a sigh
Somewhere ages and ages hence:
Two roads diverged in the wood, and I—
I took the one less traveled by,
And that has made all the difference.

—*R*obert Frost: The Road Not Taken.

Our life, in our twilight years, reflects the choices we made on the way. One misstep leads to another; short-term gain is often long term pain. I remember with gratitude the old sailor who advised me against going back to sea. While my life has had its share of missteps, that "road" I did *not* take, and it *has* made a difference.

After a half-hearted attempt at returning to school, my restless spirit got the best of me again. In 1960, I again left Norway for Canada.

PART II

CHAPTER 4

Emigrating to Canada

Canada and Norway have many similarities. They are both northern countries, with cold winters, snow and mountains, sea and lakes. Except, in Canada, the distances are huge, and in between mountainous littoral western Canada—which has some topographical similarities with western coastal Norway—and the eastern Canadian coast, lies a vast plateau that has nothing at all in common with Norway: the Canadian prairie. The immense distances of the western plains, leaves one breathless upon first seeing it. There it was that several of my relatives settled and homesteaded in the early nineteenth century—moving from tiny mountain farms to the unending expanse of the Saskatchewan prairie. There I was to meet up with their descendants—sons and daughter's—in my own immigrant journey.

In July of 1960, at the age of eighteen, I arrived by train at the South Railway Train Terminal in Regina, Saskatchewan; alone, with only a few dollars in my pocket, very limited English and just a name and the telephone number of a relative there. I dialed the telephone number but got no answer. In a moment of panic, the thought struck me: *what in the world am I doing here*?

My journey to Regina began in June, 1960, following my stint in the merchant navy. I was at home when my father's cousin, Malvin, arrived from Canada, to visit the country his parents left when he was only one year old. He was now fifty, and back in the "old country" for the first time, but speaking the language fluently. Malvin was a farm boy from Saskatchewan, but had moved to Prince George, British Columbia to become a lumberjack, and was a bit of a bumpkin. Some things that he said and did were quite comical. He had been told by his parents that in Norway, people were very polite, and that it was custom to shake hands and say "thank you" for the meal, when eating at someone's home. However, when he walked up to the waitress in a cafe in Bergen and shook her hand, thanking her for the excellent meal, my brother, who was with him at the time, found it necessary to take her aside and explain to her that Malvin was an "American". She smiled and nodded that she understood. Everyone knew that Americans, and by association, Canadians, were quite eccentric in their behaviour.

He told us that as lumberjack in Prince George, he made the astronomical sum of $ 50.00 a day cutting trees with a chainsaw. With over seven kroners to a dollar, it was unheard of pay in Norway then. Although I had considered settling down, gong back to school and become a teacher like my father, my adventurous spirit was rekindled and I impetuously decided to go to Canada to make a small fortune and return back home with money and perhaps even a car! In spite of my parent's misgivings—they had some reservations about my going to a foreign land with a relative we barely knew—I agreed to go with him to Prince George to work in the bush with him. Like Molly Brown, I was unstoppable. I used all my savings to buy the ticket and was on my way.

Almost everyone in Norway has relatives in North America. When word got around that I was going to Canada, some of the townspeople would ask me to carry greetings to an uncle or aunt in "Amerika": one had an uncle in Chicago, another New York, Vancouver or Minneapolis! They had just no idea of the size and geography of North America.

It reminds me of a story told here, about a fellow living in Vancouver, B.C. whose niece was coming from England for a visit. The itinerary was boat from Liverpool to Halifax, thence train across Canada. On departure from England, the father telegraphed: "Daughter leaving today. Please meet her in Halifax". The brother telegraphed back: "You meet her—you are closer!"

Immigrants were required to travel directly to a Canadian port, not via another country, so Malvin went back on a Norwegian liner to New York City, while I traveled to Liverpool, England, where I embarked on the Carinthia, a

Cunard Line passenger vessel, which was to take me, in seven days, to Montreal, Quebec.

I was assigned a cabin below deck in second class, with two Englishmen who were Korean War veterans. We became quickly friends, in spite of my limited English. We passed the days playing cards for cigarettes, or just chatting. They would tell me some stories from their Korean experience, or just talk about women.

There were six people at my table in the dining room, and the first evening out of port, the table was full with happy travelers, mostly English and Canadians. The second day, well into the Atlantic, we encountered some rough sea, which I didn't pay much attention to, until I came for dinner. Not a soul at my table! In fact, for three days I ate pretty well alone, and I ate like a king, with superb service, as the lone diner at table number ten.

There was a lounge in the ship, and an orchestra played dance music. One evening I was asked to dance by a well endowed, slightly overweight girl. I bravely ventured onto the dance floor. She asked me questions which I could little understand with my limited English, but I will never forget one: "what do you do for a living?" she asked, and I felt I had to tell her something, although I did not really have a vocation. I had been a sailor for fifteen months, worked in a tourist hotel one summer, and as a waiter's helper or busboy in a Bergen hotel, but I thought I would promote myself to waiter for this occasion." I am a *waiter*", I replied. "A *writer*? How interesting!" she jovially exclaimed. Realizing the mistake, caused by my heavy accent, I attempted to correct the error: "No", I remonstrated, "not writer—waiter!" Her jolly smile froze, her mouth dropped slightly, and I perceived her face turning pale. She mumbled something and left the floor, leaving me standing there by myself, feeling just a little embarrassed. I realized that there is a definite difference in status between a *waiter* and a *writer.*

LEAVING FOR CANADA: JUNE, 1960

THE CUNARD LINE'S CARINTHIA—Arriving in Quebec City.

We arrived outside Quebec City early in the morning, and anchored in the St. Lawrence River just outside the city. It was a beautiful, sunny day, July 1st, 1960, Dominion Day, and we watched the old city, nestled atop the river escarpment. After awhile, Canada Customs officers came onboard to process us, which took several hours. Later we proceeded up the river, and landed in Montreal in the evening. The "redcaps" took our luggage to the trains, and in a few hours, I was on a CPR train bound for Vancouver, having barely caught a glimpse of Montreal lights in the dark. I was off to Regina, Saskatchewan, where I was to meet up with Malvin at his sisters who lived there. The porter came around to make up the beds. The top berth swung up from below, and he put a small ladder there for me to get up into bed, drawing the curtains close in front of me. I slept well on the train, on my first night in Canada.

By the time I awoke, we were entering Manitoba and soon we were rolling along the prairie. I watched the immense plains of golden wheat stretching out before me, with those narrow, tall buildings in silhouette against the sky. I struck up a halting conversation with an old Saskatchewan farmer and his son, returning from a trip "down east". I asked what those tall buildings were. "Grain elevators", the old man replied. I was puzzled. I knew what an elevator was—it was the same word in Norwegian, but there the elevators ferried people up and down between floors. What grain was doing in an elevator I could not comprehend, but asked no more about it, lest I seem stupid.

The two farmers were very friendly and talkative. The old man punctuated every sentence with the phrase "son of a gun". Another conundrum. I translated in my head: "son of" … OK I got that, but "a gun"? How could someone be the progeny of a gun? Later, I asked my relatives what "son of a gun" meant, but no one had the answer. "Just a saying", they said. This was my first introduction to American idioms.

In 1992 I was in Boston, Mass. and took a tour of the old eighteenth—century American battleship, the Constitution. There, the guide told us: It was the practice for officers, when the ships were in port, to bring their pregnant wives onboard, since the ship had a doctor, which was free for the crew and their families. The wives, who were soon due, were brought onto the gun deck, and a cannon fired to induce labour. Anyone born onboard was referred to as a "son of a gun", even if it was a daughter.

I was eating sandwiches all the way, buying it at the stations or on the train, because I could not afford the meals at the dining car. Or so I thought. Long after, I found out that my ticket had actually included meals!

I had just nine dollars left when I got to Regina.

It was evening and dark when I arrived at the Regina railway station, or *South Railway* as it was called then. I found a telephone, and attempted to call my relatives. I had this strange number, which began with LA (Lakeside) and then five numbers. The telephones had both letters and numbers on the dial, which puzzled me. After some study, I managed to dial the number, and it rang, but there was no answer. At that time, there was a central switchboard in the station, with an operator, and I asked her for help. Somehow she got the neighbour's telephone number and called them. The neighbour said my relatives were at another relative's home, as their brother, Malvin, had just arrived from Norway. She got their telephone number and called them. "Here is a young fellow from Norway looking for you," she said. They soon were there to pick me up, and the evening had a happy ending. I had never met them before, of course, but when they spoke to me in my Norwegian dialect, I felt I was at home.

Some times in your life someone does something nice that stays in your memory forever. I am sure the lady at the railway station thought it just another incident in her life of service, but to me, she was an angel. I was in a strange country, speaking little English and feeling lost and alone. I never forgot her kindness.

The old railway station is now a casino.

I did not go to Prince George. I have been in beautiful British Columbia many times, but never in Prince George. I sometimes wonder what my life would have been, had I gone with Malvin to work for MacMillan Blodell. My relatives in Regina, his sisters, would not let me go. "You are not going to live with Malvin in the bush" they said, "he lives in a shack and eats from tin cans!" So I stayed.

Their mother still lived on the farm with her son, Chris Roset. It was in mid-July, a warm and clear evening, that I saw the farm for the first time, bathed in the moonlight. The open prairie stretched as far as the eye could see, with just a few hills breaking the monotony. The distances between neighbours were incredible. You could see the lights from the homes dotted across the landscape, like ships on an ocean, kilometres apart. Malvin, who was driving, stopped the car and pointed to a hilly part of the rolling prairie, and there, in silhouette, was a lone coyote. What a contrast to the compact towns of mountainous western Norway, where I grew up.

I was surprised at the lowly living standards on the prairie. Their homes were plain and utilitarian. My cousin, Chris, lived in the house his father built when he homesteaded in 1915. It was, essentially, a rectangular box. At one end was the door leading into a small foyer, then another door to the kitchen, which contained a coal stove, a sink, a long-table and bench. A door led into the main room, which was a combination living and sleeping room—beds were lining the far wall and sides in a u-shape, with curtains that could be drawn around each bed. The beds served as "sofas" during the day. At the other end stood a potbelly oil-fired stove, and as of recently, a TV. The furnishings were drab and Spartan, with overtones of gray. In this environment, the parents worked from sunup to sundown, raised seven children, and raised them well. The mother was still living, and she was as content and happy as if she was the queen in a castle.

She was never happier than when her children with their families visited her on the farm. I once went with the three sisters and their families from Regina—there were ten adults, plus eight children and me, all sleeping in the one room. The three older boys and I slept in one bed, two by two at each end, feet to the middle, just like the Vikings used to sleep in their long houses.

Most farms were small,—just a few acres. Anyone with more that a section was considered a large farmer—my relatives were not. In Norway, the farms were much smaller, and the farmers were fairly poor, but their homes were large, and designed for two families—the oldest son's family and the old parents. The barns were built to keep the milk cows warm in the winter, and the hay dry. The hay on the prairie was baled and stored outside, but of course, the climate was much drier. Still, I had expected a more luxuriant life style on the fertile plains of "rich America". Even among the better off farmers, with large farms, housing was of little concern. They lived in modest homes and drove tractors and combines worth much more than their houses.

Another thing surprised me: the cattle, or steers, were not kept in barns (only the milking cows were), and during the winter, they would huddle against a wooden wall, or "lean-to", in 40 degrees below. You could see the steam rise from the clump of cattle.

I spent a couple of weeks living on the farm run by Chris. I worked a while for a neighbour and relative, Oscar, hauling hay-bales to the town of Herbert. Oscar was a talented musician, but an indifferent farmer. The half-ton truck I was driving required several turns of the wheel to react—it had worn-out kingpins, and I had a difficult time keeping it from running off the narrow, graveled country road. I had an international driving license, and once the local town policeman stopped me to check on my license. When I showed him the document, he scratched his head and grunted, but let me go. I think he did not want to take a chance on looking unsophisticated not knowing what an international license was.

The guy at the corral in Herbert kept referring to a dollar as "a buck". This puzzled me, and I had to ask him why. He took out a quarter and pointed to the deer head on the quarter coin. "That's a buck," he said. I still didn't know why he called the dollar a buck, not the quarter, but thought it best not to pursue that line of questioning at the time.

Now I know. It is a North-American abbreviation of buckskin, which was used as a unit of trade with the Indians in the Frontier days.

Les Solberg, Oscar's eldest son, who was about ten at the time, tells me a rather amusing anecdote. The first day I visited them, I asked his mother, Thelma, where the W.C. was (W.C. is an old English term for water closet, meaning toilet). She thought I was asking where British Columbia (B.C.) was, so she answered that it was far away, and I would have to travel through Alberta to get there! Even on the prairies, that's a long way to go to pee.

I have always been curious about origins of words and phrases. In Quebec, I asked French-Canadians what the slogan on their license plates meant (je me souven). Most could not tell me what they meant by "I will remember". Once I was driving around Pennsylvania on vacation, I noticed their license plate slogan "The keystone state". I asked everyone I met what a keystone was. I asked gas station attendants, waitresses and hotel employees. No one could tell me. Finally, I got to Gettysburg, and went to the town tourist centre. There I found out. It was the capstone joining together the top arch of the old Pennsylvania Dutch home's semicircular windows, and from the state's geographical position in the thirteen original colonies. A dictionary would have told me that, but I was amazed at the lack of knowledge they had about their own state slogan.

Oscar let me have a riding horse to get back and forth, and I learned to ride, cowboy style. I bought myself a cheap plastic cowboy hat, a western shirt and Lee jeans. I still have a photograph I sent to my mother, in that silly cowboy outfit. Chris taught me to throw the lariat, and I became quite apt at it. One day, I thought I had graduated to lasso real cattle, so I jumped on the horse and rode over to the corral where he had some steers. I threw the lariat and caught a big steer around his neck, just like the cowboys did. Then the fun began. The steer took off, pulled the rope from my hands, and I fell off the horse. The horse ran away, and so did the steer, right through the corral fence, disappearing down the lone prairie.

Chris later fetched the steer with his pickup, and I gave up on the cowboy life. To his credit, he never berated me or made fun of me for it, and when I brought it up many years later; he pretended he could not remember the incident.

Roset Homestead

The community had a party-line telephone system, so everyone could hear the other's conversations and for whom the call was by the number and length of the rings, or "ring-downs". When the phone rang, and it was a relative (which included most of the community), they would pick up the 'phone receiver and listen in for a while. Then, if it were anything of interest, say someone was coming to visit, they would tell the rest of the people in the house. This way, they kept well abreast of the goings on in the community. Sometimes, when too many people would be listening in, it affected the quality of the sound, and the receiving party would ask the neighbours to "get off the line" so he could hear the calling party.

The local newspaper was also quaint. The "news" was primarily about the neighbour's activities—which were visiting whom, where and when and for how long. Out of town visitors, like me, were front-page news.

Foods have quite an ethnic connection, and some foods did take me awhile to get used to. The first time I was served corn, I would not eat it, as I thought it was "chickenfeed". However, my relatives took me to the Regina Exhibition and there they convinced me to eat corn on the cob. To my surprise, I liked it. Another strange food was peanut butter, which I did not like—it took a few years before I got used to that taste. Saskatchewan blueberries (Saskatoons) and crab apples I never did get used to. It also took me a long time to be able to drink the Regina water. It tasted of alkaline, and I would mix *Kool-Aid* into it to mask the bitter taste. I could even taste it in coffee and tea.

There were some cultural differences. My parents had taught me, that as a guest, you always say no thanks when first asked if you wanted more food. Then, after a second, or even third prompting, you could take more, if you were still hungry. This was quaint even then, and is now history, but in the days of food shortages, it served a purpose of not embarrassing the host, while preserving the appearance of hospitality.

I visited a cousin in Midale, Saskatchewan, Doreen and Ted Rinas. They were hospitable people, but very North-American and casual in their manners. At mealtimes, they would offer me a second helping, but when, in my tradition, I declined, they would not offer it again. I almost starved before I got the courage to accept a second helping on the first (and only) prompting. I ate ravenously, having starved myself for a couple of days, and Noreen commented on my sudden appetite. I decided to tell her about the Norwegian custom of refusing a second helping until prompted a third or fourth time, and they had a good laugh on me. "Here", they said, "you eat until full, and don't be shy". I liked that custom better.

I have many fond memories of that first summer with my farmer relations in Saskatchewan. It was at the end of an era, when farms were still small and the community was close-knit and self-reliant. Yet, they were depending on each other in both work and play. They played musical instruments; fiddles, accordions, mouth organs and guitars, and all sang together; old gospel tunes and folk songs, in Norwegian and English, or watched Don Messer's Jubilee on the new-fangled black and white television. They were simple, kind and caring people.

They are almost all gone now. The farming community of Gouldtown is no more. The town of Herbert is the centre for the few farms left. Some of the Roset's and the Solberg's descendants are still there, mixed with the general populace. Though the old community is gone, like the Phoenix, a new order has risen from the ashes, keeping many of the old traditions and adding new ones. Like good, blended wine, it is fragrant and getting better with age.

Oscar Solberg died as had lived—serving others. He was playing his violin for the elderly at the Herbert Retirement Home, when he had a massive stroke and died with his cherished violin in his hands.

CHAPTER 5

The Regina years

Two weeks later, I went to Regina and attended at the "Immigration Office" at the address given to me in Norway. It was a hole in the wall, on the second floor—a single, small office, with a desk and a bespectacled man behind it, his feet on the desk and a copy of the Regina Leader Post in his hands. "I have come to find a job", I said, for I was told by the Canadian Consulate in Norway that this office would help me. I showed him the papers I had been given in Norway. "You want a job?" he asked, seeming surprised to see me. "Here". He spread the newspaper out on the counter, pointing to the "help wanted" page. "You call these", he said, "and you can keep the paper".

I stayed with my relatives in Regina for a couple of weeks, until I got a job as busboy at a place called Drake Hotel. Later, I got the same job at the Hotel Saskatchewan, for a little more money, but ended up washing dishes. I was making nine dollars a day, and walked to work and back so I could save the ten cents bus fare.

I rented a room on Rose Avenue; on the second floor of an old house. The room had a single bed, a table, a chair, and a hot plate. There was no fridge and the bathroom was shared amongst three other roomers. While employed at the hotel, I was getting free food while working, and that was a definite bonus, because I could not cook, even if I had had the equipment. I had a frying pan and used it for frying eggs and bacon; otherwise, when at home, I ate mostly cold sandwiches and canned foods. In the fall, I keep milk cartons cold between the inner windowpane and the outside storm window. It just fit, and worked well until winter came and it got too cold and the milk froze solid. Fortunately, on weekends I was able to sponge off my relatives, taking "turns" visiting them for dinner.

Later on, I took room and board with a Rumanian-Canadian couple, and was well fed, with pirogi and other East-European fare.

My first acquisition was a small radio for my room. Later, I bought a cheap guitar, and tortured my fellow roomers with my playing and singing. I got a library card and borrowed a book by P.G. Woodehouse, as I had enjoyed his books translated into Norwegian; but to my chagrin I could not read it, my English was not adequate. I tried some simpler mystery books, but made slow progress. I borrowed a "whodunit" book about Perry Mason: *The Case of …* something or other, but I didn't even get past the title. I knew a case was a kind of box, but couldn't connect it with the story title. For some reason, I did not get a dictionary. Either I did not know what it was, or perhaps I just did not think of it. It took me another year or so before my reading skills were good enough to read books and magazines, and I bought myself a dictionary. Since those early days, a dictionary has been my "bible".

I went to the Regina Exhibition that first summer, and had two interesting experiences: one was tasting corn on the cob—I had never eaten corn before, in any form, and the second was my introduction to North-American hucksterism. A guy sold me a "21-jewel watch" which stopped working shortly afterwards. I took it to a jeweler in Regina, and he told me it was junk. I pointed out that it said "21 jewels". He explained that there were 21 jewels all right, but they were set in a cluster and had no function except misleading me and protecting the manufacturer from a charge of outright fraud! I vowed to never again get caught in such a scam, but a couple of times I still did.

I spent much time alone the first winter in Regina. I had no TV so I went to the movies often. It probably helped me learn English, so the time wasn't all wasted. I saw some good movies, actually: Hitchock's *Psycho, The Magnificent Seven, Elmer Gantry*, all which turned out to be "classics."

I was watching *Sink The Bismarck* a Saturday afternoon, when a man struck up a conversation with me. He was quite friendly, and he invited me to have dinner with him after the movie ended. I accepted readily, as I had nothing else to do, and dinner in a restaurant was something I could not afford by myself. This guy was some kind of traveling salesman, and seemed to have a liberal expense account. I was quite flattered and impressed—as well as incredibly naïve for someone who had been around the world.

After dinner, he invited me to his hotel room for a drink and a look at some "photographs" he wanted me to see. Well, the photographs were of young men in various states of undress, and I realized that this was a queer on the prowl.

Thinking back and analyzing this experience has made me understand how sexual predators can entrap young boys, or young girls. I did not know what to do or say—I was scared, but uncertain about how to handle a situation that I had never before encountered.

I was fortunate that this particular gay man was not a sexual aggressor; he sensed my discomfort and anxiety, and after a while he offered to drive me home. I accepted with great relief, thanking him for a nice dinner! The incident really scared me, and made me very cautious of homosexuals.

I now know that such behaviour is not limited to homosexuals—any young person, man or woman, who is accosted or importuned in the same way can easily get into trouble, especially if they are alone and vulnerable. Someone with money and/or prestige can easily overwhelm their resistance and caution. I was lucky, not smart.

Just before Christmas, I got laid off from the Hotel Saskatchewan.

I don't think I was a good busboy or dishwasher, and they probably laid me off rather than firing me outright. I was depressed about the job loss, and did not quite know how to look for work. I thought I would go to school to learn a trade, and enrolled in an evening course at a school in Regina. However, my English was not good enough; I remember studying Ohms Law, but could not understand half of it. The teacher was very nice, and told me I should try again after I learned some more English. Then, I saw a recruitment ad for the military, so I went to the recruiting office and took the standard I.Q. and aptitude test. They told me I did O.K., but the only area open at that particular time was the paratroopers. However, I was again stumped, for I didn't pass the physical for paratroopers and was told to wait for something less strenuous. I gave up on the military.

I applied to work for the Hudson Bay Company at one of their remote trading posts, but I struck out there too. Then I saw an ad for a used car salesman, and applied for that (!), but the job was at my cousin's husband, Andy Salloum's firm, where Andy was the used car Sales Manager, and it was his ad. Andy told me that I was not ready for sales, but when I told him that I was getting frustrated without a job, and that I was contemplating giving up and going back to Norway, he said "No", "don't give up", "I will see if I can help you". He did. He had sold a car to a fellow who was a senior manager at the newly formed Inter-provincial Steel and Pipe (IPSCO), a "pipe dream" of the Saskatchewan NDP (Tommy Douglas) government that turned out to be a pretty good "dream." Andy called up this guy, by the name of Stanley Pridmore, and asked him to hire me, and he did! Andy must have been some salesman, that a customer would hire me on his request.

In retrospect, it shows my lack of direction and life plan that I would aimlessly apply for whatever job came to mind. I was fairly intelligent and a quick learner, and motivated when I decided upon a goal, but my opportunistic approach to life would continue to hamper my career choices and my future. I was young and inexperienced, but more than anything, I lacked, and would continue to lack, someone who could guide me with a firm hand, and give me advice. Young people are their own worst guidance counselors. It is surprising that I managed as well as I did, considering my "rudderless journey". I think the responsibility thrust upon me by an early marriage at twenty, and the subsequent child (another unplanned act) did settle me down, ending my rather unfocused life; but it introduced other problems, where the same failings and lack of external guidance and support continued to frustrate and handicap me.

IPSCO (Inter-provincial Steel and Pipe) has an interesting history. Someone had the bright idea to start a "mini-mill", before mini-mills were common, in the middle of the prairie. The nay-sayers, of course, said it couldn't be done. However, the promoters (and the government) knew that the farmers had a lot of old, worn-out cars, tractors, and other farm equipment, all good scrap steel, lying around the farm yards, and they would go around to the farms and buy this scrap very, very cheaply—the farmers were happy to get rid of the junk. It was a brilliant idea, and it worked—eventually. However, the mill had real problems the first couple of years with producing quality steel. For some reason, the steel plate would be pitted, and they had us sitting with air grinders for hours grinding to smooth the pits away. This, of course, degraded the steel, and reduced the prices they could charge.

They eventually brought in a fellow from Texas, by the name of O'Connor, who discovered where the problem lay: they were heating the steel ingots too quickly, causing small air bubbles to form inside the ingots. This would cause blisters, or pits, when they rolled the ingots into steel plate. Once they fixed these problems, they were, literally, on the roll.

They trained me to be an overhead crane operator, at the fantastic wage of $ 2.25 per hour. I was assigned the "scrap crane", which loaded cut steel scrap with an electromagnet, picking it up and dropping it into the steel melting furnaces. It was pretty hot up there, as this crane was not air conditioned, but it was still one of the better jobs. Trouble was, every time the mill was down, and it was often the first two years, I would get laid off, or assigned odd jobs cleaning up. They would put us down into the "soaking pits" with picks and shovels, breaking up steel slag and loading it into buckets. The temperatures were about 140 degrees Fahrenheit down there. I remember going outside in the ninety-five degree sunshine to cool off! More than one guy passed out from the heat.

Another awful job was using a jackhammer to break up chunks of carbon. The carbon would get into the nostrils and ears, making me look like Al Jolson on stage. I took much effort and time to clean up.

My broken English made me the focus of much levity and practical jokes. One was especially funny: I was working with a crew, shearing plate steel, when the chain broke on the transfer bed. The lead hand told me to go to the stores and get a *skyhook* and a *chain stretcher*. I did, and the stores man, who must have been in on the scheme, gave me a box, which he filled with an old chain and some other scraps of steel. I lugged the heavy box back to the transfer bed, to the hilarious enjoyment of the whole gang. I don't recall getting upset over it, I thought it was quite comical myself, when I understood the joke.

IPCO supporters in the government were getting a bit of political flak over the continuing problems and cost of the poor steel produced, so they came up with an ingenious way of showing the plant's importance to the local economy: we were paid in cash each two weeks, and one payday we got paid in two dollar bills. This flooded Regina merchants with these easily recognizable bills, and the message got through loud and clear.

I, however, got fed up with the constant layoffs, and just before they fixed it, I quit. "Stupid is who stupid does."

I still had serious problems with pronunciations, especially words containing either *th* or *v*. I could not hear the difference in the sound of *w* and *v*. *G* and *J* was also a problem (and still is today). Sometimes, it would put me in an awkward situation.

I had just bought my first car, a 1952 Mercury Meteor. It cost four hundred dollars, most of which Andy loaned me. Once, I was proudly driving my movie-date home, and had trouble finding *Third Avenue* (in Regina, the avenues are numbered). "I can't find *Turd Avenue*", I told her. She began to giggle and laugh. "Which avenue", she said, laughingly. "*Turd* avenue", I replied, somewhat nonplussed. This scenario was repeated a few times, I would say *Turd Ave*, and she would break out in laughter. I became rather frustrated. "What's so funny?" I asked. "Do you know what you are saying?" she inquired. "You are saying *Shit Avenue*!"

There was another idiom I could not understand. The term "two bits", denoting a quarter dollar, or twenty-five cents. No matter whom I asked, they could not tell me why a quarter was called "two bits". I could have looked it up in almost any dictionary. It originated as a Spanish coin worth 1/8 of a peso.

I would send home tapes (spoken letters) to my parents in Norway, and my relatives would speak greetings and tell about themselves in Norwegian. However, they were all born here, so their Norwegian was quite mixed with English words. One time, Alpha, my cousin, was explaining what her husband did for a living. He sold cars, but she didn't know the word for car in Norwegian, so she used the English word, but made it sound Norwegian—karar. Unfortunately, it sounded as the word for *men* in Norwegian, so my father wrote back asking what actually did he do with *men*. I don't think he thought Andy was involved in the *slave trade*, but we got a good laugh from it anyhow.

Those letters and tapes between us meant much to me in those early days, and helped me bridge the gap between my "old" and my "new" life. I still remember the warm feeling I got whenever I saw the blue airmail letter from my mother. It was my link with home. Those letters kept coming until my mother died, but they were especially crucial in those early days. After her death, I found most of my letters and photos amongst her personal belongings. She had kept them all that time. A mother's love is forever.

In those days, there was a public dance hall in Regina, called the *Trianon*. The hall was ringed by seats alongside the walls, where the ladies would sit, and the men would go to a girl and ask her to dance. It was a good way to meet girls. One night I danced with this very cute Chinese girl, and asked if I could walk her home afterwards. She readily agreed. She lived with her parents above a Chinese restaurant they ran, just a few blocks from the dance parlour.

Some days later, I decided to call on her, and went into the café where her father was working the counter. I asked him if his daughter was home. He got very angry and told me to get lost, never to come there again! I was very disappointed, but after talking with friends about it, I realized that the Chinese were afraid of losing their child to a "westerner". It was my first "culture clash". I can't say I blame the Chinese father.

In between layoffs at IPSCO, I worked in a shoe store, *Agnew Surpass*, in downtown Regina. My immediate supervisor was Bert Lommerse, and we became very good friends. There was a hypnotist calling himself "The Great Raveen" entertaining people at a Regina theatre, and we went to see him. Raveen would initially test the audience's suggestibility by having them put their arms above their heads, then telling them they could not lower their hands. About a quarter of the audience would be caught, and Bert was one of them. He was incredibly suggestible, and became the star "performer" on the stage. Every day he would get a set of free tickets, and we would be back in the same routine. However, one day, Bert did not come out of his trance, and when he returned to his seat, I realized something was wrong. He was stiff and unresponsive, staring straight ahead. I had to take him back stage, and Raveen came and snapped his fingers in front of his face and said, "Wake up!" Bert did, and we went home. The strange thing was that Bert did not remember anything, and did not believe me when I told him about it. I have never met anyone as suggestible as Bert.

I had a few friends where I worked, and one fellow, Johnny, almost got me in serious trouble. One Saturday he arrived in a "new" car, a 1957 Ford Galaxy hardtop, two tone red and white. It was a beautiful car, and I readily agreed when he asked me to come for a ride. We headed down the highway, past Moose Jaw, and he decided we would visit his parents on a farm near Swift Current. We stopped at a gas station in a small town and fueled up, but when it was time to pay, Johnny stepped on the gas and took off without paying. A local policeman gave chase, but when we got onto the highway, he turned back. Johnny thought we were safe, but later the RCMP stopped us. They arrested Johnny, took the car away and dropped me off in town. I managed to hitchhike back to Regina, and later found out that Johnny had stolen the car from another fellow staying at the same boarding home.

It was a "wake up" call for me, telling me to be more careful with my associations.

Another time I almost got myself in serious trouble. It was in January, and I decided to take a trip with my "new" car, a 1952 Ford Meteor, to visit my relatives on the farm. I was driving along the farm road and it was snowing quite heavy. I hit a clump of ice on the road and lost control, careening down the road and into a snow bank. The snow was so deep I could not even open the doors.

There I was stuck in the snow in forty degrees below, late at night in the dark, in the middle of the prairie, far from anyone.

Fortunately, the engine was still running and I had almost a full tank of gasoline. I climbed out he window to clear snow from the tailpipe, grabbed a blanket from the trunk, and settled into the front seat for the night, with the engine running and the heater at full blast, the window slightly open to guard against carbon monoxide poisoning, and went to sleep.

A farmer on his tractor awakened me in the morning. He towed me onto the road, and I continued to the farm. It could have been a disaster; I could have frozen to death or died of carbon monoxide poisoning. I realized I had been lucky.

Once I was driving back from the farm when I was caught in a snowstorm. I could not see anything and drove with my head out the window, in order to follow the white stripe in the road, barely discernible in the whiteout. Prairie winters are unforgiving.

I have fond memories of those two years I spent in Regina. I still think of Regina as my "hometown", and of my relatives as substitute parents. I was always welcome in their modest homes and I developed an eternal bond with them. Andy would come home late in the evenings, about nine or ten, after finishing work at the car lot. I would drop by, and we would have coffee or tea and a snack that his wife, my cousin, Alpha, would prepare. On weekends, I would drop in, unannounced, to my two other "families": the Kasics and the Nordlanders. The three sisters all lived in close proximity in the same neighbourhood. I was always welcomed—and fed. The winters might have been cold as ice, but their hearts were warm as the sun.

In winter, we would plug in our cars at night, running cables from a house power outlet to the cars. All the parking lots had power outlets for this purpose. When you started to drive after a cold night hiatus, the tires would be frozen flat on the bottom, and your car would go "hump-hump" along the road until the rubber warmed from friction and the tires returned to its proper round shape.

All municipal parking lots, and most company ones, had electric outlets where you could plug in your car in the cold winters. There was a story in the Regina newspaper, The Leader Post: An American tourist, visiting in the summer, wrote to thank the city for its hospitality. She was especially impressed with the power outlets in all parking areas, allowing her to plug in her house trailer and cook her food!

Toronto

My English improved, but the Saskatchewan winters did not. I also missed the mountains, the water and the trees, and fresh fish. Fish, I was told, is something Catholics eat on Friday.

I also saw no end to the frequent lay-offs at IPSCO, so I decided to move on, either to British Columbia or to Ontario. Fate again intervened. One of my friend's mother and her sister were going to Windsor, Ontario to visit their brother there, and they told me that if I was going east, they would hitch a ride and pay my fuel and motel rooms. So it were, that in the summer of 1962, I traveled from Regina, Saskatchewan to Windsor, Ontario, with two "old ladies" as passengers, my belongings in a suitcase and my guitar in the rear window of my 1952 Mercury Meteor. At Sault Ste. Marie I crossed, illegally (I was not even a *Canadian* citizen—had I gotten into any trouble I could have been deported back to Norway!), into Michigan and drove down Interstate 75 through Detroit and crossed into Windsor through the underwater tunnel.

I stayed in Windsor a couple of weeks, with the "uncle" there. I almost got a job as policeman in a small town outside Windsor. They must have been pretty desperate for a policeman in that town, but when they realized I was not a Canadian citizen, they could not hire me.

Windsor was rather depressed, economically, still suffering from Ford Canada's move to Oakville in the late fifties. I decided to drive to Toronto, the big city, to try my luck.

I arrived after dark, driving along the then two-lane 401 and missing the city all together. I turned back on highway two, or Kingston Road, and somehow ended up on the Gardiner Expressway, again bypassing downtown and turning off at South Queensway, finally ended up on Queen Street. Tired and hungry I spied a sign saying, "Rooms only $ 3.00 per night". I turned into their parking lot and registered at the *Spadina Hotel*, a dump of a place, even then. Such was my entry into the city that was to be, except for a short hiatus, my home until now.

Toronto was a different city then. It was still rather "waspish", and both small and large "c" conservative. You could not buy liquor or beer on a Sunday, even in a restaurant; stores and even most movie theatres were closed Sundays; the city all but rolled up the sidewalks Saturday night. The main group of non Anglo-Saxon immigrants were Italians, who mostly lived around the St.Clair and Oakwood area (they would later move "uptown" to Weston, and the Portuguese would take over downtown, painting their homes in the rainbows colours).

I thought I would try to get on the Great Lakes ships, having sailed in the Norwegian merchant navy. I went to the hiring hall of the famous S.I.U. (Seafarer's International Union). This was the time of *Hal Banks*, and the union was not exactly a Boy Scout club. Hal Banks was the union president who escaped to the U.S. after being charged with racketeering and violence on the Toronto waterfront. I walked into this hall where a bunch of men were sitting, and spoke to the hiring officer. "No problem", he said, "just pay $ 250.00 dues up front, and then wait until we call you." "When might that be?" I queried innocently. "When all those guys you see there have jobs," he said. "Maybe next season."

I didn't become a sailor on the Great Lakes. I spent the next few days looking in the papers for a job—any job. Once, I read an advertisement for a Customer Service Representative, and called the man whose name was listed in the ad. After listening to me briefly, he exclaimed: "you want to be in customer service? You cannot even speak the goddamn language!"

He was right, of course, and I promised myself I would learn this "goddamn" language,"and learn it well, even if it killed me. I did, and it didn't.

I got a "job" selling pots and pants to young girls for their "hope chest". Young girls did have these then, in anticipation of future marriage. We would stop girls on Bay Street at lunchtime, offer them a "free gift" (talk about an oxymoron: "free gift") if they would let us give them a demonstration of this fantastic "Queen Anne" cookware. I later found out that you could buy the same thing at Sears for a third of the price.

Next, I graduated to selling storm windows and doors. In those days, builders did not include storm windows and storm doors with new houses, so there was a active after-market for these items. Once, in Guildwood Village, then a new development in east Scarborough, I knocked on a door of a large home. The owner opened the door, listened to me for a moment and yelled "not another goddamn salesman!" Then he slammed the door right in my face. I continued on to the next house.

I spent two weeks at the Canadian National Exhibition. The aluminum company had a booth there, and we were flogging our storm windows and doors. I found the Exhibition exhilarating and exiting, but I didn't sell much. I did, however, meet a good-looking native-Indian girl, and I kept company with her for a few weeks, before I got in trouble by stupidly calling her *Big Chief*. With my poor English, I didn't know any better, but she took exception to this and required extreme unction.

Fall arrived and the aluminum door and window business died. I had pretty well used my savings, and was living on eggs and bacon, which I purchased at 50 cents a meal from a local eatery on Castle Avenue, where I lived in a rooming house. Someone told me I could collect unemployment insurance because I had worked for a couple of years at IPSCO in Regina, so I decided to apply. The man who saw me said I could have applied long ago, and probably pitied the poor young fool. He backdated my application two or three weeks, and the cheque I got helped me survive until I got a job a couple of weeks later. Sometime you find a human heart, even in bureaucrats.

I sold shoes for *Bata* on Yonge Street (the store is no longer there) for a few months, but did not set the shoe world on fire. I was in the men's department downstairs, and was making about sixty dollars a week, not much even then.

Bata was a strange place to work. It was in the centre of downtown, on Yonge Street, just below Dundas, so we got some unusual patrons. One day a gay man came in to try on platform shoes. He also wanted inserts, so he could be "taller than his dancing partner". Though Toronto had a fairly large gay population even then, it was much less open than now, and I was particularly troubled about how to deal with them. I remember being very nervous and afraid of embarrassing the man, though he seemed quite nonchalant and untroubled about it.

Sometimes we had "sales" on shoes that were out of fashion. They were called "spiffs", and while some pairs were indeed reduced, some shoes were actually increased in price and put in with the sales stock.

Some of the "inmates" were also peculiar. The department supervisor, a skinny little middle-aged man with an out of proportion large head, was a fellow with many vices and proud of it. He had been a friend of Ronald Turpin who had been condemned to hang for the murder of a policeman, but they had apparently had a falling out when Ron threw him through a plate glass door in a fit of rage during a party. Turpin's girlfriend, a heavily painted Clairol blonde, used to come in and commiserate; complaining about what they were going to do to poor Ronnie, but when she was gone, the fellow said, "I hope they hang him".

They did in December, together with Arthur Lucas. Lucas was a black man from Detroit who came to Toronto for a contract killing. He killed a couple and was caught, and executed with Turpin, hung back to back at Don Jail. It was the last hanging in Canada.

Their crime: murder. Their punishment: death. Shortly after midnight on Dec. 11, 1962, two cop killers faced death by hanging. The execution at Toronto's Don Jail would be Canada's last. Ronald Turpin, 29, was convicted of shooting a Toronto police constable. Arthur Lucas, 54, was convicted of murdering an FBI agent and his wife.

I turned twenty-one in February, and thought I could now sell cars, like my relative, Andy, in Regina. Andy had told me that if I could sell cars in Toronto, I could sell anything, anywhere!

I was hired by Rootes Motors, at the corner of Eglinton and Warden in Scarborough, selling British Hillman and Sunbeam cars. Foreign cars, with the exception of the Volkswagen Beatle, were not exactly hot sellers in those days, so an English import was just about as low as you could go in the car selling business, at least for new cars. Selling used cars on the Danforth was at the very the bottom of the automobile "food chain".

I was quite successful for a while—don't ask me how I did it—with an accent so thick you could slice it with a knife. I sold British cars to naïve Brits who had recently immigrated and had always wanted one of those cars that they could not afford back home in Britain. The cars rusted like mad, and would not start when it rained or got too cold.

In those days, you could call the Vehicle Registry Office with a license plate number, and they would give you the name and address of the owner. It was then an easy step to get the telephone number from information (again, free back then). I would spot a rusty old Hillman or Sunbeam sputtering along the road, take the number, and then call the owner in the evening, telling him that I had been looking for a good used car just like his, and would he by chance be interested in trading it in? Would he! He had probably tried every domestic car lot in town. Usually, the ruse worked well, and the prospect would appear in the showroom eager to trade the old lemon in for a new one.

We also sold used cars of all kinds—my boss would go to the car auction and buy these "junkers" and then put them on the used car lot as "trade-ins". They would rewind the "clock" (turn back the odometers) to an appropriate level, then re-groove the used tires, spray paint them, and put the car on the lot. This was common practice in those days, especially on the Danforth, where such crooks as "good-hearted" Ted Williams and Ted Davey operated. "Good hearted Ted" used to advertise on the radio that if you could drive your car onto his lot, he would give you $ 100.00 in trade-in and donate $ 50.00 to the church of you choice. This way, you could unload your clunker and be a saint at your church at no cost to yourself. Ted Williams finally went too far and got caught. They sold a 1960 Chevy Impala to a fellow, saying they would deliver the car to him after they had done a mechanical check on it. Well, they switched cars, drove a "junker" of the same year and model to the man's house and handed the keys to his son when he opened the door, then left in a hurry. After this, the Government of the day decided they had to do something, so they appointed Ted Davey to head a Used Car Commission to regulate the industry. Talk of having the fox guard the chicken coop. Not long after, Ted Davey was charged with fraud—I believe he ended up in Michigan and never saw the inside of an Ontario jail, but it was the end of his tenure as guardian of the used car buyer.

Once, I sold this "dog", a 1960 Ford with an underpowered six-cylinder engine, to a service-station mechanic. At the point of sale, as he was getting ready to sign the cheque, he hesitated: "perhaps I should take it to my mechanic" he demurred. I could see my commission cheque fluttering away, and quickly used some applied psychology (God knows where I learned that):"*You* are a mechanic," I said stoutly. "Why would you ask another mechanic to check your car?" "You're right" he said, and signed the cheque. As usual, I would run to the bank to "hammer" (certify) the cheque, before the customer could change his mind and stop it. Two days later, he came back, complaining about several items. I asked my boss, general manager Ron Kramer, if we could do something for him, and his reply, I can still hear it, was "who are you working for, me or the customer?" (Mr. Kramer ended up as the Canadian CEO for Nissan, a major Japanese automobile manufacturer).

We would make the highest commission on used cars, and I would volunteer to work Saturdays at the used car lot (in today's euphemistic world it's called "pre-owned" cars. Same bird, different name).

Some guy came in and said that that he had been next door to the Golden Mile Chevrolet ("you don't walk away, you drive away, from Golden Mile Chevrolet"), and they offered him just two hundred dollars for his car (which is what it was worth), but he "would not consider taking less than five". He had seen a car on our lot that he was interested in, and asked me how much. I added the three hundred dollars difference to the price of our car and gave him his five hundred dollar for his trade in. Voila! Another happy customer.

Young Italian men, and I mean no disrespect, seemed to like cars of a particular colour combination. If you had a two door hardtop or a convertible, with black paint and red interior, or conversely, red paint and black interior, you were sure to sell it to an Italian youngster. One Saturday afternoon, I was sitting in the car lot office, when a young Italian male came in. He had seen a black 1960 Impala convertible on the lot, and was interested in buying it. I knew he really wanted it, so I did not reduce the price at all, even though it was incredibly overpriced. He decided to buy it, but I could not take a personal cheque from him, and the banks were closed (this was 1963 and banks were not open Saturdays or evenings). He left, but came back in about one hour with his whole extended family. Some brought their pay cheques, others cash, even coins. After a while, there was a pile of cash on the table, the full amount—I think it was about $ 2,500.00. He went off in his car, happy as a lark, and I went home that day in a similar frame of mind.

The work was unethical. I still remember the common phrase used by the used car hucksters: *Would you if I could?* (Translation: would you buy if I could get you the deal you want?). We would put up a show of "fighting" with our boss, the terrible grouch, to get this wonderful deal for our customer, and sometimes we would go back and forth several times, each time bringing another "offer" from the customer to the boss, and often managing to "bump" the customer to where we wanted him in the first place. It is incredible how many times it worked. I still remember a sale that made me decide to leave the business. An immigrant couple from England wanted to buy a new Hillman car, but their trade was not worth much, so their down payment was not enough. We dealt with a couple of finance companies for such cases; one I remember was called Reliable Finance. They would take almost anyone, and I remember their rep coming and listing all their furniture as collateral for the car loan. The details of these loans were deceptive, and written in small print on the back of the promissory note. What it said, and what was not explained to the customer, was that the interest shown was based on the interest on the original amount, and no credit given for the declining balance after monthly payments. In this way, a five or six percent published rate was actually closer to twenty-four percent, or just under the limit set by usury laws.

I decided to try a domestic dealership, and I got hired by Frank Rowland, of Frank Rowland Mercury on O'Connor drive. I thought this would be an improvement, and in many ways it was. Frank Rowland was quite ethical for the times, but I did not fit in well in the rather staid dealership. I had been ruined to a degree by the slick operators at Rootes Motors. One day, when I detected a couple of "shoppers" (people Ford Motor Company sent in to see if their products were being sold properly), I dropped them in favour of a more promising "prey" in the used car lot. Frank got very angry, and fired me. He promised to give me a good reference, as long as I stayed out of the car business. I did, and he did.

Belatedly, I came to the realization that if I was ever to get anywhere in life, I must have an education. So I enrolled in the Ontario Department of Education's correspondence school, intended to get my high-school diploma. Eventually I did, but that's another story.

I had gotten married shortly after arriving in Toronto. It was a "shotgun" wedding, though the shotgun was a "virtual" one in my mind—my conscience. These were the days before birth control. The girl was from a poor Saskatchewan farming family, so it was not an auspicious beginning for an immigrant with halting English and no education. I don't think a betting man would have gambled on me. I know I wouldn't have.

We lived first on the third floor of an old house on Castle Ave in east end Toronto; later I got a second story flat on Hastings Ave, off Gerrard St.

The home on Hastings Avenue was owned by east European immigrants, who rented out the upstairs to several people. The second floor was occupied by us, and by a drunkard living on welfare. One day while my wife was in the bathroom, he pushed open the door and came in, flailing his arms. When I got home, she told me about it, and I went to his room to see him. He was lying in his bed with a half-finished bottle of cheap whiskey on the night table. I poured the booze over his head and told him if he ever did that again, I would kill him. Then I saw the "landlord" and told him to get rid of the guy. However, the welfare cheque was regular, and the landlord did not want to kick him out and lose the income, so I ended up moving, not him.

I had just gotten the job selling cars in Scarborough, so I rented an apartment in the low rental area of Kennedy Road below Eglinton. We did not have any furniture of our own, so I purchased the basics, including a TV. set on credit with a consumer credit company called Household Finance, at exorbitant interest rates. Fortunately, my income from selling cars was quite good, and I paid them off early, even though I had to pay the full two year interest.

The building was full of party-animals, and it was hard to sleep in the summertime when you had to have the windows open in the non-air conditioned building. Music was blaring, car horn blowing and people shouting all night.

We moved first to a quieter building in Victoria Park Ave, another low rental building (subsidized by the city), and then to another one on Weston Road, a two bedroom apartment with no balcony renting at one hundred dollars per month. After a year or so there, following the birth of my second child, I bought my first house in Bradford, Ontario—one of many to come. I paid $ 16,500.00 for the 950 square feet bungalow in the summer of 1967. It was on the first street in the first new subdivision in Bradford, built by John Zima of Luxury Home Builders, and the street name was *Luxury Avenue*! We lived there for over three years, before moving on.

An American comedienne/actress, it might have been Ethel Merman, once said that she had been rich and she had been poor, and rich was definitely better. Well, I have never been rich, but I have been poor, and let me tell you, being poor is an experience we can all live without.

Citizen

In 1965 I qualified for citizenship (you had to wait five years then), and I decided I wanted to partake fully in Canadian society, which included voting in elections. I went to the Citizenship Court on St.Clair Avenue in Toronto. There were about twenty or thirty of us getting our citizenship that day, and each of us was questioned independently in an office before the ceremony. I was asked to name the three levels of government, and managed without too much difficulty. Then we individually took the oath. However, when I was asked to swear allegiance to Canada and the Queen, I committed a verbal faux pas: I swore allegiance to Queen Elizabeth and her *hairs* (heirs)! I don't think the Judge even noticed. I have always maintained that I did not swear allegiance to the Queen—just her hairs.

One experience that awoke my patriotism was the "Great Flag Debate" of 1964-65. I remember the various design proposals and the partisan arguments for and against. The Conservatives and Diefenbaker led the faction against the flag the Pearson Liberals were trying to introduce. The issue became highly politicized and polarized.

I came from a country where the flag was a revered symbol of national pride; where the flag was treated with respect and honour, used for all holidays and special occasions; where every home had a flag pole, and you dare not let the flag touch the ground when hoisting it on the pole. I could not fathom why a people—Canadians, would not want their own symbol of nationhood. I recall speaking with a war veteran, a really nice fellow, who told me that he had fought with the Union Jack and would die with it. Such were the sentiments of some. I recall seeing Union Jacks on lawns and buildings. Toronto was very much a British enclave at the time; you had certain advantages being British: you could vote after one year of residence, and some jobs were only open to Canadian citizens or British subjects. In many government jobs the British were hugely over-represented. How things have changed!

I was not anti-British, on the contrary, I had (and have) great admiration and affection for the British and the democratic civilization they brought with them. However, I could not understand why Canadians, born here, would prefer British hegemony and its colonial symbol, the Union Jack.

Those feelings have moderated in the ensuing years. I don't see the monarchy as an impediment to Canada's nationhood. In fact, it might be our bulwark against unwanted American influence, but that early experience, and especially Lester Pearson's determined fight for the flag, formed my political attitude and cultural beliefs for the future. I don't think the Liberals walk on water any longer, but Lester B. Pearson is still my hero!

A few years later I had just returned from a family reunion in Norway, and I had made a video recording of the trip. In reviewing the tape, I heard myself say, "Tomorrow I am going home" referring to departure day for Canada. Suddenly it struck me: In the past, I always referred to Norway when I spoke of "going home". I realized that I was finally integrated, emotionally as well as physically. I was going home indeed—home to Canada.

After achieving my high-school equivalency by correspondence school, I worked a short while for the Allstate Insurance Co. I was hired as a "customer service representative", but the job was mainly trying to up-sell life insurance to current customers who called in about their car policies. I didn't set the insurance world on fire, and got fired after a six months—my first step backwards.

The Canadian National Railways

My next job was with the *Canadian National Railways* in the "operations office". My very first assignment was at the "Don Yards" at the foot of the Don Valley Parkway. As a junior, I was put on the "Spare Board", which meant I got sent to various local yards to cover for whoever was absent, usually as a "checker". The checker did just that—walking around along the tracks with a clipboard recording the railcar numbers and the track number where they were located. I arrived for the four o'clock afternoon shift and just sat around until six p.m., when the dayshift and other workers were gone home. There was just one clerk left, and he gave me a clipboard and told me to go and check all the cars on all the tracks, and not to bother him when I returned, as he was going to get some sleep. He said to be sure to wake him before midnight when the next shift began and a new clerk and checker arrived.

There were about ninety thousand employees working for the CNR in 1964 when I started, probably a third of them redundant. But it was a government-owned railway, so who cared? Today, there is less than a third of that number, thanks to technology, and getting rid of their LCL (less than carload) business, and later, the caboose; but also to better management. With new ball bearings on the car wheels instead of journal boxes, which did catch fire now and then, the jobs of conductor and helper in the caboose became superfluous. Until finally eliminated, it was a real sinecure.

I soon moved on to the new marshalling yard ("hump-yard") in Concord, and stayed there for five years, in various clerical jobs. It was not a bad experience; I rather fondly remember it. We were mostly young men, and there was certain camaraderie among us. Bashing the CNR was a favourite past-time, and I remember a story typed and posted on the bulletin board about a worker who was getting married, and was worried about telling his fiancée and her family about his own troubled family: his sister the prostitute, his brother in jail, his parents on welfare, and worst of all, having to tell them that he worked for the CNR!

Some of the guys were gamblers. They would bet on horses and played poker in the rooms set aside for the train-crews lying over, and in a lounge upstairs, sometimes staying up all night playing poker. On one occasion, one guy had won a fair amount from the timekeeper, who paid it off by giving the winner several hours of overtime at time-and-a-half. It was plain theft, but he got away with it—no one would say anything.

The night shift was particularly unproductive. One fellow, Louie S, used to bring an alarm clock to work, and then disappear for a few hours snooze. We tried, but could never find his hiding place. One night he fell asleep with his feet on the desk, so we tied his feet together with his shoelaces. Then one guy stood behind him with a blown up paper bag, and exploded it behind the sleeping fellow's ears. He jumped up, then stumbled and fell flat on his face to the tremendous enjoyment of the rest of the gang. Everyone skulked work to a degree, but his blatant indifference to his duties was too much for us.

Ron Grimmer was an inveterate gambler. One day he told me about this horse, Eric Lee that was good at running on turf, and we went to the upstairs lounge to watch him on the TV. Sure enough, Eric Lee won. Ron told me he would go to the track next time the horse ran, and asked me to go along. I declined, but told him I would put in a few bucks. When the horse ran again, Ron went and I gave him two dollars to gamble for me. The darn horse won again, and I got twelve dollars for my two. Ron got a lot more.

The next time the horse was running, Ron asked if I wanted to put money on him again. For a moment I could feel the gambling "fever"—the temptation was great, but I said no. I have always been careful about gambling—too many people's lives have been destroyed by it. Ron went, and the horse lost. He spent all the money he had won and then some.

One day Ron came to see me. He wanted to borrow some money, telling me he had lost his pay cheque. I offered to help him look for it, but he told me he had not really lost it physically, he had gambled it away, and was afraid to tell his wife! Gambling is a terrible affliction.

Ron was killed in a head-on accident on highway fifty south of Kleinburg a few years later. He was in the passenger seat, with no airbags or even seat belts in those days. He was horribly smashed up, but when I went to see the corpse, he had been made up and reconstructed; yet I could barely recognize him. It struck me as a macabre custom in North America, to stuff a corpse and put it on display, euphemistically calling it embalming and the undertaker a Funeral Director.

For a few years, I would hunt deer in the fall at a place called Coopers Falls, not far from Gravenhurst, Ontario, with two friends, Dennis Findley and Peter Salezski. I never did shoot a deer, but enjoyed the wilderness and the open air. Dennis had a small house trailer that we hauled as far as we could into the woods. One year, during the big blackout—I think it was 1965—we were tracking deer in the bush, and crossed a small creek by walking on a beaver dam at the end of a small lake. After several hours of walking and paying little attention to our surroundings, we realized that we were lost. It was overcast, and we could not find our directions. We did not have the foresight of bringing a compass. We walked and walked for hours, until we realized we were back at our starting point—we had walked in a circle! We were getting tired and hungry. Fortunately, Peter had a couple of chocolate bars in his pocket, and he shared them with the two of us. Dennis was so tired that he wanted to throw away his rifle, but I managed to talk him out of it by offering to carry it for him. Just before dark, we saw a power line, and realized that if we followed it we would eventually come to a populated area.

Finally, we saw the lake we had crossed over, and followed it until we found the beaver dam. We arrived back just as it was dark. Tired and hungry, we stumbled into the trailer, went to bed and immediately fell asleep.

After a couple of hours, I awoke to the smell of food cooking. Dennis had got up and was cooking up a storm. We had boiled potatoes, wieners, canned beans and sauerkraut. I don't think I ever ate so well in the best hotel. Later, I got out my accordion, and Peter got out a bottle of sacramental wine (yes—sacramental wine was just that, and could be purchased very cheaply at the liquor stores). There we were, the three of us: a "Russian", a Norwegian and a Canadian, drinking and singing and having a whale of a time. We didn't shoot a deer, but who cared—we had a good time anyhow, after surviving a near disaster.

When we returned to "civilization" we heard the lights had been out for a couple of days in a major blackout.

I had to work shifts, including weekends. This played havoc with my social life; especially the afternoon shifts and working weekends with two days off in the middle of the week. I eventually managed to get Friday and Saturday free, but it mattered little, for I usually worked an overtime shift on Saturday (I also drove taxi Friday nights and Sundays for an outfit called Rexdale Taxi, and occasionally worked as a labourer and driver for Tippet Richardson Moving, at the foot of the Don Valley Parkway; driving from Bradford, Ontario, about an one hour drive). Sometimes we would work round the clock, twenty-four hours straight (I don't think it is legal any longer), but when I fell asleep at the wheel driving home one morning, barely avoiding running off the road, I decided that I would limit it to sixteen-hour shifts.

The railway had a "spare-board", a list of people who were willing to work overtime. When they called, you had two hours to get there, and you had to accept the job then and there, or you got dropped to the bottom of the board. At time and a half it was hard to refuse, and many an evening I answered the phone and said *yes,* but really meant no, dreading the very thought of driving from Bradford to work an overtime shift, and then usually my own shift in tandem. It was easier when you were at work all ready—you just stayed on. Years later, after I had normal working hours, I would react when the 'phone rang at night.

Something good came from it. Whenever I could, I would work overtime driving the yard bus. This bus took train crews back and forth from the diesel shop to their sleeping quarters above the central office complex, the Administration building where most of us worked our regular jobs. Driving the bus was not a popular job, because it was so incredibly boring. I found it useful, however, for at each end I had about a fifteen minutes wait, and I would bring a book to read. I read classics, like *Moby Dick* and A *Tale of Two Cities* to improve my vocabulary. I had a small dictionary, and would look up new words, then cross-reference them in the margin with words of similar meaning. Thus, I created my own Thesaurus, before I knew what a Thesaurus was. By doing it the hard way, I learned a lot of new words. I would construct sentences in my head, using my newly learned vocabulary, and I would then practice on my coworkers, to their consternation. They must have wondered what kind of weirdo was this pompous foreigner with the heavy accent using all these highfalutin words.

After five years there, I got promoted to "management".

Even the occasion of my promotion was weird. I had an argument with the guy responsible for the bus operation. He told me that I had been speeding past the pedestrian crossing tunnel (under the rails). It was posted ten mph, which I said was too slow to keep my schedule. We got into an argument, and I got in trouble for he charged me with "insubordination". This was a formal affair, with a hearing where I was represented by a union rep. (Jim Hunter, who was eventually to become a senior official in the CBRT&GW union). A secretary took shorthand and typed up a transcript, which was then sent to head office.

After a week or two, I was called in to the Superintendent's office. He said that he had heard from the Toronto Head Office (for Ontario), who told him that my defense was so eloquent and intelligent that they thought I could be management material, and he wanted to know if I was interested.

I was, and an appointment was arranged with Emmett Murphy, the Regional Sales Manager, and someone from Personnel. I was offered a job in Sales, which I accepted without too many reservations, though some of my fellow workers suggested that they were promoting me to get rid of a "burr in the saddle".

Now, I thought, I would really be able to achieve something, what *Abraham Maslow* called "self actualization" in the management literature of the day.

Disillusionment wasn't long in coming.

My first assignment was in the CNR Sales office in Barrie. It was located in the Barrie railway station building, above the platform. I shared an office with the Sales Manager, Ken Callen. He was a very nice man, about sixty and getting close to retirement. He didn't do much beyond reading the mail and watching the people in the passenger train that stopped there briefly. We could see right into the little bedrooms in the sleeping cars, and sometimes when the curtains were open; he would catch a glimpse of a woman in a more or less state of undress. This was a "show" he seemed to enjoy immensely, but when I commented on his little peccadillo, he denied any prurient intentions, saying, "Sex is an overrated pastime!"

I was sent off to a sales training course run by the railway at Cuttle's Tremblant Club, Mont Tremblant, Quebec. There were about thirty of us in the two-week seminar, where we had a good time but learned little. When I returned I made out my expense account and presented it to Ken for his approval. He rejected it, because I had not put in for enough expenses. "You will make the rest of us look bad" he told me, then helped me to find expenses I had never thought of, or incurred. Ken missed his calling; he should have been a politician.

North Bay

After about six months in Barrie, I was transferred to North Bay, Ontario. I bought a house on Joseph Street in the suburb of Ferris. I remember arriving by car in February and watching the homeowners shovel snow from their rooftops! Snowfalls were heavy in North Bay; I ended up with snow banks so high that by late winter I could not throw the snow over them any longer. But, the snow came and stayed, and you got used to it. The summers were wonderful, with two lakes, Trout Lake and Lake Nippissing nearby; and from my house, we could walk to the beach in five minutes.

Only one thing marred my enjoyment of North Bay. I decided to close in the carport to make it a garage, but when I applied for a building permit, I discovered to my surprise that I could not do it because I needed four feet distance from the edge of the garage to the neighbours property, and there was only one foot between us. I called the people whom I bought the house from, and they told me that the neighbour had put up the present fence, and taken extra space for his driveway. They had not wished to make an issue of it, as the neighbour was quite forceful, and they were rather timid. I hired a surveyor, and found, indeed, that I owned another three feet of the property, front to back. I asked the neighbour to help me move the fence so I could get my permit, but he refused and got quite hostile.

The long weekend in May the neighbour went away, and I dug eighteen fencepost holes with a hand auger, and moved the wood fence. I then put a chain-link fence down the paved driveway along the proper demarcation line, which meant he lost three feet of his seven-foot wide driveway—not quite enough for his pickup truck. He returned, just as I was finishing up the chain link fencing between us. He got very, very angry, yelling and screaming at me with mailed fist waving in the air. He would surely have hit me if his wife had not stopped him by clinging to his raised arm.

That evening he and a buddy got quite drunk, and they were in the driveway shaking my new fence and yelling insults. It was almost amusing: they thought I was German, so they were yelling that they had been fighting us Germans in the last war, and now we came here to take their jobs! I called the cops, and when the police car arrived, the neighbour's friend dropped a bottle of booze on the driveway so it smashed right in front of the policeman.

They charged him with being "a public nuisance" and he had to post a peace bond. They say that fences make good neighbors, and though I cannot vouch for that, I *can* confirm that this neighbour did make a *peaceful* one after that.

North Bay had one strange peculiarity: "Shad flies". For about two weeks every summer in July, there is an invasion of these fish-flies from the lake, swarming so thick it looks like snow, especially in the car lights at night. Downtown in the mornings, the storeowners would be outside sweeping the shad flies from their store windows and sidewalk, and the whole area smelled fishy.

North Bay was a pleasant interlude in my life, a two-year hiatus that I still remember fondly.

That, however, is more than I can say about my stint at the North Bay Regional Sales Office of the Canadian National Railways. It must have been the nearest thing to office Hell the railway could devise.

There were just a few people "working" there: one Sales Rep, a rather happy go lucky guy; a Rate Clerk, also a pleasant guy, the Office Supervisor, an older fellow, quiet and content; an Office Manager who said little and was deadly afraid of losing his sinecure; a "statistician" who had an "office" with a half-wall to hide behind, and the office secretary, an "old maid" with the personality of a snake, who slithered about the office, pulling files in the morning and replacing them in the afternoon. In between, she typed letters or filed her nails. She took an instant dislike to me when I had the nerve to ask her to do something for me—I have forgotten what it was, but she hissed at me and treated me with obvious contempt. It became mutual.

The boss, the Area Sales Manager, was a rather humorless and intellectually challenged fellow by the name of Fred Rohem. He was rather typical of railway management in those days—arriving at his station in life by tenaciously hanging on to his job until eventually pushed upwards by sheer inertia from below. Freddy had a door to *his* office, the only one with a full wall enclosure, which he hid behind most of the day. The CNR practiced "rug ranking" and the top dog got an office with a door, number two an office without a door, the next in line a half wall with an open doorways, and the plebeians were seated in the general office. This group of "happy campers" with little or nothing to do was hidden away there in their Walden Pond, hoping no one in Head Office would pay too much attention to them. Then there was me, inexperienced in the art of feigning work, trying to look busy. I asked the Office Supervisor what he did with the stack of files on this desk, that seemed to re-appear each day, looking about the same, and he told me he was a "pilot"—as in "pile it here, pile it there". One day, old Fred was in a particularly bad mood, and when Brunhilda came with his files, he complained that she had put elastic bands around the bundle. "You know I don't want elastics on my files!" he yelled.

Fred would go shopping with his wife during working hours and keep away from the office when he could, to the relief of all the staff. Once he ran into our salesman, who was also doing some "shopping-work." The salesman, of course, told the whole office about it.

I soon realized that they all were deathly afraid for their jobs, or more properly, *sinecures*. There was almost no useful work to do; all were well-paid management employees, living the good life, hoping no one would discover their own *Shangri-La..*

It became harder and harder to pretend to work, I began to hate going to the office. On my way to the office in the mornings, I tried to think of something I could do to make the day pass. I pined for the month end, when I would get reams of useless statistical computer printout that no one read. My job was to make reports for the boss, taking printed data and converting it to hand written summaries, so that he would not have to shuffle through the raw data. This would occupy three to four days. Sometimes, with a little luck, I could stretch it out to one week. This should have been the job for the "statistician", but he was to busy with other things—God knows what. Regardless, I was grateful for the work. Thus, my "challenging management career" limped along, month after month in an ever-deadening nothingness.

This was 1970-71, and Canada had a short recession. The CNR, being a Government agency, had to do its part, and asked the NOA (Northern Ontario Area) office to reduce expenses. Consequently, Mr. Rohem did his duty, and cut my job. I was given two weeks notice and the choice of returning to the rank and file in Toronto, or be laid off.

I chose the lay off. In other words, I quit. I did not want to leave north Bay; I loved the place and intended to stay, somehow.

I lucked out. The salesman told me of a new plywood mill starting up there, under the auspices of a northern area government subsidy for business startups. To put it bluntly, the government gave a bunch of money to a few opportunists who promised to perform economic miracles in the depressed northern Ontario area. In this particular situation some British Columbia expatriates with softwood lumber plywood-manufacturing experience started up *Champlain Industries*. I was hired as a Traffic Manager, but soon ended up doing anything that required a high-school education, like production statistics, using a *comptometer* (a pre-electronic calculator relic) for calculations. To no one's surprise, the plywood business went bust after devouring the government's money, and I had no choice but to sell my home in North Bay and return to Toronto. It was one of the saddest things I ever have had to do in my life. I still miss North Bay.

Return to Toronto

—Xerox

I worked for a short while as a salesman for a transportation agency called Highway Transport Brokers. I was the top producing salesman there, though I really was not that good a salesman, I just worked harder than anyone else.

Fridays, we had to go in to the office located in the TD Centre, with our sales reports. Most of the sales people would "knock off" the whole morning or perhaps make a single call on the way in. I would work right until the afternoon, before going to the office. Thus, my success was due largely to the law of average, not any particular sales skills. I found the work rather tedious, so I looked for something better.

I landed a job with *Xerox of Canada* as a Traffic Supervisor, later Traffic & Transportation Manager. It was pure luck; I was not really qualified for the job, though I had almost completed a college-level Certificate in Distribution—but I learned fast and the four years I spent at Xerox were the most productive, educational and rewarding years of my business life. Xerox was a very progressive company; it invested much time and effort in training its employees at all levels. I managed the company's Canadian logistics operation, and developed a reputation as a "fixer". When another department got in trouble at the Distribution Centre, they gave it to me to fix, and I did. I was responsible for all the satellite distribution warehouses and machine installations across Canada, and got to travel the Country on company business. It was a great time for me. Of course, like all ambitious people, I didn't think my pay cheque truly reflected my contribution, conveniently forgetting that I made twice as much as my former fellow workers at the CNR, and that had I not been given this opportunity by Xerox, my inherent skills and abilities might never have been put to the test. Like many ambitious and driven people, I rationalized my narcissism.

The beginning was a bit unsteady. My boss had a drinking problem, and so had the warehouse manager he hired. A third manager did not, but he went along with the boss when he wanted to go to the pub for "lunch". I went along once, to a "strip joint" in Brampton, and realized that my boss did not go there to eat—he just drank beer. So did the warehouse manager. After that, I refused to go with them. It was just as well, because my boss was fired and so was the warehouse manager. Not for drinking—for incompetence. I don't know what came first—the chicken or the egg—if his incompetence was a result of his drinking, or the drinking was a result of his knowing he was over his head. However, he hired me, and for that I am grateful.

Xerox was my first "real" management job, and I learned the "craft" there. At first I was quite nervous: I had to hire staff for a brand new department, as Toronto had taken over Montreal as the National Distribution Centre (because of Bill 101, part of Rene Levesque's legacy). I managed to hire some really good people, and used applied psychology to motivate them. I relied almost exclusively on what I had learned in school and from books about motivating human beings—and it worked. In the beginning, I would hold short daily meetings to discuss the best ways to approach a given administrative or technical problem, hear everyone's suggestions and build a consensus before implementing the procedure, or make the change. I used "group dynamics" and "consensus building" before it became in vogue, and built a strong, effective and motivated department from "scratch".

I will relate another short anecdote. I had been on vacation in Norway for three weeks, and the first day back, I called my secretary to my office to take dictation.

Lorna Decca was of the "old school" of secretaries, and could take dictation very fast and accurately. It was very efficient, in the days before personal computers.

I began to dictate to her, and could see that she was hesitating; her pen was still on the pad. After a while, I stopped and asked if there was something wrong. She hesitated, then said "Mr. Roseth, I don't understand a word you are saying". I had been dictating in Norwegian!

During the mid-seventies, Xerox had some difficult times with the Japanese competition in desktop copiers, and my immediate opportunity for advancement was, at least temporarily, blocked. My head had swollen appreciably from the success and positive feedback I had received from my superiors at Xerox, and I was quite anxious for a "well deserved" promotion. I had expected a shot at managing the new distribution centre then planned for Calgary, but because of the financial setbacks facing them, that project was shelved. I then made one of the most stupid decisions of my life: With the promise of "running my own show" and quite a bit more money, I accepted an offer to run a Branch of a transportation company, Cottrell Transport. To this "horror story" I now turn.

Cottrell Transport—*cauldron of machinations*

Cottrell Transport was a freight forwarding company, utilizing the CNR's equipment, railway cars, tracks and even buildings. The railways had gotten out of LCL (less than car load) and were "farming" this business out to the independent forwarding companies such as Cottrell, Muirhead (later Clarke), Trans-Western and Howell Forwarding. These outfits, for a while, made piles of money with little investments, riding the railway's rails using railway equipment and buildings. The railways had wanted to get out of less than carload freight (LCL) in the late fifties, and individual, independent businesses or *forwarders* were given contracts with either of the two main railways. In Cottrell's case, the CNR built their terminals, which Cottrell then leased back at a very good rate. Larry Wilson once told me, in "complete confidence", that the business was a "money machine".

When the original owners, the Cottrells, retired, a few of the management employees bought the company from them. The main shareholders were David Trudeau, C.E.O., in Montreal, and Jack Farley, CFO, in Vancouver. Larry Wilson was hired, as General Manager. He had been a minor functionary with the CNR'S Liquid Cargo division in Concord. Larry was brought in after the company was unionized by the Teamsters, Local 419, and the management had screwed up the whole process to an extent that they faced a strike. They folded, and signed an impossible contract with the union. In spite of the sweetheart terms for the union, the flames of hate that the management actions had kindled were not extinguishable, at least by the original protagonists. So, Larry was brought in to smooth things over. Larry was "silky smooth", but silky talk didn't do the job either, so he hired me. I knew Larry as a fellow graduate from the Canadian Institute of Traffic and Transportation (C.I.T.T.), but I did not know much more about him, and almost nothing about Cottrell, except that I had some minor dealings with them at Xerox.

I should have known better, but I didn't. Cottrell was a rat's nest, thoroughly fermented with union machinations and management duplicity. The management, initially, had threatened the work force rather shabbily, and as a consequence, the company got unionized. Not only unionized, but unionized by the Teamsters union, Warehousemen's Local 419, at the time the most rabid and antisocial union Local in the country. It was headed by a demagogue called Jack Robinson, who had as his life mission to attack anyone remotely connected with the "business class". Something must have happened to him when he was younger, for his class hatred went far beyond anything that could be explained by the normal conflicts in industrial relations. His histrionics were legion. He would sit in on a grievance meeting (the guys would file grievances for almost anything, and grievances were used to bog us down in these meetings—it was a tool, a weapon he used with élan), and when we did not go along with his suggested solution, he would stand up and shout "I am calling a walkout—you can sue me if you want!" Then he would look around at his troops, taking in their admiring glances. I would just stare at him, say nothing and await his next move. Then, as suddenly as he had gotten up, he would sit down again and change the subject, as if nothing had happened. I think he could have made a fairly dramatic actor.

The unionization was spearheaded by a Jamaican immigrant by the name of *Moe Richards.* Moe had a chip on his shoulder and a confrontational attitude, which got him in much trouble with management, and, as a result, he approached the Teamster's Union. From there on, he became the main protagonist in the Cottrell/union saga, and the objective of management's efforts to escape the union's grip.

In some cases, management is less sensible than the people they are managing. The Cottrell owner-managers were a particularly foolish lot. When the union certification notice went up, they tried to argue that the firm should be unionized through the Federal Labour Department, not Ontario's. This was a pure stalling tactic, and they managed to keep it going for a year, spending a fortune on high priced downtown lawyers and creating a stalemate that progressively ratcheted up the bad feelings existing among the employees, even the more moderate ones. Management went to great lengths trying to intimidate the main protagonists, in particular Moe Richards. They had him digging ditches in the yard in the hot summer sun, then, filling it in again, something right out of a Steve McQueen movie. I could envision the Branch Manager, Harold Scott, saying, "What we have here is a failure to communicate …" The result was predictable: the union got certified, Moe Richard, "cool hand Luke", became Chief Steward, and the relationship between the men, their union and their employer was one of hatred, suspicion and fear.

This, then, was what I inherited at Cottrell Transport.

Larry Wilson, among his fellows at the Transport Institute, was known as "Slippery Larry". He had perfected an avuncular, amicable persona, with a polish that could have been the envy of any politician. He had little formal education, but was well spoken and intelligent. When on the C.I.T.T. Board, he manipulated, cajoled and "glad-handed" until he got his way. To be fair, at Cottrell he did not have an enviable position; he was an outsider, trying to steer a political course between Dave Trudeau, the President and major shareholder, located in Montreal, and Jack White, C.F.O. and second in command, located in Vancouver. Trudeau, however, called the shots. There were some disgraced former managers still hanging around as "staff" people: Dale MacDonald, a former Operations Manager and alcoholic, who survived by Trudeau's good graces as his staff assistant in Montreal; his brother Richard, the Pricing Manager; Harold Scott,[1] Ontario Manager, Mel Bigelow[2], Marketing Manager, and Red Swan, Toronto Sales Manager and nominally reporting to me. They shared a common bond of resentment and hatred for the usurper, Larry Wilson, and later, for me. They were supposed to be "support staff", but "fifth column" would be better description. Having thoroughly screwed up the operations in Toronto and got

---

1. *Harold Scott* quit soon after I was hired. He bought a local cartage company, "Jessan Cartage", which he operated until he retired. He never gave me any trouble at Cottrell.
2. *Mel Bigelow* stayed on in a staff capacity, but he never interfered in the operations, and I was not aware of any shenanigans on his part.

the Branch unionized, they lurked in the background, hoping to see us fail. The tension was palpable, and I was the cheese in the middle of this unholy sandwich.

This kind of organizational arrangement is often favoured by insecure autocrats. My first test came soon. Dave Trudeau was visiting, on occasion of my employment, when word came of a work stoppage on the floor. Moe Richards had had words with one of the foremen, as he was won't to do; he put on his histrionics in the middle of the floor, waving his hands shouting "Stop work! Stop work!" The Operations Manager came running, huffing and puffing (he was a rather corpulent man) into my office. Dave Trudeau was there, and so was Larry Wilson. Trudeau was very nervous, not knowing what to do. I told him to stay in the office, grabbed my copy of the Ontario Labour Relations Act and told the Operations Manager to bring the men to the lunchroom. I had never faced this situation before, but knew instinctively that I had to "face the music". I also knew, from my experience on strike at the CNR, that things can quickly get out of hand if a demagogue is allowed to hector a crowd.

When they were seated, I read the relevant parts of the act and told them that anyone or all not going back to work would be fired instantly. I buttressed my words with a bit of rhetoric about "a new day" and some other platitudes. They bought it and went back to work when I promised that no one would be punished. I had studied some psychology in school, but this was my first practical experience confronting a hostile group. I learned much more about human behaviour the next three years—I had to.

I realized that the present Operations Manager would not make the cut. He was older and tired. He was also not very bright. I knew I had to fire him, the sooner the better, but he had a family and I had never before fired anyone. He had been hired because he was a former football player—quite former—the thinking being that he would demand respect! It was one of the most stupid reasons for hiring someone that I had ever heard, and now I was left to correct this one of their many bad decisions.

I called him in to my office and told him straight. He took it well—I think he had expected it. Since then, I have been on both sides of the "firing line", and I dislike both about the same. There is little protection for middle managers, no "golden parachutes" or "golden handshakes". In fact, there is no gold at all. It's truly Darwinian "survival of the fittest".

I hired a young fellow, Paul Publow, just twenty-four years of age, and full of piss and vinegar. He was green as hell, but had tremendous stamina and was quite bright. Larry Wilson was aghast at me hiring this youngster, but I insisted. Youth was an asset as we were to endure grueling hours of tremendous stress before we got the place under control. Trouble was, Paul was also quite arrogant and abrasive, and I had a hard time in the beginning, keeping him from overstepping his bounds, or from being "eaten alive" by the union.

I recognized there was one fundamental problem I had to face right away. The foremen were poorly paid and totally without training in supervision. They knew nothing about labour law or the Collective Agreement. I rented a large boardroom at the Woodbridge Board of Trade and set up a classroom there. I brought the eight foremen in on five consecutive Sundays, lecturing them on the Collective Agreement and supervisory tactics. We did role-playing and drills, and I brought in an Industrial Relations expert for one session. I promised them that management would support them come what may, as long as they did their best and acted in an honest and truthful manner. This was a revelation for these guys who had been treated as scapegoats for managements and offered up on the union altar whenever they got in trouble with any of the men. Moe Richards was used to have a foreman for breakfast.

I told Larry Wilson what I had done, and he had no choice but to support me. I wanted uniforms and raises for all the foremen. He hesitated, but gave in after a little chat by telephone with Dave Trudeau in Montreal.

Now I was getting ready to take on the union, and the opportunity was not long in coming.

The next thing I did was refusing to let grievances go to senior management (me). I would make the steward deal with the head shift foreman. This put Moe into a frenzy. He hated not being able to sit around my office chatting about trivial grievances that he generated so he could get away from work for a while, for Moe was also very lazy. Once, we even had a grievance from a worker complaining that he had been refused a "gas" mask, meaning a dust mask, which he had requested because his fellow worker was farting in the boxcar they were loading. I refused to deal with the absurd "grievance", and I think even Jack Robinson found it too much, for he quietly dropped it. However, it does tell something about the mental state of Moe Richards, that he would encourage and process a "grievance" of this nature. It also says something of the atmosphere existing at the time.

I think Jack Robinson felt a bit slighted having to deal with me instead of Larry Wilson, for he assigned a union agent to me, a man by the name of John

Kehoe. John was not your average Teamster; he was polite, well spoken and sincere. I think he found it refreshing to work with someone who had no "axe to grind" and were not part of the company history. I think he also believed me when I said I wanted to reform and renew the relationship between the company and their union, and develop a professional bond based on mutual trust and respect. I remember John telling me that I was an unusual person to find in a managerial position. Naïve and idealistic would perhaps have been a better description. I had a framed copy of the *Serenity Prayer* on my office wall, and he asked if I was a former alcoholic. I said no, and he then told me that he was, and that the Serenity Prayer was recited every time at the *Alcoholics Anonymous* meetings he attended regularly.

John and I were making steady progress cleaning up grievances and improving communications between management and union. However, this scared Moe Richards, who feared being sidelined and losing power over the men, and he prevailed on Jack Robinson to get rid of John, claiming he was too friendly with me. At a union meeting John was confronted with trumped up and phony charges of collusion with management and dereliction of duty, and was given the "opportunity" to resign! It was a classic union coup. John went back to Nova Scotia, his home Province, where he apparently started a small business! Perhaps his heart wasn't really in the union work in the first place, but I still think the Teamsters lost a fine human being with more class than the rest of them put together.

To replace John, I was assigned a manipulating, underhanded rogue who was too discreditable even for the union. He quickly brought the relationship back to square one, but somehow he did not get along with Moe either. I think Moe did not want anyone between himself and Jack Robinson, his mentor and hero, so this fellow, whose name I cannot even recall, was removed in due course. That's when I decided on a strategy that eventually brought direct confrontation and ultimately, the demise of Moe Richard and the end of "union rule". I realized that I needed to go directly to the men on any major issue, and instituted a series of company/employee meetings in the lunchroom. This infuriated Moe, who insisted that he was the only spokesman for the men, and that I had no right to approach them directly. I told him that on non-union matters, the Company had every right to communicate directly with its work force, and in this I knew I had the law on my side, for whatever that was worth in that environment. I knew I had only so much time to turn the situation around, a short honeymoon period, before Dave Trudeau would panic and cave in, which meant my own demise (and probably, Larry's). This was industrial warfare in its simplest form.

Before "declaring war" on Moe, I wanted to try once again to overcome his hatred. I had a long meeting with him, and told him that the despotic leadership he was exhibiting could be used more productively, if not in a union setting, then with management. I offered him a job as foreman with an ironclad, written contract so he would not have to fear termination after losing his union membership. Moe was a vain son-of-a-bitch, and he was for a moment considering it. However, I think he was afraid to be viewed as a turncoat, and he "chicken-out." Later, he told the men that he had been offered a management job, but had turned it down as a sacrifice to "the men" and his union! What a wonderful speech. I saw my attempt as partial victory; though he had turned me down, the fact that he had even listened to me probably put a question mark in the mind of some of his troops, and I could say with veracity that I had tried everything before giving up on him—a regular Neville Chamberlain, looking for "peace in our time".

Moe had told me some of his background. He grew up in Jamaica without a father, and he said he had been discriminated against all his life. He didn't particularly blame white people, but I think he must have gotten great satisfaction from being the leader of a predominantly white group of workers (though we had about seven or eight Jamaicans working there, they were *not* his main supporters). One thing I am particularly proud of, and I will return to this subject later, was that not once in this struggle was there ever any suggestion that I was attacking Moe on any kind of racial grounds—not even by Moe himself.

I wanted to find out what Moe was up to, and who his most avid supporters among the men were. Larry Wilson suggested I use an undercover detective from Wackenhut Investigations; they had been using that firm during the unionization drive to try, unsuccessfully, to discover what the ringleaders and the union were up to. We got a former policeman from Jamaica by the name of Tyrone. He was put on the payroll and quickly befriended Moe. Every day he would send detailed written reports to my home address, detailing Moe's shenanigans, but there was little in it I could use and that I didn't know or suspect all ready (we did discover a Marijuana drug dealer among our men, and I called the drug squad who came and arrested the poor guy, catching him right in the act). Then one evening he called me to tell me that Moe had confided in him that he was tired and needed a couple of weeks off on compensation. Sure enough, the next day Moe booked off sick—he had hurt his back! Of course, he got a doctor's note suggesting he stay off work for a few days (doctor's notes were a dime a dozen; doctors loved Compensation Board cases, as the Board paid more than OHIP and they paid much sooner). Now the fun began. Moe asked his new "friend" to go with him to the *Mercury Club* in downtown Toronto, at the time a hangout for West Indian immigrants. There he danced the Limbo and had a great time on the Compensation Board's expense, and his "friend" on ours. No one thought to take along a cameraman. Later, I called the Compensation Board in, and showed their representative the written but unsigned report. He told me flatly that as it was unsigned, I would need the detective's personal testimony. Tyrone refused, saying that he could never work undercover at a union shop ever again if I blew his cover. I was hopping mad and told him I would subpoena him anyhow, but then the Board rep. said he had interviewed Moe's girlfriend (Moe was married with two children), who stated unequivocally that Moe had spent the night with her. I gave up and fired the detective. One thing I did find interesting: nowhere in the detective's report did I find any incidence of collusion or support on behalf of the other Jamaicans for Moe's behaviour, in fact, they usually steered clear of him. That was encouraging. His own nationals did not support him (in fact, long after Moe was gone for good, I had the pleasure to promote one of them to foreman, and he made a fairly good one).

After Moe returned to work, he was even more obstinate, as he knew from the Compensation Board rep that I had tried to nail him. I knew he was about to blow.

I warned Larry Wilson that a climax would ensue presently. I had prepared the foremen as best I could. I think Moe by now had seen the new professionalism exhibited by the foremen and it made him nervous. He was feeling his grip weaken, as his whole raison d'etre was to protect them from a "viscous and arbitrary" management.

One thing I had drilled into the foremen was that refusal to do a job was a serious offence for which they could suspend (not fire) a worker on the spot. In support of this, I posted a notice to this effect on the employee bulletin board. This was a new and immense responsibility for the previously emasculated foremen, and in giving them such power I took a calculated risk. Moe Richard was the only one to my knowledge that would refuse an assignment. I knew it would not be long before it would happen again—he was getting anxious and needed a confrontation to maintain his power and control over the men.

Then it happened, as if choreographed. Moe had a particular dislike of the head foreman, Hilton, a short, wiry man from the Maritimes. One day Moe was checking off a load (he had "super seniority" as a Chief Steward and could pick his jobs, usually the "checker" job—it was, physically, the easiest job there), when he took exception to something or other and refused to continue checking. Hilton asked him, clearly and politely, in front of several witnesses, to continue working, but Moe screamed that Hilton was a bigot and had called him a "nigger"(there were never any corroborating evidence that Hilton had uttered this word). When he refused the third time, Hilton suspended him and told him to go home. Moe did his usual gig: "Hilton fired me! Stop work!" he yelled, and everyone did, as usual. It was a routine they knew well. Soon, Moe would be pacified, and work would resume after a nice rest for the men.

Not this time. I had Moe removed—he was told to leave the premises or be charged with trespassing, and after hanging around outside for a face-saving while, he did. Then I called a meeting in the lunchroom. The men wanted to know if Moe was fired, and I told them no, not so far, he was suspended, and the normal legal procedure would determine if he would be returning (I had already decided that his return would be "over my dead body"). Act two of the drama was now set; I knew the union would not take this lying down, and expected a confrontation soon.

It came the following morning. I had not contacted Robinson, nor did he contact me. He was lying low plotting his next move, behind the scene, so to speak, but his options were limited. He was a man foreign to diplomacy or compromise, and he chose the only way he knew.

I got the call about five a.m. The night shift was out on a "wildcat" strike, blocking the entrance gate. When I arrived, I drove through the gate, between the striking men, without an incident and proceeded to my office where I met Paul. Larry Wilson was hiding at home and could not be reached, as was Dave Trudeau in Montreal. I decided to go it alone. I grabbed my copy of the Labour Relations Act and opened the page on *Illegal Strikes*. I told Paul to take the Polaroid camera and follow me, taking pictures of any one acting aggressively. We drove back to the gate to confront our workforce. It was a cold January morning, and the car windows kept fogging up, as did the camera lens. At the gate we got out of the car and faced the crowd.

The scene was something right out of "On the Waterfront". The men were milling around in the cold January morning, tired after a nights work and probably wanting to be anywhere else; carrying hastily made-up placards saying things like "The Company is unfair" and "Bring back Moe Richards". I knew I had to get them back to work before the day shift showed up, or I would lose control completely.

Jack and Moe had made a major mistake: they had called the men out too early, giving me time to act before the next shift arrived. I literally read them the "riot act", reading directly from the Labour Relations Act of Ontario while Paul Publow ran around snapping pictures of anyone that moved (later that day we found that I had forgotten to put film in the camera, but by then it was immaterial). I spoke of their families and their responsibility to them, and to us. I cajoled, begged, praised and implored them, and assured them that Moe would get his fair hearing in Labour Court (arbitration), and that they would not be punished. Slowly they began straggling back, first one or two, then several, until all but a few were heading back to the warmth of the building. I knew I had won the day, if not the battle. Two or three of the "hard core" supporters still hung around. I walked up to them and gave them fifteen minutes to return or be fired, then left. That did it; I could see from my office window that they were slowly walking back toward the building. A few days later, one of the three cornered me in the washroom and thanked me for saving his job.

Jack Robinson was wild but not crazy. I told him I knew he was behind it, and would charge him and his union before the Labour Relations Board if he did not back off immediately, and take the legal route. He did. I was served with the appropriate paper and we were heading off to arbitration a few months later. But first, I had work to do. I needed to mend fences, reassess authority and develop a measure of trust between workers and management, knowing well that the hyenas I worked for would devour me if I failed. I sincerely wished to make the workplace more humane, but that was my own personal goal and not one necessarily shared by the owners. I saw this battle as not one between good and bad, but between bad and "badder"; there were times I was not quite sure who was worse—the union or the owners. One thing I did know: this was a power struggle between the company and the union, I was in the front on the "firing line" and the workers were the pawns in this game. We all would pay the price of failure.

Human organizations are predicated on conflict and self-interests, even our parliamentary political system is based on conflict within rules and balancing of interests. Unions are a legitimate force against arbitrary and self-interested behaviour by management. That's the way liberal democracies work. It is not perfect, but the alternatives are worse. We need these countervailing forces: unions in industry, newspapers and news media in politics, government and business. Sometimes, such as where a union is strong and the company small and weak, (or the other way around), things are out of balance and do not work well. However, the survival of the firm is also in the union's interest, neither party wins if the company goes bankrupt. When there is reasonable honesty and fairness on both sides, the relationship works. In fact, a union shop in many ways is an advantage to management, at least in larger organizations, as the collective agreement gives structure, guidelines and directions to the relationship, making it easier to manager the labour force. Management and union can point to the Agreement for guidance. Decisions, especially unpopular ones, can be made more rational and less subjective. It can be a win-win situation.

There was a hiatus of six months or so while the Moe Richards arbitration case wound its way through the bureaucratic "red tape" and an arbitrator of mutual acceptability was chosen.

I used the interregnum to work toward establishing control and effective communications with the men. Fortunately, Jack kept away most of the time. Larry refused to see him and he was probably too proud or angry to see me. He appointed another business agent who never did manage to establish effective rapport with the men, he was rather ineffectual, but Jack left him there and that was all right with me. I think Jack was expecting that he would win the arbitration case and Moe would soon be back with "guns blazing". However, I think most of the men were actually happier with Moe gone.

One of the laziest guys, after Moe, was another immigrant, Fernando, who, of course was appointed Chief Steward by union fiat. However, Fernando was not able to win the men's trust, and he gave me little trouble, though he tried once.

Payday was on Fridays, and it had been the practice to give the nightshift their pay cheques on Friday night before they started their shift. This had caused problems, as the men would look over their cheques, and finding a mistake or error, would hassle the foreman about it, even writing up grievances. I decided to have the cheques given out Saturday mornings after the shift, and posted the required notice about the change. That evening I got a call from the night foreman. Fernando had called a work stoppage, and was demanding that the pay-cheques be distributed right away. I told him to hang tough and drove there as soon as I could. It was now about one o'clock in the morning, and the men were standing around waiting for me to arrive.

I got up on top of the dock operations office's stairs, overlooking the dock area, and spoke to the men. I reached back into my memory of psychology and human relations theory for guidance. I told them that the change was permanent and would not be rescinded. I explained, again, the reason for the change, and that it had no real effect on them, for any errors would only be looked after on Mondays anyhow, as there was no office staff on the weekend. It was a non-issue, and I think they knew it. Then I performed my final act. I pointed to Fernando who was standing at the foot of the stairs. "Fernando", I said, is it you that have called this *illegal* work stoppage? Do you not know what happened to Moe? Are you prepared for the consequences? Do you really think the union is going to protect you from the consequences of this *illegal* action?"

Fernando slowly slunk away, moving towards his workstation, and the men did likewise. The emergency was over, and I had learned two valuable lessons: first, communicate carefully any changes, especially if it has to do with money, and second, single out the ringleader of the crowd, and attack him directly. If you can break him, you have won.

Fernando was feeling the pressure of his exalted position. I was making sure we kept him working so his temporary Chief Steward's job would not turn into a sinecure. He then tried to collect compensation by claiming that he had hurt his back—the old Moe trick. It didn't work. I had found out that he had a previous claim for the same ailment at his last employer (a little bird told me), so I went to the Workers Compensation Board. It took several months and a meeting with the "Full Board", but I managed to get his claim referred to their "deferred compensation enhancement fund".

This first entailed a meeting with the Chairman, who had an office at the top of their building on Bloor Street. He had a bed in his office, where he had his naps, as he was a "rehab" and needed to rest often. In my mind, he was another example of the wasteful and highly politicized Workers Compensation Board, staffed with lazy and incompetent bureaucrats of the worst ilk, all of whom, over the years in management, I learned to loathe with a passion.

The foremen were also getting better at their main job, the job of keeping freight moving to the right destination. There had been a problem with freight going to the wrong city, and of freight being overlooked and left behind on the dock. They had tried everything, using little flags on the skids of freight, to bring it the attention of the foremen. Nothing worked. In talking to the foremen, I suddenly realized why it was happening, and I had a solution. The foremen, including Paul, the Operations Manager, were not making any notes, relying on their memories. I had long ago learned the value of keeping a notebook in my pocket, and I bought them each one and told them to use it. It fixed seventy-five percent of the problems, and Paul later told me that he was amazed how much more he remembered once he had written it down! Supervision and management isn't rocket science, but when you have not been properly taught, even small things can make a huge difference—like making notes.

Productivity increased greatly, and there was labour peace—or at least a truce. I am sure Jack Robinson had a few sleepless nights. I tried to understand him, and made efforts to be friendly. Paul and I took him and the stewards to dinner in an expensive restaurant downtown, but he spent the whole night relating how terribly the company had treated the men. I realize that friction and tension were what keep people like him in power, but in Jack's case, it was more than just that—he really hated all business and management, or "capitalists", his preferred term. An uneasy, symbiotic relationship, I realized, was the best we could expect from him, though even that was in the future, if and when Moe Richards was gone.

Then the letter came. We had an arbitrator and a date. A boardroom was booked for a week at the Hotel Toronto, at that time a favourite "hangout" of the legal beagles. The arbitrator was *Master Dunn* (he was a *Master of the Court*). We had a lawyer from Hoskins & Harcourt, a top-line law firm with a specialty in labour relations. The management team was Larry Wilson, Paul Publow and myself. The union had Jack Robinson, his shop rep, their lawyer and five union stewards, all on *our* payroll, making zero contribution to the process.

The main issue soon boiled down to proving that Moe had called the illegal work stoppage. While he admitted telling the men to stop working, as he was wont to do, he denied the more serious allegation that he called a "wildcat" strike. We had an informer who would not testify, because he feared for his safety, to say the least. We knew that one Bill Touckas had carried the message from Moe to the men to strike at five in the morning, which they did. Bill was just the messenger, a simple bumpkin, and no radical union man. I think they were afraid of putting him on the witness stand. We knew that Bill was holed up at home, and we made a bold decision: we would subpoena Bill Touckas as *our* witness. It was a risky move. If Bill was a hostile witness, we could not force him to tell the truth, and if he lied, we would surely lose. Paul volunteered to personally deliver the subpoena late in the evening before the scheduled testimony of our witnesses. The union side did not know of our action.

The following morning we were having breakfast in the large, open cafeteria on the main floor of the hotel. The union guys were sitting at the other side of the room, when Bill marched in. He walked directly over to us, waved to his compatriots as he passed by them, and shook hands with all of us, looking quite happy and cheerful. To say we were surprised is an understatement, and in the Union case, they were practically in shock, and left the cafeteria presently.

When the hearing resumed, the union lawyer asked to see the arbitrator and us. They folded. Admitting culpability, Moe asked for "another chance". He got none. I could not risk it, though it is hard to tell, perhaps he could have reformed, but I doubt it.[3]

The arbitration hearing alone had cost the Company $13,000.00 (a lot of money in 1976), the Union's cost was somewhat less. What a waste of energy, money and effort on both sides.

Moe tried one more time. He went to the Human Rights Commission and charged me with discrimination! A young man of East Indian decent was the investigator. He went to see all eight black men on the floor and asked them if I had ever discriminated against any one of them. They told him never! Whatever my faults, bigotry was not one.

The last day we met in my office and he gave me a verbal report.

On the way out, I introduced him to my private secretary, a young immigrant from the Philippines. The investigator smiled and winked at me as he left. Without any words, he acknowledged what I was telling him.

I heard later that Moe had gotten a job with another transportation firm as labourer. He was not a union steward. No one at Cottrell missed him, or had any contact with him again.

Bill Touckas had more brains that I had given him credit for. He quit and bought a Taxi, which he operated in Scarborough with his wife. One day he came to my office to solicit donations for his Bowling Club. I gave him a cheque, and he invited me to be "guest of honour" at the club's annual do. I went and enjoyed myself. I could hardly recognize Bill. The man, who had been a marginal worker and a slave to Moe, was now the perfect small businessman, and acted the part. I guess the moral of his story is "never underestimate human potential".

---

3. Those that wish to read the arbitration case can find it in Law Reports: *Cannet Transport vs. Teamsters Local 419*, 1975-76. The case was also published in a book by Bruce Young and The Canada Labour Views Co. Limited, in June, 1984, called *Beyond Discharge* (see also two earlier books "*A State of Suspension*" and "*At the Point of Discharge*").

Having achieved labour peace, or at least a truce, I could now concentrate on other areas of business. I hired a credit and collection person to clean up delinquent accounts, and began doing operational studies to increase gross car revenue and eliminate "bottlenecks" in the process.

The Credit Manager I hired was a young man called Ajay Veermani. He was from New Dehli, India, and a pretty quick learner. His father had been in the British army and was an educated and intelligent man. Ajay was getting married, so his father advertised for a bride for him in New Delhi. The ad described a successful man, a manager in Canada, who would bring his bride to Nirvana in the Promised Land, Canada. I met his father when he was in Toronto to discuss marriage options with Ajay, and I remember telling him that I questioned the brazen commercialism of advertising for a bride. The old man told me something I will always remember: "You westerners," he said, "put more efforts into researching the family tree of your dogs than in finding out what kind of people your wife's family is from". He was absolutely right, of course.

Ajay is now the owner of a air cargo company in Toronto.

One area had to be dealt with in the upcoming contract negotiations. There was a clause in the present contract, which had no other purpose than to generate unnecessary work. The clause, number twelve, said, "There shall be a Checker at every door". This was a case of the Collective Agreement usurping management's rights, and it hamstrung the operation by slowing down activity through this "bottleneck". It was a totally redundant position, but a desirable one from the workers point of view, for it involved almost no physical activity. We did a study to estimate what could be saved by eliminating just that one clause, and it was substantial. I resolved to make it the key management demand in the upcoming contract negotiations.

Larry Wilson, who had been lying low when the "war" was on, now took a leading role in the contract negotiations. Clause twelve became a stumbling block. It was a strike-issue, and as we approached the deadline, Larry wanted to cave in. Of course, he did not have to face the problems of managing around it. He could blame *me* for operational costs, but if the union struck, it would be *his* head on the block. Dave Trudeau did see the problem as a monetary issue, and was more supportive. However, I had no illusion about him taking a strike. I knew that, and Larry knew that. We were not exactly negotiating from strength, but having lost the arbitration, Jack and the gang did not want a strike either, and I think Jack did not know for sure if we would call his bluff.

The union had taken a strike vote as usual, and had this "mandate" in their pocket, using it as a club with which to hit us over the head. The last meeting came to an impasse. I told Larry that if he "folded", I would quit. He was cornered. Jack said "so it is a strike then!" as our meeting broke up. I knew Jack had tried to call Dave Trudeau in Montreal, but Dave did not take the call. He complained to Dave's assistant that I was holding up a settlement and dissuading poor Larry from settling with him. I was certainly guilty of that. But that 'phone call told me something else: Jack was clearly averse to a strike, and we could possible bluff it through.

As Larry and I walked across the parking lot to our cars after the meeting ended, Larry' face was ashen gray. "When Dave finds out, he will fire us both and settle with Jack" he said. At that point I didn't care. If that was the case, I did not want to work for him anyway, and I told Larry so. I don't think it made him feel any better.

When I arrived at the office, there was a call from the union rep requesting me to call him back. I knew we had won! I waited a reasonable time before returning his call. He wanted to settle. We drove back to the union office, and with a few minor adjustments, signed the new Agreement. Clause twelve was history.

People like Larry Wilson are the smart ones. They know how to keep away from the firing line; how to hire people like me to do the dirty work while they take the credit and benefit from other peoples sweat and tears. Larry got the kudos for the new Contract. Paul and I did the spadework.

The Teamsters gave us little problem after that. Grievances were minimal. I made sure we communicated with weekly meetings, taking written notices of complaints and ensuring that all suggestions were considered, if not acted upon. Jack seemed to have gotten over his paranoia about me speaking directly to the men. Perhaps he just gave up. I would invite the Union rep to all meetings, and Jack himself attended once or twice, behaving himself admirably. I made sure the Union would not think I was trying to circumvent them—on the contrary, I involved them whenever I could. Discipline was handled objectively, reprimands were recorded, and the few times we had to terminate an employee, it would come as no surprise, being a "culminating incidence". In fact, there would usually not even be a grievance.

We had some problems with alcoholics—they tended to miss work on Mondays, and since alcoholism must be treated as an illness, I had to expend much effort to try to get them to seek treatment. However, I don't remember anyone who did, and after a fair try, I began issuing warnings each time they missed work. I would keep a strict record of average absenteeism, and give them three months to align themselves with that average. After that time, if no improvement was noticed, and it seldom was, I would fire them, and that was the end of it. I learned another lesson there: unions do not really want to spend time and money supporting bad and troublemaking employees if the unions own security is not at stake. Jack's shenanigans were driven by insecurity—partially justified—but his confrontational tactics left me no choice but to meet him head on.

Jack Robinson died some time after I had left Cottrell. A fellow by the name of Sean Floyd took over as President. Jack had been a bastard, but he was a fairly honest bastard. This guy Floyd and his sidekick got in cahoots with some supervisors at Consumers Distributing's distribution centre in Weston (Consumers is no more, they went bankrupt in the early nineties) and stole a small fortune of merchandise. They eventually got caught and Floyd ended up where he belonged: in jail. I lost contact with Local 419, but many years later I did have dealings with them. They seemed to have settled into mid-life blandness, their "wild youth" behind them. We all mature, eventually.

Item: Toronto Star, Tuesday, August 12,2003: "… Union angered over hiring of ex-racketeer (Sean Floyd) …"

D6 • TORONTO STAR • TUESDAY, AUGUST 12, 2003

Business

Unions raise objections

► Floyd From D1

Since his release, Floyd said, he has worked with various unions in consulting and "trouble-shooting." He would not identify the unions.

But the retail division of the United Food and Commercial Workers Union said on its Web site that it achieved some recent organizing successes in Eastern Ontario because of Floyd's efforts. It described him as "a labour activist in southern Ontario who has a long-standing relationship with the RWDSU in the province."

Floyd had worked for a small union that represented the Satisfied Brake workers before jumping over to the United Food union's retail division earlier this year. The small union is no longer trying to retain representation at the plant after the CAW agreed to provide services for workers there last fall.

Robin McArthur, president of the retail union's council in Northern Ontario, said he wasn't sure Floyd was the same Teamsters leader who ran into trouble in the 1980s.

"I imagine it is, but I don't know," he said. "I never really asked him. I don't do background checks on a temporary organizer. Why would I?"

McArthur added even if Floyd was the same Teamsters official from the 1980s, he had paid for his crimes through jail time. And as long as the same Floyd had no access to any labour funds except for money in card signings and travel expenses, nothing should hold him back from working for a union, McArthur stressed.

Floyd noted he doesn't negotiate contracts or talk to employers.

Rival unions said although Floyd has served time and his past record should not impede him from employment prospects, he shouldn't be anywhere near a labour organization.

CHRIS WATTIE FOR THE TORONTO STAR

United Food and Commercial Workers Union has hired Sean Floyd, right in a 1985 poster, to help sign up Satisfied Brake workers at this Cornwall plant.

Wayne Fraser, Ontario and Atlantic region director for the Steelworkers, called the retail union's use of Floyd "despicable" and charged there are already signs of a cosy relationship with the company.

"We can't get near the company's property but the RWDSU (retail union) is allowed to hand out free union jackets with the name Satisfied Brakes on the back to workers in the lunch room," Fraser said.

Colin Heslop, a national co-ordinator for the CAW working on the organizing drive, added the retail division of the United Food and Commercial Workers can hire whomever it wants.

"It's their business but the workers in the plant will ultimately decide which type of union they want to represent them," Heslop said.

Floyd said he is confident that the retail union will win bargaining rights at the brake plant.

"I've organized four groups for them," he said. "Satisfied (Brakes) will be five when the election is over."

Unions angered over hiring of ex-racketeer

Sean Floyd helps organization drive

Cornwall plant centre of battle

TONY VAN ALPHEN
BUSINESS REPORTER

Sean Floyd, a notorious labour racketeer here during the 1980s, is back in the spotlight again — working for a major union.

Floyd, who spent time in jail for tax evasion and extortion, has acted as an organizer and "consultant" for a division of the United Food and Commercial Workers Union in the Cornwall area for the last five months.

"I've tried hard to be a model citizen," he said in an interview late last week. "I think, to a large extent, I've accomplished that ... Geez, I haven't had a parking ticket in 20 years."

Floyd, 58, is currently working for the UFCW's Retail, Wholesale and Department Store Union in a fierce organizing battle to represent about 500 workers at the Satisfied Brake Products manufacturing plant in the city.

He said the Canadian Auto Workers and the United Steelworkers of America, two other unions seeking bargaining certification at the plant, will use his past criminal record and activities for political purposes to win votes.

"It's sad," Floyd said, clearly uncomfortable about any public exposure about his past and any possible impact on his family.

The three unions are preparing for the start of a 90-day period later this month where they can sign up to 40 per cent of workers and then immediately apply to the Ontario Labour Relations Board for a certification vote.

Even before the intensive sign-up period, the three unions have been accusing each other of skullduggery in the battle to win the favour of workers. Floyd, whose past popped up in the leaflets, said he told members about his previous union activities and his criminal record.

Floyd, former president of Teamsters Local 419 in Toronto, spent four months in jail in 1985 after pleading guilty to evading taxes on $250,000 of secret payments from Consumers Distributing. Consumers, which closed after declaring bankruptcy in 1996, paid a fine of $125,000 for falsifying records to conceal the payments.

A judge also convicted Floyd and an accomplice for an attempt that year to extort money from the president of Consumers. Floyd served a jail term concurrently with the first sentence.

"I was a kid who allowed himself to be used by some Teamsters," he said about the tax evasion and extortion capers. "I was a whole different Sean Floyd back then. I worked for some very strange people. It pretty well ruined my life."

Furthermore, Floyd confessed at the time to a role in a theft of $200,000 in goods from another warehouse. He spent four months in a halfway house for that crime.

"All I got out of that was a bicycle and a barbecue," he recalled.

➤ Please see Floyd, D6

et tu, Brute!

With the threat from the union a distant memory, the Company's struggles became internecine. Fighting the Union had been, for me, a straightforward proposition, right and wrong, good and bad. However, the management's habitat was a cauldron of conspiracy and machinations for which I was ill prepared and poorly equipped. It had never ceded, just gone underground while I battled the union. There would come a time when I truly wondered if I had been on the wrong side of the equation. I had carried the battle for a bunch of ungrateful hyenas, and I was to find out that in their world you are only as good as your last success, and the word loyalty is not in their vocabulary. Larry was basically a decent man. Though ambitious, he was caught in the middle, with Trudeau & Co. dangling the carrot of the presidency before him. I think Dave figured I was pushing Larry too hard from below, so he sent his henchman Dale MacDonald there under the pretext of "assisting" us with our time and motion study. Dale was a slippery eel—"vertebrally challenged".

The sales manager,"Red" Swan, had a chip on his shoulder and an irascible temperament. Nominally, he reported to me, but because of his long-term friendship with Dave Trudeau, he would go over my head, and also Larry Wilson's, to deal directly with Dave. He had convinced Dave that if he left, he would take every customer we had with him. The truth was that the only customer "friend" he had was the Traffic Manager of FAG Bearings, a rather substantial client. Red would be hauling him around to all Traffic Club and other customer functions, plying him with booze and telling the same stupid jokes. In his office, Red had photos of naked women plastered all over his walls, which I suggested he remove lest a customer see it and take objections. I also thought it was puerile, and I told him so.

There was natural tension between the departments—Sales did not understand the problems of Operations, and Operations did not fully appreciate the pressures that Sales was facing. I tried to have weekly meetings between Operations and Sales, but these meetings became a forum for Red Swan to attack Paul, who became defensive and retaliated verbally, as only Paul could. I realized that Red was a festering problem that I had to deal with if there was ever to be a more cooperative atmosphere between the two departments. I discontinued the meetings. I spoke with Larry about the problem, but I think Larry was afraid of "rocking the boat", and basically, told me to "let sleeping dogs lie", which I did, for the time being. Larry had a "if it ain't broke, don't fix it" attitude, and in retrospect, he was probably right. However, I saw it as a brooding, festering problem that would soon be exacerbated if not checked. In that, I was correct.

Paul had begun to act strangely, complaining that I was taking Red Swan's side and not supporting him properly, considering what he had gone through with the Union. Dale MacDonald had been working with him on the dock, doing boxcar-loading time and motion studies. We were trying to optimize the per car net revenue. Paul was getting more and more vocal in his criticisms and complaints. I considered it, on a very small scale, akin to the tensions that often happen after a major conflict, familial squabbles and irritations come to the fore, whereas you had other preoccupations when the arrows were flying.

One day, I asked Paul to have dinner with me so we could discuss any problems he might have with the Company or me. After dinner and not a few drinks, he confided in me, telling me a story of conspiracy and deceit that I had never, in my wildest dreams, thought possible, considering that I had really saved the Corporation from its own folly.

Dale had set his sight on recapturing his lost position, now that the place was safe. He told Paul that he could handle Red Swan if he, Dale, was to become General Manager, and that he would give Paul my job, if he would help him topple Larry Wilson and myself. The way to do it was to create a confrontation with me, which he would support when it came to a head, and in so doing, would put Larry Wilson in an untenable position of having to take sides, thus exposing himself to criticism if he defended me, and equally if he did not. For Larry Wilson, it would be a Hobson's choice. He told Paul that several of the "old guard" supported him, including, of course, his brother, and Red Swan.

Paul was ambitious, young and naïve. He swallowed the hair-brained scheme, but then got cold feet, and perhaps a bit of bad conscience. He decided to tell me all, and he put it down in writing.

I decided to bide my time and find another job. This I managed quite soon, I got an offer to manage the Toronto and area branch of Brinks, an armored car security firm.

The day I got the written job offer, I resigned from Cottrell, giving them three weeks notice. I thought that would be the end of it, but it was not. Dave Trudeau flew up from Montreal and wanted a meeting with me in a downtown Toronto hotel. I was stupid enough to agree, being somewhat curious about what he was going to say. Larry Wilson was there also. I spent the whole day saying no, but I was alone against the two, and they kept upping the ante. They promised me the

General Manager's job when Larry became President, within a year, and an immediate raise of six thousand dollars, a large sum in 1976. Dale Macdonald would be removed, never to again grace the doors of the Toronto office (Red Swan got off, he denied any involvement, and Paul had only Dale's words against his), and I was offered a written three-year contract with four-month payout should they decide they did not want me. I caved in. The money they offered me was above anything I could earn anywhere else, including the job I had just accepted with Brinks. I told Larry he would have to call up the President of Brinks and tell him—I was too embarrassed to do so. He did. With a signed contract under my arms, I thought I was safe for the next three years anyhow.

I was wrong! For the second time, I had made a major career mistake.

The next several months were uneventful at work. We made steady progress in all areas, except the Sales/Operations relationship. Paul and Red were still not getting along well, and it was mainly caused by Red's hostility. I think he felt threatened somehow. I kept putting off dealing with it; I was tired of conflict, and I had my own, personal struggle to deal with.

My wife and I separated, and the split was not amicable. There were many reasons, but the incessant problems at work certainly contributed. As well, I had continued my studies at York University. In addition to long, stressful hours of work, I spent weekends bent over textbooks. I think now that it was a kind of escape from work, and perhaps also from my wife. Long afterwards, my daughter told me that what she mostly remembers of me during that period, when I was home, was of me, sitting bent over a textbook.

I ended up living in a rented apartment in Agincourt. I think I developed a "devil-may-care" attitude, which affected my work in a sense—I was willing to take unnecessary risks with my career. I decided to go into the lion's den and confront Red Swan.

I gave him a choice: Change his attitude towards the operational side of the enterprise, or face dismissal. His response was to become directly insubordinate and abusive. I fired him.

Red was on the 'phone to Dave Trudeau as soon as he left my office. Larry came to see me, asking me to reconsider. I told him I had tried everything possible, but Red was not going to change, he was just too proud. Dave Trudeau came on the 'phone, saying he was afraid Red would go to the competition and take several of our major accounts with him, in particular FAG Bearings. I told Dave that I had fought the battle for him with the union, and in spite of his misgivings then, I had done the right thing. Furthermore, I had stayed with the firm, in spite of the machinations of Dale Macdonald and probably Red Swan. This was the only thing I could do if I was to keep "peace in the family". Trudeau, of course, could not care less about internal peace, as long as the money rolled in, and he had the affront to suggest I fire Paul instead! I refused, and told him that it was either Red Swan or I. It was an ultimatum, and he knew it.

A few days went by, and I heard no more. I knew the issue was not resolved, but bided my time, and kept busy with the daily routine.

It was I. The operation was running smoothly, I had made myself expendable. Dave Trudeau was not prepared to stand on any principle, but took the easy route. They cancelled my contract. No "thank you". Just good-bye, and a cheque.

Red Swan did not have the last laugh——Paul did. Paul was appointed to my job, and a few months later, he fired Red Swan. This time there was no reprieve; Trudeau could not very well fire Paul also, in order to retain Red. The irony was that, again, I had been right. Red did get a job with another transport company, but not one of his customers left Cottrell. The salesman's importance is often overrated in business. Beyond obtaining the business, for which the salesman, of course, is the key person, if the customer is well served, he is not likely to switch just because the salesman has changed jobs. I knew that, from being a buyer of transportation services at Xerox. In business, loyalty is ephemeral, and everyone is, eventually, expendable.

Larry Wilson eventually retired, and Paul got his job—for a while, until a "palace coup" dethroned him. He started his own "consulting" firm.

Larry Wilson died in 2005.

Painful interlude: Unemployment

The five months following my departure from Cottrell were brutal. I had no vehicle to drive, as the company immediately took back the company car (later, I arranged to buy that automobile from their leasing company).

I took the bus to the unemployment office (as it was called then, now it is euphemistically named *employment* office), and waited to see the official there. There were zero chances of me finding a management job there, but they did allow me unemployment insurance pay, after the appropriate waiting period.

I worried that someone I knew would see me there, but no one did. I was very embarrassed at being unemployed. I now realize how caught up one can get in ones identity with work. I recall being uncomfortable going to my bank branch to cash my unemployment cheque, feeling that the tellers would look askance at me. I would avoid the apartment building's superintendent, so he would not see me at home during weekdays and realize that I was not working. I avoided people, lest I be asked what I was doing for a living.

I had child support payments of $ 750.00 a month, a fairly large amount at the time. I had handed over the house to my wife as part of the settlement, but kept some savings, which I now used partly for living expenses. The unemployment cheque did not go very far.

It was a depressing time in my life. Most of my acquaintances had been work-related. Now I shunned them—and they shunned me.

I kept busy applying for jobs and studying at York University. I was in my last year of an Economics Degree. However, it is not easy to find a managerial position when you are not working. No matter what you have accomplished in the past, there is the stigma of "failure".

Clarke Transport

After an agonizing hiatus of about five months, I got hired to "fix" problems for *Clarke Transport.* The Cottrell experience should have taught me a lesson, and kept me away from small transportation companies with their never-ending management problems, but it didn't. As a "hired gun" you are paid well, and the exhilaration of "fixing" problems is like a drug—it gets in your blood. Perhaps I had a "Napoleonic complex"—I enjoyed the challenge of planning strategy and executing tactics in the corporate chess game, and the satisfaction of "winning", otherwise known as achievement—forgetting that Napoleon ended up on St.Helena.

After Cottrell, Clarke was a walk in the park, until 1981 when the recession hit and destroyed most of the structure I had put in place.

A few years earlier, Clarke had purchased Muirhead Forwarding, which like Cottrell, utilized the CNR rail and infrastructure. At the time, they were located in Mimico West-Toronto). Graham Muirhead, the owner's son, stayed on as General Manager, and hired me to straighten out their Toronto operations, their main terminal. Larry Wilson, God bless his soul, had recommended me for the "cleanup" task!

Graham Muirhead was one of the kindest people I have ever known, and the best boss. He worked out of the Montreal headquarters, and left me mostly alone to do my job.

Clarke had a productivity problem, not a union problem. They had hired a bunch of "consultants", Hay Partners, who had done a time-and-motion study and devised an elaborate scheme of recording every single thing they did. The result was a mountain of forms and reports, which no one read and much less knew what to do with. The reports were scrupulously done, but the work was not—productivity was dismally low, both in Operations and Administration. Loading errors were high and quality low, resulting in high levels of claims. There was a weak credit and collection function, with the concomitant slow revenue stream.

The first thing I did was to throw out the old reporting system. Graham Muirhead was a bit nervous about that, the Company had spent a lot of money with the consultants, putting it together, but he trusted me enough to let me go ahead. I set about replacing a couple of ineffectual and lazy managers and promoting a couple of bright lights. Then I trained them and trained them. I reduced written reports to a minimum and kept those for the people that needed them (remember, these were the days before personal computers and the internet). I travelled across the country to see destination terminals and view the loading quality of the boxcars they received from Toronto, and then corrected the loading methods back home. I changed the workflow and improved productivity. It was a breeze, really—just common sense. In Operations, I had a reasonable and rational union to deal with, and no real problem-workers. The union was the Canadian Brotherhood of Railway and General Workers (CBRT&GW); I had been a member years before when I worked for the CNR. I found some very good talents among the employees, "diamonds in the rough", and trained them. One of them, Dave was eventually appointed General Manager of the Company's trucking operation in Newfoundland, Newfoundland Transport. I had put forward his name as a candidate. Graham wrote me a very nice note after that. It said "you took Dave from the ranks, nourished and trained him, and gave him to the Company. We have had our differences, but this time my hat is off to you!" Those words meant much to me; I cherished them for a long time.

Bringing out talent in people has been my forte and the greatest personal satisfaction in my management career. I did it at Xerox, and in every firm for which I worked thereafter, not always with the recognition I got at Xerox, or which Graham gave me. Many years later, out of the blue, I got a letter from one of the foremen, Jim, who had worked for me at Cottrell. He told me how he appreciated my faith in him and my support and training. It filled me with joy to hear that, I have kept that letter (Jim was a draft dodger from Minnesota, and after the amnesty, he went back home). The greatest reward is to have meant something for another human being, and contributed something positive to another's welfare.

A fellow called Harry Steele bought Clarke Transport from the Clarke family. Harry Steele had purchased Eastern Provincial Airways from the provincial government for a "song", and sold it for a tidy profit to CP Air. He used part of the loot to buy Clarke, by then floundering in the 1981 recession, but mostly from a bloated organizational structure. Harry was quoted in the papers as saying "if you have an accountant that is not giving you 200 percent, fire him", or some such drivel. In any event, he was a totally ruthless son-of-a-bitch. The old man Clarke had built his life around the company and had many friends among the management employees. I think he just could not bring himself to do the cost cutting and "downsizing" that was needed, and he sold out. Harry Steele brought in a corporate executioner and began chopping. Graham Muirhead was fired without notice, as were most of the "old guard". Much of my efforts were undone, after four years of hard work. Eventually, I was also swept out with the tide. "Nothing personal". But, I did get a "glowing" reference letter.

Some people never learn …

Losing my job this time was a little easier on the ego, because I knew that it was nothing I could have done or not done; I didn't make a mistake or do anything wrong. I got caught up in the recession and a corporate economic crisis. My salary was high and an easy target, especially after I had straightened out the organizational structure. That's the way of the "hired gun". I was unlucky, my timing was wrong, my "hand was too slow".

However, I had just gotten married again, and it was a shock to my new wife, who had two children and was not working. We had also bought a new house together, so the pressure was on to find suitable employment.

Fisons Plc.

The opportunity came presently. This time it was a "head hunter", who put me in touch with a British agriculture products company called *Fisons Plc.* It had purchased a western Canadian peat moss producer, Western Peat Moss. Fisons saw it as their gateway to the North-American market for their processed potting soils and other organic products. They also owned a small pharmaceutical firm, and operated peat moss plants in B.C., Alberta, Manitoba and New Brunswick. Product distribution was a major expense; peat moss is a bulky, low value commodity that needs to be transported a long way from the harvesting and processing plants to the end user markets. Theirs were predominantly in the southern and southwestern United States. Peat is an important product in the water-short southern states, where it is used by the many plant and flower-growers, as well as other agricultural users.

I was hired to manage distribution in the eastern North-American market, with an office in a most unlikely place, Niagara-on-the-Lake, Ontario, mostly known for tourism, fruit and wine—not peat moss. It didn't seem to be much of a challenge, but I needed a job after Clarke, and the pay was fair. I did hedge a bit, I stayed put in Mississauga, driving the 100 kilometres to work each day.

Nothing is easy. I should have known. The local manager, Fred Kuchan, resented having to report to me, and looked at me as a threat. I know that my bosses at Fisons head office in Vancouver knew it, and counted on me to resolve *their* problem. Fred had his whole family there: his daughter as office manager, his son-in-law as operations supervisor and his cousin as operations manager. The reason the office and depot were located at Niagara was that they depended on truckers returning empty to Florida where they picked up loads of produce and flowers for export back to Ontario and Quebec. Peat moss had a preferential tariff (subsidized rates) with the railways, as it was coming mainly from the Freight Tariff Reduction Area of Eastern Canada, in this case New Brunswick, so the cost of landing it in Niagara was relatively low.

Fred had total control; if they had fired him, there would have been no one there who knew what to do; he had kept it to himself, in the family, so to speak. There were hardly any records. I had to start from scratch.

We needed to decentralize the operation, to catch trucks crossing at other border points such as Montreal and Windsor, thus lessening the dependency of Niagara.

I set up a depot at Windsor, Ontario and hired people to look after it, and then did the same in Montreal, Que. This allowed us to catch returning trucks crossing at the Quebec-New York border, as well as Windsor-Detroit. I traveled around Florida to make arrangements with flower growers for backhaul trucking.

I visited our depot in Tampa and did an audit. I discovered that the manager was using fictitious shipment in collusion with the regional sales rep there. The inventory was still at the depot, damaged beyond salvage. Peat bales are packaged in plastic bags, and as they were stored in the hot Florida sun without cover, the plastic broke down. So we fired the two dishonest employees and closed the Tampa depot, shipping directly from Niagara.

Back at the Niagara office, Fred was frantic. He saw himself losing control, and it scared him. I tried to get him onside, but he did not trust me. He knew, I am sure, the real reason the Company had hired me, and I began to see it too, but it was sink or swim—again.

I terminated Fred. His daughter and son-in-law quit the same day, but head office sent me some temporary help until I could hire new people, and we muddled through. I hired an operations manager, new to the business. He did very well, and last I heard, he was promoted to plant manager at their peat moss processing plant just northwest of Edmonton.

Later, I traveled to Caraquet, New Brunswick, where Fisons had a peat moss operation, to learn about peat moss harvesting and processing. Caraquet is a quaint little town on the eastern seaboard, in the heart of Acadia. Everyone fished for lobster for three months, then lived on unemployment insurance the rest of the year, and they live quite well. I have never seen so many new cars in a small town.

Our plant there was unionized, and I saw a strange Collective Agreement: it had "reverse seniority". The workers with the highest seniority had the right to be laid off first, if the layoff came in the spring during the lobster fishing season, so they could go fishing lobster.

The plant manager told me a quaint story: when he was a child, he went to school with lobster sandwiches in his lunch box, because his family was poor lobster-fishermen. He would hide his sandwich, and eat it in secret, since he did not want the better off kids to see that he was eating lobster sandwiches. They, the richer ones, were having bologna sandwiches!

When I returned, work settled down to a routine. There was some consideration of expanding the depot at Niagara, but it came to naught.

The President and C.E.O. for *Fisons Canada* was a fellow by the name of *Donald Triggs.* He was originally from Manitoba, but had worked for Molson's Breweries in their wine subsidiary, Bright Wines, and most recently had been in charge of their California operations. Triggs was a photogenic, intelligent and driven man. He would fly from Vancouver to London, England for a meeting at the head office there, then right back again. Once I met him in Montreal, on his way back from London, England. We had a meeting at a hotel there (I had just opened the Montreal depot). He was so tired that when he tried to pour a glass of water, the water spilled all over the table. Yet, he carried on, finished our meeting and was off to Vancouver. He was the kind of guy who when traveling on business abroad, would visit museums and galleries in his spare time. I had a dinner meting with him in Toronto once, and I complained that I had little chance to reach "the top" in management. He was very supportive, saying that though I had probably about a ten-year late start, I could still make it.

Some years later, after I had "thrown in the towel" in corporate management and started my own business, I spoke with him in Toronto. He and a couple of other investors had purchased the winery business from Molson's. After the government lifted the direct subsidies to Canadian wineries and growers, the brewers got rid of their winemaking business at fire sales. They expected the business to fail, but they were wrong, and Don Triggs and his partners proved it. Theirs firm, Vincor, is now the most successful wine operation in Canada, and world-renowned.

Vincor was recently sold to another, large operator, and Don Triggs resigned as President. I don not know where we went or what he is doing, but I doubt he is resting on his laurels.

Cochrane-Dunlop

I decided I had little long-term future at Fisons. I did not want to move to Niagara Falls, and I saw little chance of moving into head office in Vancouver, so when a friend in Toronto told me about an opening where his brother worked, I was interested, and went to see them. The company was *Cochrane-Dunlop*, an old hardware distribution firm, with a chain of retail hardware stores called *Dominion Hardware*. I was hired as Director of Distribution, reporting to the President. The company had been purchased from the Cochrane family by a high-flying entrepreneur by the name of *Dolliver Fredrick*. Dolliver was from Alberta, and had a pair of cowboy boots sitting beside his desk in his office. He had been involved with Global TV in some way, and, according to himself (one of his favourite people), had made his money in that business. He had great plans for his acquisition.

Cochrane-Dunlop was housed in an old, converted munitions factory on Bloor Street in the west-end of Toronto. It was a very inefficient facility from a workflow point of view, operating on three floors and two buildings connected by elevators and manual roller transfer beds. They were in dire need of a new facility. Here I met my old friends Teamsters Local 419 again, but with a new crew. They were fairly tame, though there had been a brief prior strike.

The President was a German immigrant by the name of *Wolf Gruber*. His forte was the buying function; he had been a buyer at Simpson-Sears for many years prior to arriving at Cochrane-Dunlop. He had all the attributes of a P.O.W. camp commandant, a narcissistic Colonel Klink out of Hogan's Heroes, and just about as silly. He was about fifty-five, tall and still handsome, with a mane of thinning, long, white hair, which he combed carefully and often. He had a Cheshire cat's grin that would quickly turn to a frown, and he would go into fits and yell to his buyers so the whole office floor would hear him. He terrorized his subordinates, but crawled obsequiously before Dolliver Fredrick, and courted his approval.

The first week of the month was worst. The monthly P*rofit and Loss* statement would be issued, and it was usually *loss*. Gruber feared Dolliver's reaction, and would browbeat the whole management group, trying to find a scapegoat. Managers would scurry about, trying to avoid him. Lengthy reports would be demanded. Any department head that could not explain and justify any cost overrun would be browbeaten in his office, you could almost see the steam rising from under the doorjamb.

Cochrane-Dunlop was building a new distribution warehouse in Aurora, with money borrowed from the TD Bank. I had an interesting experience working with their design-build engineering consultants, Giffels, developing the warehouse.

They had purchased a western Canada hardware distributor owned by The Bay, and had convinced the TD Bank that they would become a countrywide hardware retailer, competing head on with Home Hardware. The Bay was happy to get rid of the money-losing stinker, and sold it for a little cash and a whole lot of I.O.U.'s. That purchase, and the building of a new distribution warehouse, brought down the Cochrane house of cards.

We had an annual inventory count, ostensibly audited by their accounting firm, but there was little auditing done. I found that thirty percent of the inventory was missing, and that shortages had been accumulating for several years. The company had covered it up, for if the bank knew, they would have "pulled the plug" (as they did eventually). I had a "row" with Gruber over this, and shortly thereafter he fired me. I sued, and settled for fifteen thousand dollars. It was lucky I did, for just a few months after, the TD Bank called their loans and they were bankrupt. As far as I know, the other employees got nothing.

I never heard what happened to *Dolliver Fredrick.* Like *Icarus,* he flew too close to the sun. Perhaps he *landed* back in Alberta from whence he came. He could charm a snake out of his skin. I am sure he went on to build other sandcastles, one day, somewhere.

Wolf Gruber went to Singapore for a job; later I heard he surfaced in some capacity at the now defunct Cashway Lumber. Perhaps he is sawing logs.

He was a big man with a small heart.

I was again without a car, having had a company vehicle at Cochrane. I bought an old Chrysler Plymouth and used it for the next while. One day I was stopped at a subway station in Toronto, when the radiator hose came off and the coolant spurted out. I reattached the hose, but the radiator was dry, so I was stuck. A taxi driver saw my predicament and came over with a large can of water. He said he always kept one handy for his car, and told me to keep the can and refill the radiator on my way to the garage. It was a nice thing for a taxi driver to do for a stranger. He was a Sikh with a turban on his head, and I got thinking about the occasions I had joked about "turban-twisters". I never again made jokes at the expense of minorities or generalized about people that happen to be different. You find a good person in every race and creed.

A.T. Kearney

I was speaking with the consulting engineer at *Giffels*, and he suggested I do some consulting in Logistics. I tried on my own, but it is very hard to try to obtain business and then do projects at the same time. Some people can do it, but I did not succeed in getting anything worthwhile. I thought I would work for a consulting firm, and did obtain a job as an Associate Consultant with A.T.Kearny, an international consulting firm of some renown. I was hired as their logistics consultant in Toronto. I did a couple of interesting assignments at large Canadian firms. One was with the *Sifto Salt* division of Domtar. I knew nothing of salt, so I spent a week at the main Toronto library, reading everything about salt deposits and salt mining. I visited their salt mine in Goderich, and spent time at their facility in Chicago. It was an interesting experience, but I did not really enjoy the political aspect of management consulting. I found that to a large degree, you collected information already available to the firm internally, massage it and deliver it in a nice package to senior management who hope it will support their own opinion. In some cases, management is using the consultant to support a decision they are afraid to make. They can then say that this well known consulting firm's conclusions agreed with their decision. The consulting firms, who want to continue working for the company in the future, are reluctant to make suggestions that are too contrary to the perceived wisdom of management who hired them. To this degree, the consultant is compromised. It is not only senior management that is using the consultant to their advantage. Middle management also tries to get their point across, using the consultant as the medium. It was amazing how much information I could get from various managers, who were often happy that anyone would listen to their opinion. Thus, in a highly politicized management structure, an outside consultant might be useful in bringing out important information hidden away in various departments. The problem is, will senior management listen, and if too contrary, will the consultant dare to present it unedited?

After a little more than a year, I left A.T. Kearney. In the short time I was there, I learned a lot, but I had decided to start my own business. In the fall of 1985 I began what was to take me on a roller—coaster ride in the world of small business entrepreneurs.

PART III

Chapter 6

Entrepreneur

The new venture will also outgrow its capital structure … as the venture grows, private sources of funds, whether from owners or from outsiders, becomes inadequate … during the early years the cost of staying in business is always larger than the surplus from yesterdays operations … the growing venture must invest every penny of operating surplus to stay alive.

—Peter F. Drucker: Innovation and Entrepreneurship (1985).

Many people think that running your own business is nirvana—freedom from control, freedom to act, financial independence and so on.

The reality is rather different. Most entrepreneurs spend long hours at work, and often live their work at home. Yes, you have some independence, and some freedoms, but while you have no direct superior giving you orders, you have the demanding market, employees and banks, suppliers, equipment, accidents, unremitting stress, and the ever-present possibility of failure. You cannot just quit your job and go on to something else—your job is your life and your life your job. You are never free from the demands of economic life whether a business owner or a wage earner. However, the big difference is that as an owner, you cannot quit. Your whole existence is tied up in your business, emotionally and financially. While, if you do well, you can build a "nest-egg" for your retirement, you can also fail, and you have no company pension on which to fall back.

To this reality I was partially blinded, wearing the rose-colured glasses so typical of entrepreneurs.

To that story I now turn.

MOVING EXPERIENCES

The business

"Call us for a moving experience"

—Slogan on our moving trucks

People have moved with their belongings since they settled in communities and began to accumulate goods. In North America, for hire moving originated in cities and towns several hundred years ago, when it was done with horse-drawn wagons. The first long-distance moves were by ships, on oceans, lakes and rivers; oxcarts and horse drawn wagons and coaches. Later, the railways moved settlers and their belongings overland. Rail was the prime long distance "mover" until roads were adequate to carry trucks over longer distances, later in specialized, air-cushioned vans. It has now come full circle, with the railways recapturing some of the long-haul household goods transportation from trucks. However, local moving is still done the "old" way.

There are hundreds of "movers" listed in the Yellow Pages of large cities, ranging from a one-man operation to large commercial corporations. The majority, however, are still small, family operated companies. Out of all these, about ten percent belong to one of the four largest van line operations in North-America: Allied, Atlas, North American and United Van Lines. The same group owns Allied and North American; United Van Lines and Atlas Van Lines retain the agency-owned structure. United is the largest one, Atlas second. Van line agents are mainly long distance movers, but they also compete for the local moving business, generally charging a premium over the independent movers.

The van line operation is peculiar to North America. It originated after the first world war, when several small moving firms combined to handle long distance relocations, by coordinating origin loading, long distance hauling and destination delivery services. Temporary storage was also part of this service. This way, a smaller, individual moving company could operate as if it had large, countrywide operations. With the rapidly growing highway network and the growth of trans-national corporations and their need for transferring employees, the van line business took off. Canadian van line operations are offshoots of U.S. firms, with the U.S. and Canadian partners cooperating in cross-border traffic. Long distance moving by van lines grew rapidly after World War II, especially after the interstate and trans-Canada highways were completed.

The van line operators have experimented with domestic containers, with limited success. The containers face the same problems of returning the units, as do the trailers. Only in cases where the customer requires short-term storage at destination is this mode advantageous, as they need not incur the extra labour of handling the furniture twice—in and out of the destination agent's warehouse. Otherwise, there is little cost savings for the operator, and no "environmental" advantage. *Mayflower* experimented with "self-loading" of containers, placing them at the customer's residence for the customer to do his own loading and unloading, but while this saved labour costs for the customer, it did nothing for the moving company's "bottom line."

Ocean containers are readily available, but not suited to furniture transport. They have steel sides and roofs, making it very difficult to secure the load. The lack of springs or other cushioning systems causes a high level of damage, something Allied found out when they tried this method. Transporting trailers via rail on "flatbed" railcars—"Piggyback"—is a better solution, and is likely to become a major method of furniture transport. It allows the safe stowing of household goods, with protective padding and securing on air cushioned trailers, as well as protecting against the impacts from the railway shunting. However, it does not solve the major problem of returning the trailer units, especially in Canada, where the imbalance in east-west traffic, especially in household goods traffic, is substantial. This problem is not easily rectified, and will continue to contribute to the high cost of long distance moving in the foreseeable future.

The *local moving* business in the large centers, such as Toronto, has become a "free-for-all," unregulated collection of small firms, from the "mom & pop" operator, to the large, multi-branch van line agent. The majority, the "average" moving company, however, consists of a ten to fifteen square feet warehouse, half a dozen trucks operated locally, and perhaps two or three long-haul tractor trailer units.

The size and flair of their yellow pages ads, the main source of local moving prospects, has no relationship to quality, quantity or price of service. It is truly a situation of *caveat emptor.*

The business of moving people's household goods has to be one of the most difficult and problematic commercial activities ever contemplated. Moving services are ripe for conflicts and litigation. The mover is exposed to liability for which he is only partially protected by insurance coverage—if he can get insurance at all. He must show up when agreed, and do the job within the estimated time without damaging the furniture.

These small firms, with limited resources, face an increasingly competitive market and marginal profitability, for reasons many and varied. The customer often choose a moving services as if it were a commodity—deciding mainly on price, and expecting perfection. Movers, no matter how well intentioned, have to face high employee turnover, equipment breakdowns, inclement weather, and other factors that are nearly impossible to control. Government regulations regarding hours of work and driving time, as well as safety, add to the mix of economic pressures facing a mover.

Moving is stressful—for customer *and* the service provider. Customers are often nervous and emotional—moving all your belongings is a major undertaking. They also are concerned with "closing" times and other problems involved in the multiple transactions of selling and buying a house, as well as the move itself.

Times are changing for moving companies. Deregulation in the early nineties opened up the field for anyone with a truck and a driver's license, and the ensuing chaos caused many problems. The free-for-all competition has forced down rates and many truck transportation and moving firms often operate below fully allocated costs. Movers have the additional problem of seasonality, earning half or more of their annual revenue in the three summer months June, July and August, and half their monthly income in the last week of the month. They hemorrhage money during the winter months, and many wear out their assets until they eventually give up; sell or close their business. To some extent, this can be attributed to a lack of business skills by the small, unsophisticated operators facing laissez-faire competition, but even large firms have gone bankrupt when revenues did not cover total costs in the long run. Effective rates (prices) today are below what they were before de-regulation twenty years ago. Discount from published tariffs (list price) is very high, especially "off-season," and makes a travesty of published prices altogether.

In addition to the problem of seasonality, moving firms are especially sensitive to economic contractions. While they can lay off people, overhead costs continue.

No one has yet found a satisfactory way of utilizing equipment twelve months of the year, and never will, as long as people prefer to move during the summer. The school year has a large impact on move timing. The Federal Government, and Military's contractual commitments put added stress on van line agents, who must handle the majority of their relocations during the summer months.

Operating without covering depreciation and overhead has been endemic in the moving business since deregulation, probably contributing to road accidents and public endangerment. Provincial Governments were slow to react to these problems, but have recently become more vigilant in monitoring highway trucks. Had they set stricter financial and safety standards at the time of de-regulation, many of these problems could have been avoided, and many "fly-by-night" operators would not be on the roads.

Having had difficulties dealing with deregulation, moving companies now face re-regulation in the form of increasingly stringent safety measures and enforcement. Beyond regulations and safety, they must also deal with the public and do so with employees who are uneducated, rough, and have a tenuous attachment to working life. Until (if ever) the moving business can demand the income needed to attract a better class of people, this will always be so. Who would want, given an alternative, to work in an environment where you lift heavy furniture and appliances all day, carrying them up and down stairs and over steep ramps into trucks, working in all kinds of weather; bitterly cold in winter, steaming hot in summer! Add irregular working days and hours, and you have a major *disincentive* to work. Many factors cause delays and extended hours, and often, exhausted workers must listen to the customer complaining about the time it took to do the job. Another problem is seasonality. Irregular and occasional work in winter, overwork in summer. No wonder you find outcast, drug abusers and illiterates gravitating to this kind of work. Movers, by default, get the dregs of society, and are lucky to have and retain a few dependable workers among its work force. Good workers are scarce in any business; in the moving business they are rare.

In the last few years the scarcity of qualified drivers has become serious. You get men with a brand new truck-driver's license—often obtained through unemployment "retraining" programs—that are poorly motivated and often barely competent to drive. They cannot get a regular trucking job until they have some experience, and as soon as they get it, they are gone. Why slug furniture when you can sit in a highway truck and just drive, and have the people at the customer's warehouse load the truck for you? It is amazing how often I have heard the potential employee responding to a help wanted ad and after enquiring about the pay scale, asking if there is heavy lifting involved. When they hear that there is, they say "no thank you." You dare not hire a "temp driver" from an agency lest they endanger your equipment and the lives of your employees, not to mention having to appease the irate customer who expected a "professional" driver and now wants a "discount."

In this environment, an honest moving operation struggles to survive. The moving business is *economic Darwinism* in its purest form.

I remember once, in the early nineties, during the recession, when I attended a meeting of the mover section of the Ontario Trucking Association. One of the members complained that during these slow economic times, people often did their own moving. Another fellow, who was about to "throw in the towel" in his moving business, had not lost his sense of humor. His response was that he could not see why anyone would do their own moving when all they had to do was to call in a mover, give them a "rubber cheque," then put in a claim for damages! We all laughed, but we should have cried, for the joke was on us.

So *why* and *how* do movers stay in business? Well there is really no market for selling a small moving business. Families, who have done this work all their lives and know nothing else, operate most of these small moving companies. Usually they have inherited the business from their parents. They survive by running down their assets, and underpaying themselves. Eventually, they give up, close down or sell, if they are lucky and have some value in equipment and warehousing. Their children, having watched their parents struggle, want nothing to do with the moving business, and who can blame them.

This, then, was the business I entered in 1985. It's been quite a trip, you could say a *moving experience*, but having now sold the business, I can at last sit back and objectively reminisce on days gone by, feeling a bit like a survivor of a shipwreck.

A&S ROSETH
MOVING AND STORAGE

Atlas
Van Lines
Atlas
Van Lines
A&S ROSETH

Tabula Rasa

After the Cochrane-Dunlop debacle, I decided that I would go into business for myself. I wanted to buy a trucking firm, but found it was beyond my means, so I got the "bright" idea of starting a moving company from "scratch", starting with a "clean slate." I chose moving because it was fairly easy to get into that business, even in those days of regulated operations.

I bought a couple of used trucks at an auction and spent most of my savings fixing them up and obtaining insurance. I set up an "office" in my basement, and advertised for helpers in the local newspaper. I arranged with a gas station operator to park my two trucks on his lot in return for having him look after repairs for us, and buying fuel for the trucks from him.

I had to learn to manage people all over again, as I had never had to deal directly with people who had, no commitment, little or no education and very, very little self-motivation of any kind. Most of them came from dysfunctional home situations that put little value on education and personal betterment. When I managed larger businesses, I had many people I could lean on—to discuss problems, strategy and plans. I could delegate to various subordinates, and I usually had a reasonable time frame in which to make decisions. Not here. There was no buffer between my workers and me, and many decisions had to be made instantly. Management principles went out the window, offered on the altar of expedience or urgency. I was poorly suited for this environment.

In retrospect, I realize that my naiveté was astounding. I knew nothing about the business of moving. The first call we got was from someone wanting to move a piano. We had no prices worked out, so I quoted them $ 50.00 on a guess. I got together my "new" employees, a couple of local kids, and we practiced a bit by moving my own piano from the basement family room upstairs and down again! We managed to move the customer's piano without smashing it to bits, even though we had to take it downstairs to their basement. I collected the fifty dollars, but after paying the help, I had nothing left! I realized we must have more compensatory prices, and 'phoned around to various local movers to obtain a sense of the competitor's rates.

I did not know how to properly estimate a job, and guessed all over the place. This, of course, got me into further trouble. Luckily, most of our customers in those early days understood. I guess they figured that since our rates were so low, they could put up with some underestimating. We did not even have Bills of Lading in the beginning, but recorded names, rates and costs on little index cards!

Eventually, I had Bills of Lading typed up and used carbon paper to create a copy for the customers.

We got busier, and had problems getting drivers. I got the idea of using local firemen. This worked very well in the beginning. The firemen were all good drivers, fairly intelligent and presentable. The problem we had was juggling their days off. I had colour-coded calendars showing the days off for the guys, and I managed for some time. Eventually, however, it got too cumbersome, and I gave it up. I must say, though, that I never did have better drivers than those Mississauga firemen!

I learned a few hard lessons in those early days, like, don't take personal cheques, and that there is such a thing as a *claim.* I arranged to accept credit cards, which largely solved the "bad cheque" problem, and I hired a furniture repairman to look after smaller damages.

We lost a few jobs because we did not have storage facilities, so I took a gamble and leased a unit in an industrial plaza. At that time, I also bought a new moving truck. The business grew (the housing market was "red hot" the last part of the eighties) and I bought two more trucks that year. I did the office work myself; answered the telephone (*both* lines), typed the Bills of Lading, paid the bills and issued pay cheques on a manual "one-write" ledger. I also bought a small photocopier and a stamp machine for mailings. My office "staff" were a dog and a cat, and their pay consisted of free room and board. Thus, overhead was very low and I actually made money the first couple of years—enough to pay off the three new trucks I had bought by then.

I applied for an expanded license at the Ontario Highway Traffic Board, the governing body that issued operating licenses at that time. I went before the Board again and again, each time getting a little bigger slice. The "big boys" would be there with their lawyers opposing the application, stating that there was no "public need and necessity" (as the terminology was) for granting a license. At last, I managed to obtain the coveted open license (C-class operating license), allowing my little company to operate in all of Ontario, with some restrictions. I remember well the kindly judge that granted me the license. He said, "I wish you luck. We don't get many of your caliber here". That was the high point of my moving career! The following year the government de-regulated the transportation business, and my hard-won license was worth nothing.

After obtaining a C-class operating license, I decided to join a van line. The license was a requirement for joining, as van lines are primarily concerned with long distance moving and depend on member agents for equipment and manpower. The smallest van line at that time, Mayflower, took us on, and thus started a whole new experience and a brand new learning curve.

Some "War" Stories

We had some interesting moves over the years. We happened to get a contract with a company scheduling filming crews, and got work temporarily relocating the people living at the filming location, so the moviemakers could use their homes for props. The first movie we worked with was called *In the Jaws of Evil;* another one was *The Santa Clause.* The producers used a townhouse in Oakville and they moved the owners to a hotel and had us move their furniture into our warehouse. Then, after the movie was finished, they re-decorated the house for the owners and we moved them back. I watched them spray artificial snow on the premises in July! We also moved furniture from a nursery school, located in an old, former police station in downtown Toronto that was being used for that movie.

I lost track of my "movie" contact. I found out that these free-lancing "consultants" pop up and disappear all the time, in unison with whatever films are shooting here, and what jobs they can snare.

We moved a few "celebrities" over the years, and I will relate the stories of a few of them.

We got an order from a lady; I believe her name was *Barbara Hershey*, a sometime actress, to move her to her ranch in California. It was a large home, and she was taking with her a grand piano and an automobile. During the move, in the late afternoon, I got a call from her estranged husband, who told me to stop the move as his wife was taking the furniture illegally. He was particularly concerned about "his car" (a Ferrari) and the grand piano. He told me his name was *David Carradine*, and when I did not react to the name, he said, "don't you know who I am?" He then told me he was a well-known movie actor and mentioned the name of a movie on which he was working*: Kung Fu: The Legend Continues* (a B-grade movie filmed in Toronto). I told him that I did not really care who he was, as our contract was not with him, but with his wife. I told him to go and speak to his wife, but he said he was busy with a TV show, and he kept threatening to sue me. Finally, I told him to go to hell, and heard nothing more from him. The moving crew told me that he did arrive at the house later, and his wife called the police. They had him sit in a chair while we loaded the truck. He did get to keep his car, however. Later I saw him interviewed on the *Pamela Wallin* TV show (on CTV—it's now cancelled) and he said he had had a drinking problem. People have problems, rich or poor, famous or infamous.

Another time we moved *Eddie Melo*. Eddie had been a middleweight boxing champion in the early seventies, but fell in with criminal elements in Montreal. Later, he moved to Toronto, and got involved providing strippers to clubs in the Toronto area. Apparently, another guy was moving in on his territory, so Eddie and a friend decided to "bump him off", but they bungled it miserably. They stopped the man's car somewhere outside Milton and pumped a few .22-calibre bullets into him, but the guy survived. His friend turned Crown's evidence and Eddie was charged with attempted murder, but the case took so long to come to court that the presiding judge threw it out because of excessive delays (this sparked a small political storm and some Court reforms, but that's another story).

I got a call from Mr. Malo and went to see him at his house in Mississauga. When I arrived he was pumping iron in the basement and I could see that he was an athlete. He told me he was moving out for a while (he was in fact going to jail) and needed to store his goods. He was a friendly fellow and I quite liked him, not knowing his background. He spoke like a kid from the Bronx, and reminded me of Sylvester Stallone. He noticed my accent, and asked what my country of origin was. When I told him Norway, he said his wife was of Norwegian descent, and we chatted quite amicably.

A year or so went by, and one day Eddie called to have his goods moved to his new apartment in a luxury high-rise on the Toronto waterfront. He said he would pay cash. When time came to pay after the move, he did not have the money. He called me from the apartment and said he would pay me later, as soon as his "friend" came from Aurora with the money. He said "I'm not gonna cheat you, Sig, honestly!" However, by then I knew who Eddie Malo was, and told the crew to stay there until his "friend" came. Amazingly, his friend showed up with a fistful of cash and we were paid, although he was short $ 170.00, which he promised to pay the next day. I think he would have paid it, except he got arrested and I heard no more from him, or of him for several years until I read he had been murdered. The murderer was not caught then, but I heard later, that a hired assassin from Montreal has been charged with the murder. I guess the adage is often true, that when you live by the sword, you die by it also. He lived in a dangerous world amongst people who play for keeps. I still wonder what Eddie *could* have been, if he had taken the "road less traveled."

Item: Toronto Star, Wednesday, October 1, 2003: "Boxer's killer gets life in prison". He shot Melo as he sat behind the wheel of his Jeep Cherokee. Pavao (his friend) was shot as he stood outside the vehicle, leaning inside, talking to Melo—"Melo was the target, Pavao was in the wrong place at the wrong time".

A4 ★ TORONTO STAR ★ WEDNESDAY, OCTOBER 1, 2003 ★

News

Boxer's killer gets life in prison

Can be released in 12 years for double slaying

He was considered low-risk parolee at time of shooting

BOB MITCHELL
AND PETER EDWARDS
STAFF REPORTERS

A Quebec man who killed former boxing champion Eddie Melo was regarded by federal officials as a low-risk parolee at the time he committed the contract killing in 2001.

Charles Gagne, 30, was sentenced to life in prison with no eligibility for parole for 12 years after pleading guilty yesterday to two counts of second-degree murder in the killings of former Canadian boxing champion Eddie Melo, 40, and his long-time friend, Jose (John) Pavao, 42, on April 6, 2001.

Mr. Justice Terrence O'Connor "reluctantly" accepted the 12-year recommendation of crown prosecutor Stephen Sherriff.

"The crown is accepting Gagne's plea to second-degree murder, in what is clearly a first-degree murder case, because of the need to call Gagne as a crown witness in order to seek justice in that related case," Sherriff told the court.

Eddie Melo's partner, Rhonda Sullivan, 37, who is the mother of his young son Eduardo, 6, and Melo's daughter Jessica, 22, wept repeatedly during yesterday's hearing, as did several other family members.

National Parole Board documents obtained by the Star indicate that Gagne was on a day

Charles Gagne, 30, is expected to be called as a crown witness in related murder case.

pass when he committed the double murders, after being given a 10-year sentence for robbing a grocery store in 1995 with an AK-47 assault rifle while unlawfully at large.

In the Dec. 12, 2000, parole board decision, Gagne was told, "The board is persuaded that your risk is not undue upon such a release."

However, when he was given his day pass, Gagne was told by the parole board, "Your criminal history includes a number of weapons offences, which involved guns on all occasions and negative associates."

Calling his behaviour "impulsive" and "thrill-seeking," the decision said, "As well, you have demonstrated a comfort with a criminal lifestyle that includes guns and negative peers who make 'big promises' of easy money."

The decision to grant Gagne day parole also notes, "Your institutional performance overall has been good, which the board takes as evidence that you are less impulsive and better able to choose your associates, … all of which suggest that risk is manageable."

He had been incarcerated at the Portsmouth Community Correctional Centre in Kingston when he received day parole. When initially arrested this past July, Gagne was an inmate of the Hull Correctional Centre in Quebec, where he was facing two new charges of aggravated assault.

The Peel police investigation revealed Melo was shot at about 6:30 p.m. as he sat behind the wheel of his Jeep Cherokee. Pavao was shot as he stood outside the vehicle, leaning inside as he talked to Melo. The two men had just left the popular Amici sports bar, located in the Cliffway Plaza, near Hurontario St. and the Queen Elizabeth Way.

"Melo was the target and Pavao happened to be in the wrong place at the wrong time," Sherriff told the Brampton court.

The court heard how Gagne made his getaway by hijacking a car from a passerby.

Sherriff said evidence against Gagne included wiretaps of telephone conversations, which contained admissions by Gagne, and money paid to him by a co-conspirator.

In an agreed statement of facts read yesterday in court, Gagne admitted he shot Melo and Pavao in the head at close range in what Sherriff described as "execution-style slayings."

"This was a contract homicide planned well in advance, and Gagne was promised $75,000 in exchange for killing Melo," Sherriff said. "There were a number of other co-conspirators. Gagne received $50,000, some of which he gave to one of his co-conspirators."

JEFF GOODE/TO

Eddie Melo spars for the camera in January, 198
turned pro at the age of 17 and later won the Can
weight championship, survived an attempt on hi

Sheriff said Gagne didn't know either Melo or Pavao.

Gagne's lawyer, John McCulligh, said his client had "renounced the life he lived" and knows with his guilty plea that "deep waters" are ahead.

Melo, who became a pro boxer at 17 and later won the Canadian middleweight championship, was the Toronto driver for Montreal crime boss Frank Cotroni when Cotroni visited Toronto in the 1980s and '90s.

There were two paramilitary officers from the Peel police tactical squad in court yesterday.

Members of the Melo and Pavao families, who attended the emotionally charged hearing, were upset and angry, but accepted the decision.

Melo's youn
39, said his b
over jealousy
ties. "It had n
bikers and it l
with mobster

Rhonda Sull
"thankful" fo
Peel police.

"At least we h
but there is sti
two people st
tonight," Sull
not a day for c
still has no fat

Melo came
age of 6 but n
zenship, and a
cessfully tried
his birthplace
criminal asso
1990s. He surv
have him kille

For some reason, in the late eighties, we encountered a number of criminal types in our warehouse. One day we got a call from a man in Hamilton who wanted us to come immediately to move him into storage. He was a couturier and lived above his shop. The men noticed that he was very nervous, asking them to "hurry up", and there were two police cars parked across the street. He gave us a cheque and a contact telephone number. Alas! The cheque bounced and the telephone number was not in service. After a few months, I sold his goods and did quite well; he had some expensive things, including several industrial sewing machines. About two years later, I got a call from a lawyer in London, Ontario, asking about his goods. I told him that I had sold them long ago. He was not surprised. I asked if his client had been in jail, and he said yes, he was now trying to *keep him out* of jail. I never heard from the customer himself. I think his transgressions were also drug-related; he was probably using his couturier-business to "launder" drug money.

This guy, Felix lost his house and we moved everything into our warehouse. He took with him everything but the "kitchen sink." I noticed that his girl friend wore very expensive clothes and they were both driving expensive cars. He always paid his storage charges in cash. Later, he moved in with his parents, but the police picked him up on the day of the move. We found out that the reason his last house was sold was that he was charged with drug trafficking and the Court ordered his house sold under legal provisions for goods obtained by crime.

I will relate just one other "criminal" story. This man, who is now probably out of jail—(he got seven years "at the government's pleasure" in Kingston)—had us move his goods into storage, and told us that "his friend" was to pay the storage fees. Well, his friend did not, and I could not get in touch with anyone who could take responsibility for the bill, not realizing the guy was in jail. After a while, I had some of the goods auctioned off to pay the storage fees, and when we moved a large desk, some papers fell out. These papers were undercover RCMP reports on meetings with this man and assorted other crooks, planning to import drugs in a big way. Apparently they brought in six million dollars worth of cocaine from Florida but got caught, no doubt with the help of the undercover man. There were more than fifty pages of detailed reports of activity and meetings. The criminals were using pagers to signal meeting places and times in code, and the bandits would do an electronic "sweep" for hidden transmitters in the meetings attended by the undercover man. My customer claimed to have connections with the Montreal mafia. He was the only one with a non-Italian name, so I doubt he was close. Probably more like "name dropping" to make himself sound important.

One day he showed up at my office, and became very upset when I told him I had sold some of his goods. He was mostly angry with his "friend" for not keeping the bargain. He mentioned something about breaking the guy's legs. I considered it a bit of hyperbole. We entered into negotiations about his remaining furniture and the amount of money owing. He wanted a certain amount of money back and I refused. He said that he had friends that could pay me a visit. I knew he was out on bail, so I did not think he would do anything too foolish. My wife was in the back office and I went there to ask her what she thought was fair. She had overheard our conversation and was terrified, telling me to give him whatever he wanted. I didn't, but we compromised and off he went, to jail.

He had told me that he had lost everything he "worked" for: his house, his large boat—almost everything he owned. What he didn't say was that it was taken by the Department of Justice as illegal proceeds of crime. I should have brought out the violin.

We also moved people at the other end of the "spectrum". We moved several church ministers over the years, and had only one problem move. This was a "tele-evangelist" whom we moved to Chicago. All went well, except the van line did not get paid, and after six months of trying, they charged the whole bill back to us, about $ 5000.00 US, as we were ultimately responsible for collecting the money. I found out that the evangelist had quit the ministry there and the Chicago ministry was discontinued. No one took responsibility for paying the moving bill.

I called their office in Toronto (100 Brinkly Street), asking for the tele-evangelist in charge. I was told he was taping a show and could not speak to me right then, but would call me back later. To ensure he would, I told them what I thought about their religious ethics and threatened to go to the press. Later that day, the man called me back and apologized profusely. What was even better, he paid the bill!

There are some unscrupulous operators out there, especially the smaller ones running a truck from a home, or using moving as a sideline for their trucks doing other work. One such mover was *Mississauga Movers.* They got in so much trouble and had so much bad publicity that they closed up. However, the same people are back under a different name.

Some years ago, at the end of June, we had a customer who we could not move in to their new home because the old owners had hired

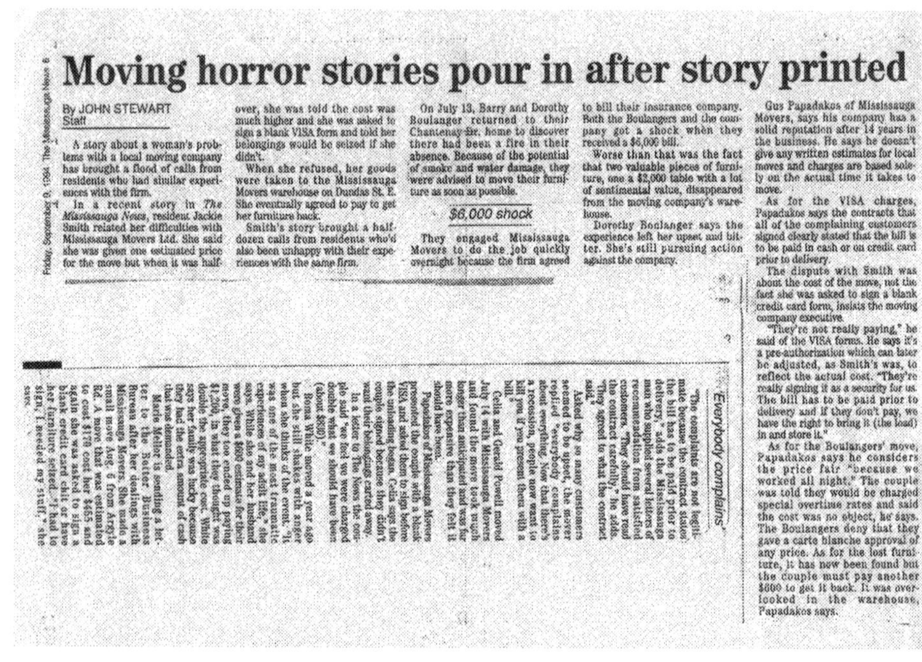

Friday, September 9, 1994 The Mississauga News 6

Moving horror stories pour in after story printed

By JOHN STEWART
Staff

A story about a woman's problems with a local moving company has brought a flood of calls from residents who had similar experiences with the firm.

In a recent story in *The Mississauga News*, resident Jackie Smith related her difficulties with Mississauga Movers Ltd. She said she was given one estimated price for the move but when it was half-over, she was told the cost was much higher and she was asked to sign a blank VISA form and told her belongings would be seized if she didn't.

When she refused, her goods were taken to the Mississauga Movers warehouse on Dundas St. E. She eventually agreed to pay to get her furniture back.

Smith's story brought a half-dozen calls from residents who'd also been unhappy with their experiences with the same firm.

On July 13, Barry and Dorothy Boulanger returned to their Chantenay Dr. home to discover there had been a fire in their absence. Because of the potential of smoke and water damage, they were advised to move their furniture as soon as possible.

$6,000 shock

They engaged Mississauga Movers to do the job quickly overnight because the firm agreed to bill their insurance company. Both the Boulangers and the company got a shock when they received a $6,000 bill.

Worse than that was the fact that two valuable pieces of furniture, one a $2,000 table with a lot of sentimental value, disappeared from the moving company's warehouse.

Dorothy Boulanger says the experience left her upset and bitter. She's still pursuing action against the company.

Gus Papadakos of Mississauga Movers, says his company has a solid reputation after 14 years in the business. He says he doesn't give any written estimates for local moves and charges are based solely on the actual time it takes to move.

As for the VISA charges, Papadakos says the contracts that all of the complaining customers signed clearly stated that the bill is to be paid in cash or on credit card prior to delivery.

The dispute with Smith was about the cost of the move, not the fact she was asked to sign a blank credit card form, insists the moving company executive.

"They're not really paying," he said of the VISA forms. He says it's a pre-authorization which can later be adjusted, as Smith's was, to reflect the actual cost. "They're really signing it as a security for us. The bill has to be paid prior to delivery and if they don't pay, we have the right to bring it (the load) in and store it."

As for the Boulangers' move, Papadakos says he considers the price fair "because we worked all night." The couple was told they would be charged special overtime rates and said the cost was no object, he says. The Boulangers deny that they gave a carte blanche approval of any price. As for the lost furniture, it has now been found but the couple must pay another $800 to get it back. It was overlooked in the warehouse, Papadakos says.

'Everybody complains'

"The complaints are not legitimate because the contract states the bill has to be paid prior to delivery," adds the Mississauga man who supplied several letters of recommendation from satisfied customers. "They should have read the contract carefully," he adds. "They agreed to what the contract said."

Asked why so many customers seemed to be upset, the mover replied "everybody complains about everything. Now that there's a recession, people now want to kill you if you present them with a bill."

Celia and Gerald Powell moved July 14 with Mississauga Movers and found the move took much longer than anticipated and was far more expensive than they felt it should have been.

Papadakos of Mississauga Movers presented the couple with a blank VISA and asked them to sign before the unloading began. Celia says the couple signed because they didn't want their belongings carted away.

In a letter to The News the couple said "we feel we were charged double what we should have been (about $830)."

Roma White moved a year ago but she still shakes with anger when she thinks of the event. "It was one of the most traumatic experiences of my adult life," she says. While she and her husband were given a $600 estimate for their move, they too ended up paying $1,200, in what they thought was double the appropriate cost. White says her family was lucky because they had the extra amount of cash that was demanded.

Marie Mellor is sending a letter to the Better Business Bureau after her dealings with Mississauga Movers. She made a small move Aug. 6 from Argyle Rd. A move that was estimated to cost $170 cost her $455 and again she was asked to sign a blank credit card chit or have her furniture seized. "I had to sign, I needed my stuff," she says.

Missisauga Movers, who did not show up. This is a serious problem at the height of the busy season, one cannot hire a mover on short notice—the people were really "stranded." We ended up first moving the other resident out, then our customer in. It took us until late at night to finish. The customer sued them, and I provided them with a factual, written statement of what had happened. They won and got $ 1000.00 from the movers. Later, I got a call from the principal of the moving company who threatened me for giving the customer the letter. I called the police and reported it and they paid him a visit. I never heard more from them, but read about them in the papers later.

In the early days, we did some work with a place that housed people with drug and mental problems. We had to stop working for them, because the guys would refuse to handle the furniture, it was that filthy. Another time we were moving a fellow who had been evicted by the health authorities. He had empty pizza boxes stacked to the ceiling, and empty beer cans likewise. The place smelled putrid and we called our cleaning crew to clean it up first. When they saw the mess, they refused to do it. Eventually, we learned to avoid such assignments, and stayed away from most welfare sponsored moves.

I have seen every kind of house and housekeeping in my days as a mover. We moved ten thousand square feet homes and we moved small hovels. It's all in a day's work (or two or three for the large mansions). But of all moves, the really filthy ones are the worst. We had to worry about contamination of the vehicles and other people's goods. Some people are so filthy it is hard to believe they can live that way. I have been at homes where I dared not sit down. Once, I was called for an estimate to a townhouse in Mississauga that smelled so awful from dog and cat feces and urine mixed with cigarette smoke and other filth that my eyes began to water and I felt I was going to vomit. I had to leave.

Amigo and Jasper (The other animals)

The first five years, while in our "old" premises, we had a German shepherd watchdog and a cat in the warehouse. I purchased the "trained" watchdog for $ 750.00, which was cheaper than installing an electronic security system. He smartly put on a show for us when we were at the dog training school where we got him, but I think he must have had "doggie Alzheimer", for he forgot everything he knew as soon as he moved into our warehouse. However, he had a fearsome bark, and we never had a break-in while we had the dog. We called him Jasper, but his papers stated that his name was Bosun von Havelsberg (meaning he was from the Havelsberg kennels in Ontario).

Just once did he display his prowess: Jasper liked to lie beside the truck while the men loaded from the warehouse. One day, a customer came by to pick up some packing materials. He came around back, and seeing our truck being loaded, came walking towards the rear door where Jasper lay. Jasper jumped up, grabbed the man by his tights and held him. He yelled, and the guys heard him and came out to get the dog off him. The strange thing was that all thought the dog had his tights in his jaws; he had not broken the skin. Nevertheless, we sent the man to the clinic, and later, a man from the health department came by to quarantine Jasper for two weeks. However, he got to sit out his "sentence" in our warehouse.

Jasper was slightly neurotic, and got into the habit of chasing his tail. I concluded the dog was lonely, so I decided to get a cat to keep him company. I went to the Humane Society's shelter to look for one. There were many cats and kittens there, and I felt they were all calling me to take them home. However, one kitten in particular caught my eye, for he had the same gray and brown markings as Jasper. "A pair of bookends," I thought, and chose him.

I was a bit worried about how the dog would take to the cat, but to my relief, Jasper accepted him quite readily. I named the kitten *Amigo*, meaning "friend" in Spanish, a friend for the dog, I hoped. Unfortunately, Amigo came with the usual kennel cold virus; he wheezed and sneezed, and had a runny nose. He also did not eat, as he could not smell the food, so I bought him a can of soft, pungent cat food. I opened the can and put it on the floor it in the office. Then, disaster struck.

Jasper had watched the proceedings, and when he smelled the food, he could not control himself. With a loud growl he jumped forward and bit the kitten's head—for a second, the cat's head disappeared into the dogs jaws. The poor cat fell over on his side, blood oozing from his nose. I grabbed his blanket and ran with him to the car, driving with him in my lap to the veterinary's office. There he got first aid and was put on intravenous support!

The following day I paid my bill and picked up the little guy. A sorry sight he was, blind in one eye due the to the concussion he had gotten from the dogs teeth, and he was walking like an old man. The vet told me his sight would probably return in a month or so, and amazingly, it did.

Jasper was feeling quite badly, so I let him be around the kitten again, watching him carefully the first while. I had Amigo de-clawed so he would not scratch the dog and provoke another attack. He improved quickly, and soon established himself as the boss in the office. I made a shelf in the warehouse above where Jasper slept and put his "bed" there, but Amigo liked Jasper's "bed" better, so he took it over and made Jasper sleep in front on the cement floor. Soon, he started asserting himself in other areas.

He got in the habit of sleeping on my desk, in the IN-tray. There he had a birds-eye view of the office and the door to the warehouse. Whenever Jasper ventured in to the office, he would wait until the dog was in front of the desk, and then jump on Jasper's back. This would initiate a brawl. Jasper soon learned that the cat had no claws, and took advantage of this. He would push Amigo around with his nose; Amigo would stand up against the wall, on his hind legs, jabbing and trying to scratch the dog with his non-existent claws. He looked like a boxer in the boxing ring, up against the ropes. Sometimes, his pugilistic would go too far, and Jasper, tiring of the game, would lie down on top of the cat, who, with his feet sticking out from underneath the big dog would scream in anger and frustration! I was sure no one would believe the spectacle I witnessed, so I brought in a camera, trying to capture the bedlam, but I never succeeded in getting the funniest acts. As soon as I got the camera ready, they would quit.

One day, a client was in the office when suddenly the ceiling collapsed and asbestos tiles came crashing down on the man's head, followed by Amigo. The cat had gotten on top of the ceiling from the warehouse, jumping onto the suspended tiles and crashing through. The customer must have had a sense of humour, for I still got the order.

Amigo would sit on my lap for hours, usually when the telephone was not ringing—which was more often than I would have preferred. Cats are usually independent creatures, but Amigo was sociable—more like a dog. I guess, living with a dog, he thought he might as well follow the maxim "when In Rome, do as the Romans do", and try to live up to his name.

One day when I was working at my desk, I saw Amigo sitting on the floor in front of me with something that looked like a moustache on his face. On further inspection, I realized that he had a bird in his mouth. I quickly grabbed him by the throat and released the bird, then opened the door and let it fly away. Amigo screamed in anger at losing his booty, and snubbed me the rest of the day.

Another day, a bird got into the office again, and Amigo took up the chase. As the bird was fluttering around the ceiling, Amigo jumped on top of the photocopier and from there into the air and caught the poor bird in flight. Again, I had to choke him to get the bird from his mouth, and to his obvious chagrin, I again, let the bird fly away out the door.

During the Christmas holidays, I got a call from the woman who did the cleaning for the pub next door. I had put a collar on Amigo, with his name and telephone number just in case he got away. As it turned out, this was fortunate. The cleaner called the number on his collar, asking if I had a cat named Amigo. I collected the little devil and paid her a finder's fee. Later, I discovered how he had managed to get there. He had climbed an insulated water pipe and squeezed through the hole in the wall where the pipe went to the next unit, where the pub was located. I always maintained that he wanted to watch the strip tease show there, but then, unfortunately, he got stuck, not knowing how to get back from whence he came. So there he was, alone in an empty pub for three days (I have known humans who would wish themselves in that predicament!).

Amigo and Jasper would be my companions for five years. When I left at night, they would follow me to the door and sit, side by side, watching me as I got into the car. As I drove away, they would turn around, Amigo in the lead, and saunter into the warehouse to patrol and guard for "bad guys"—the guard dog and his deputy.

We got a new warehouse and offices in a brand new building, and had an electronic security monitoring system installed. I could not keep a big dog there, so I gave him to a farmer in Belleville. Jasper apparently was at home on the farm, but after a year or so, I heard he died of a heart attack—he had gotten fat and his back was a problem. Shepherds have a genetic weakness with their backs.

I now had several employees, and not all were enamoured with a bossy cat in the office, so I decided to take Amigo home. At night, Amigo would lie beside my bed, where he would stay most of the night. I am certain he thought of himself as a watchdog, guarding his master's bed, yet his constant purring gave him away.

Amigo had never been an "outside" cat, but the garden around the house was too tempting, and I eventually relented and let him go outside, a fatal mistake, as it turned out. Being a "friend", Amigo lived up to his name and took to visiting and befriending the neighbours, who would feed and fuss over the friendly animal. This was to be his bane. One day as he was crossing the road to visit a neighbour, a car ran over him. Amigo was dead. When the neighbour called to tell me what happened, I could not bring myself to go out to see him, so the kind neighbour looked after the cat's remains.

I cried that day, as I never cried before, save the day my mother died. Though I have always loved animals, none have touched me as Amigo did. I still think about him at times. In fact, I still miss them both: Jasper and his Amigo.

Government agencies

I suppose every businessman has problems with government agencies from time to time. Bureaucracies can be frustrating to deal with, especially for small businesses with limited time and resources. I have found a marked improvement the last few years in the service orientation of individual agencies, but I do have some bad memories of dealing with two government agencies in particular: The (formerly) *Workers Compensation Board* (Ontario), and The Federal *Department of Human Resources*. One problem we faced in our business was workers who decided to feign back injury, and went to their family doctor claiming they hurt themselves at work. The doctor would invariably take the easy route, prescribing a few weeks off work. The WCB would, generally, accept the doctor's statement and grant the claim, which would then go against our corporate record (NEER Ratings). Even if you notated your suspicion of a false claim on their reporting form, they would just ignore it. A few times I tried to fight this, always without success. One case was kept going for more than three years. I had clear evidence of the employee's false claim, and that he was malingering, but each time I called the Board, they had lost my file, someone else had it, it was re-assigned or they had some other excuse to avoid dealing with it. I finally got to a senior official at the Board and was told an inspector was going to see me. After a long time, I called to find out what was happening with the inspector, and was told that he had visited my office but I was not available. This was pure prevarication, and I told him so, to no avail—no one ever showed up and nothing was ever done. They counted on wearing me down.

After they re-organized (and fired some of the most useless people there), now calling themselves *The Workplace Insurance Agency*, they held meetings and promised employers that things would get better. They also told us of rehabilitation program whereby they would subsidize employers for hiring handicapped individuals. This made sense to me. The individuals would get off the insurance and become productive again, and the Board would subsidize the employer for a while as an incentive for hiring the disabled. I immediately called the office to hire someone under this plan, as I needed a telephone sales/service person. They sent me a young lady to take information from me, and that was the last I heard from them. When I tried to find out what was happening, I was told the young lady was no longer there, and the "plan" was shelved! I was disappointed, but not surprised. It is a highly politicized organization. In fairness, I must say that I noticed improvements in their service orientation the last couple of years I was in the business. It could only improve.

The HRDC (Federal Human Resources) was not much better. I don't say the people working there have a mandate to frustrate small business, but they do appear to be naturally hostile towards us. Once I fired a thief, who then claimed pay in lieu of notice. I ended up paying him for two weeks. This was after he had cost me several thousands in claims for customers missing goods. What I found grating, however, was the apparent hostility of the HR officer, who arbitrarily assigned blame without much effort to get the facts from us, and at one point, blatantly lied about a letter she claimed to have sent me. I could pass this off as an isolated incidence, but it was not. Later on I had another employee who claimed for alleged overtime pay and for unjust dismissal. This time I had documented his transgressions, but the official still allowed his *overtime claim*, saying I had not responded to his letter requesting some documents. I never did receive that letter from him. Since he had registered every other letter, I could assume he would have registered this one also, so I could prove it never got to me. I think he never sent the letter, and found my "non-response" to a phantom letter a good reason to allow the claim and get the claimant off his back. The galling thing about this is that before you are permitted to appeal their arbitrary decisions, you have to pay the amount into their "trust" fund.

When these quasi-judicial departments decide to give you problems, fighting them is so time consuming and stressful that most people give up, totally overwhelmed. I am sure they count on it.

Police charge 13 in funding fraud

Scheme involved $1.484 million in federal grants

HRDC officials took secret commissions, investigators allege

ROBERT CRIBB AND DALE BRAZAO
STAFF REPORTER

Peel Region police have charged 13 people with offences ranging from fraud to accepting secret commissions involving $1.484 million worth of federal grants given to companies in Peel.

Six current and former officials with Human Resources Development Canada (HRDC) in Mississauga have been charged along with seven others as part of a sweeping 15-month investigation into a widespread bribery scheme between federal officials and companies that received government grants in exchange for secret payoffs.

"We're alleging that secret commissions, monies were paid by folks at these corporations to enable that (grant) contracts are issued to them for work in relation to HRDC business," said Detective Bob Lusty, of Peel Region police's fraud bureau.

"We're also alleging that within those contracts themselves that were issued to the different companies, that fraud occurred within those contracts."

Lusty said the HRDC project officers facing charges had influence over which companies received grants and were responsible for monitoring how the money was spent.

"When you've got people paid off who are doing that, obviously the monitoring isn't done as it should be."

Among those charged are Joan Rowe, a former senior HRDC officer in Mississauga, for influence peddling, fraud and conspiracy to commit fraud. Rowe's husband, Vinton Clarke, who was not an HRDC employee, is charged with fraud and conspiracy to commit fraud.

Other HRDC officials charged include [illegible] (fraud), [illegible] (accepting secret commissions), Rula Norman (fraud), Jason Egbuna (fraud and conspiracy to obstruct justice) and Robert Simas (bribery of an agent and fraud).

Among those charged who are not HRDC officials are Suzette Thomas (fraud and two counts of bribery), Carol Francis (fraud), Charmaine Mothersil (fraud and conspiracy to commit fraud), Whitman Solomon (fraud), Neraj Seth (fraud and conspiracy to obstruct justice) and Andre Grenier (bribery).

Joan Rowe, a former senior HRDC officer in Mississauga, and her husband Vinton Clarke are among those charged in connection with grants given in Peel.

three years ago when the federal auditor general could find no justification and little paperwork on almost $1 billion in grants.

In February of this year, Peel police charged six people — including a school superintendent, a principal and two teachers with the Dufferin-Peel Catholic School Board — with fraud involving $780,000 in HRDC grant money.

Police alleged fraudulent invoices and secret commissions were used to siphon grant money from the federal agency.

Former HRDC employees and consultants, some of whom have been interviewed by police, say there has been a systemic problem with project officers accepting bribes in exchange for awarding sometimes millions of dollars in federal grant money.

unless you knew the people and paid them," said the consultant who agreed to speak on the condition of anonymity. "That was the way it worked. That was the culture."

The consultant said project officers who routinely reviewed her grant applications asked for between 2.5 and 5 percent of the value of each grant in exchange for rubber-stamping her projects. The value of those grant proposals ranged from a few thousand dollars to hundreds of thousands of dollars each, she said.

Rowe is the most senior former HRDC official to be named in the charges. She was suspended by HRDC a year ago and subsequently fired.

Contacted by the Star at her Brampton home twice last fall, Rowe would not comment. The 13 charged are

Banks

Much has been said about banks and small business, mostly critical. Yet, I did not have many real problems with my bank, and the few I did have were mostly self-inflicted. I will say, though, that the manager you are assigned is crucial to the business relationship. If he or she understands your business and trust you, you can generally steer clear of major hurdles. My greatest frustrations were with the frequent changes in account managers, having to "re-educate" a new one. The banking system is undergoing constant change and reorganization. It seemed to me that the managers were getting younger and less experienced (or maybe it was just me getting older), with decision making becoming more and more centralized and inflexible. However, it is important to communicate with your manager, and one should not lose sight of the fact that banking is *not* a paternalistic business and bankers are not altruists. Their responsibility to shareholders far exceeds their commitment to you.

Other "Services"

Movers are often at the mercy of incompetent or dishonest mechanics. If you don't have the physical and people resources to do your own maintenance—and few small movers have, you are liable to overcharging and worse. Towing companies also have their share of dishonest operators. One example each will suffice:

I had a cube van in the shop to replace a muffler. The mechanic welded the muffler on backwards! The exhaust fumes blew directly into the cab and almost killed the crew.

Another time, our truck broke down, and I called a towing company with whom we had an account. Unbeknownst to me, another tow truck saw my truck and stopped, intimating that he was called by our office. He hooked up the truck improperly and damaged the front end. I called their office and complained, but nothing was done. I then refused to pay the bill. Later, while our truck was parked on a street, they saw it and picked it up, refusing to release it until I paid the bill. I did, and then I sued them. They had to pay for the damage, which was several times the cost of their bill.

In later years, computer repairmen and "consultants" became the modern day "car repair scammers". For the uninitiated and computer illiterate, even semi-illiterate, it is easy to get taken by these scam artists. It is particularly difficult for small businesses that cannot afford an "in-house" expert. I wasted a few thousands on upgrading computers that didn't need it and by getting poor quality parts when I did.

Claims and litigation

We moved a couple from a large ranch style home in Mississauga to a much smaller one. I realized that they had some kind of money problems, so I was careful, but they still managed to cheat me. I sued, but they got away with paying less by lying to the judge. A couple of years later I read in the newspaper that they were charged with abusing and mistreating their Filipino nanny. There is a Nemesis.

We moved a handicapped lady in a wheelchair, from her home in Mississauga to a small town outside Coburg, Ontario. We handled her with special care and empathy, but she complained a lot, and I noticed she smelled of alcohol and had a fair amount of booze around the house. She reminded me of Danny Devito's mother in the movie *Throw Momma From The Train*. After the crew unloaded at her destination and tried to collect, she told them that she was not about to "eat stale bread" for the rest of her life, and just refused to pay anything at all, and when I 'phoned her later, she told me to "get lost". I decided to sue her, but then I realized we did not have a proper mailing address for her, as it was a farmhouse in the country. She would not give it to me, so I concocted a ruse: I telephoned her, pretending I was the local hydro service, asking her, as a new subscriber, would she confirm the correct mailing address? She did, I sued, and eventually she paid up.

I was not always that lucky. We moved a fellow from Toronto where he ran a motorcycle shop to a cottage north of Peterborough. I "smelled a rat" when he was hesitant about payment arrangement, but he allayed my misgiving when his parents agreed to pay with their credit card. Well, the parents reversed the charges saying they did not move and did not owe me anything; the signature on the card slip was the son's, not theirs! The guy intentionally cheated me, the parents colluded with him and I could do nothing about it.

I got caught twice. August 27th, 1999, we moved a fellow, Mark Casseneyer, to Alton, Ontario. He signed his Visa slip with a phony signature, and then told Visa he did not sign or authorize the charge, and it was reversed. I eventually sued and got a default judgment, but I was unable to track him down. Lesson learned: a judgment is useless unless you can collect. After these experiences, I took care to ensure that we had proper destination mailing addresses on file, including, when possible, where the customer worked.

In the early days, before I got wiser, a customer "bounced" a cheque on me, and refused to make it good after numerous requests. I sued him, but he was self-employed, and cancelled his bank account, so I could not collect. I knew it would not get me my money, but I was angry with the blatant cheat, so I went to the police. They would not lay a criminal charge, saying they were not a collection agency, but I saw a Justice of The Peace who agreed to lay the charge. After one year the case came to court. The judge managed to find a technicality to let him off. Guess he figured I had it coming for "wasting the time of the court." My time, of course, was worthless.

At times, conflict is unavoidable. The customer is often stressed and unhappy with something. It could be the time it took—his perception of how long it should take, regardless how the men worked. If you estimated a time, the customer expects it to take no longer. It is very hard to estimate exactly how long it will take to load, travel to the new location and unload a household. Many factors intervene—difficulties at the origin, traffic delays and often, problems at the destination, which the sales person did not see. To look at destination access and house layout is not practical. Usually, the customer has no access to the new location, and such things as access problems are often not disclosed, even if the customer does know about them. The sales person is faced with a dilemma: if he overestimates, he will probably not get the order, for the customer will think him incompetent if other movers estimate a shorter time. Yet, if he estimates low, the company will face a problem collecting from the customer, who will often try to hold the moving company to the estimated time, regardless of the reasons for the move taking longer than estimated. In the case where you have unloaded the furniture, the customer holds all the cards, and you often take what you can get to avoid the hassles of litigation. It can take months to get a hearing at Small Claims Court, and often, the judge will bend over backwards to find a reason to side with the customer who is "fighting the big bad company." Try explaining to the judge that you are a small businessman who charges barely compensatory rates, and that giving up two or three hours of work, for which you must pay your employees, will put you at a loss!

I also learned this the hard way. We had booked a move over the telephone. The customer told me what he had in the house, quite truthfully, but forgot to mention the hundreds of boxes of books and files he had in the garage. He paid the extra hours, but later sued asking for reimbursement. The judge told me that I could have gone to see it and that he would only allow a variance of ten percent.

Another time we showed up to do a job and so did two other movers. The customer had ordered three different movers, just to be sure. I sued them for time lost (I had to pay three men four hours pay). The customer told the judge she had cancelled, and gave as proof a pack of cigarettes where she had written something on the back of the pack. The judge said he believed her, and I went away empty handed. After that, I started taking deposits.

Movers are especially vulnerable when goods are "missing." On local moves, it is not practical to inventory every item—customers will not pay for the time it takes to record everything (though it is done when goods are going into storage). One customer claimed she was missing an expensive rug. She notified us sometime after the move, and I rejected the claim. She took us to court, and the judge said he would give her the benefit of doubt, and me the shaft. Afterwards, I devised a form for the customer to sign before and after the move, stating that he had checked the truck and the house for anything left there. Fortunately, I never had to test it, but I doubt it would have stood up in court.

After a while, I learned when to contest a claim, and when to issue a claim. As Kenny Rogers sang, "you have to know when to hold them, know when to fold them". Sometimes it just was not worth the hassle, it was either too time consuming or too costly, or both.

Yet, I had some success. Once, I moved a customer who did not want insurance, and one plate of a set of dinner plates got accidentally broken. He wanted me to replace a whole twelve-piece set. I found a six-person set of the same pattern and offered to buy it for him. He refused the offer and sued me. He was a policeman and should have known better. I think the judge agreed that I had offered more than was necessary, and I remember his statement to the plaintiff: "You have no insurance, Sir". As I walked out of the courtroom, the wife screamed at me "you stole our dinner set". Sometimes you win but you lose.

Another time we moved a young lawyer and his family to Ottawa where he had gotten a job with a fairly large law firm. After we delivered his goods, he refused to pay the crew, and they returned empty-handed. I spent some time on the phone trying to convince him to pay up, but he had a hundred excuses why he should not. I finally got tired of arguing and sued him. For some unexplained reason, he did not contest it, and I got a default judgment. Still, he ignored my requests for payment, so I garnished his pay cheque at the law office where he worked. That got a reaction, and he asked me for terms. He gave me six post-dated cheques. Clearly, he had not planned to pay me—he did not have the money!

Two years later, I got a call from a bank in Ottawa. The lawyer had applied for a mortgage with them, but when they checked, they found an outstanding judgment against him from me. I had not realized that since I took the payment from him directly, the judgment was still in the court records! But, *he*, a lawyer, should have known that. The banker asked me if I thought he was credit worthy, and I replied that I had no idea what his finances were currently, but that I would not hire him to defend my dog!

Another time we moved an immigration lawyer. I accepted a personal cheque from him. Since he was a lawyer, I thought it would be safe. However, his cheque bounced. He kept promising that the replacement cheque was "in the mail." It never was, and after many imploring calls to no avail, I threatened to call the Law Society. That did it. I had the cheque by taxi. No doubt, his *trust account* was short the funds.

I have found many lawyers to be problematic customers. For some reason they seem to think that the words "I am a lawyer" is enough to scare the pants of you. What many of them fail to see is that their professional standing brings an expectation of behaving ethically. If I must go to court, I would much rather have a lawyer as an opponent than a little old lady. The old lady will get every consideration and leeway possible, the lawyer will be held to a higher standard. And so it should be. The judge knows well that for most small claims, appeals are too expensive, and he need not go exactly by the book. I have often been amazed, even when I lose, how generally fair and equitable this system is.

We moved a female "Perry Mason" and did some damage to her furniture. This woman also did not take any insurance (she would later claim it was not offered to her), in itself a strange decision for a law professional who should know better. When I offered a settlement, it was not acceptable; she wanted "full replacement value" even though our liability was limited by the contract to sixty cents per lbs. per article. Of course, she pointed out that she was a lawyer and would sue. However, instead of suing, she had the credit card charges reversed and I had to sue *her*. She counter-sued for $ 10,000.00 (which happens to be the limit for small claims court actions)! We had a pre-trial hearing with a "judge" that was not the brightest bulb in the court and I had to explain to him over and over again what a Bill of Lading was, what the Highway Transport Act was and why there was a liability limitation. He had clearly no idea what this was all about. My opponent graciously agreed to reduce her claim to $ 8000.00 (!) but could not produce any evidence supporting her claim. When she told the "judge" she was a lawyer, they began to reminisce about some acquaintances they had in common and I walked out of the room. Fortunately, when it came to trial, I faced a "real" judge and though my opponent put me through the "hoops" in court, she was not able to substantiate her absurd claim. I think she lost all creditability with the judge and wore out his patience. I can still see the look of incredulity on her face when she lost.

There are good and bad people in all walks of life. This is also true for lawyers and judges. Fortunately, I have run into really poor judges only twice, both times in pre-trial hearings. That amounts, in my reckoning, to only about two percent.

In the other case, the judge-mediator began to berate both my opponent and myself, and I walked out on him. I wrote a letter to the Attorney General complaining about the judge's behaviour. After more than a year, I finally got a reply. His *assistant* told me that *having thoroughly investigated the matter* they found there was no misconduct by the judge. Surprise! Then he, condescendingly, went on to explain to me the purpose of a pre-trial hearing.

You never know who is going to turn on you—no matter that they live in nice houses and drive expensive cars. Once I moved a person from a very nice home to another up-scale, large home in the country. I had learned my lesson about taking personal cheques, regardless of the apparent "value" of the client, and this customer agreed he would have a certified cheque for the estimated cost, and would give it to our men before departing for the new home in the country. It was Friday and I was going to friends for dinner. I did not want to have to deal with collection problems while there, so I dropped by the customer's house on my way. The wife said everything was all right and that the husband had gone to the bank to get the money order.

Later that evening, my cell-phone rang. It was the crew foreman. The customer did not have a cheque, he now said he would give it to them when they had finished unloading at the destination. I "smelled a rat". This was not what I had agreed to. I told the men to bring the tractor-trailer to our yard; I would deal with it the next day.

The next day, Saturday, I met the customer in my office. He yelled and screamed at me, waving a money order in the air, and insisted he would give it to us when we delivered. He called the police who told him it was civil matter, but then I let the policeman talk me into agreeing to deliver his goods and collect the money when we arrived. Big mistake!

The boys arrived at his country "estate" and backed the tractor-trailer into his long driveway. When they asked for the cheque, he said he would pay them after they unloaded. They called me, and I drove there. It was now about midnight. The guy had driven a cube van in front of our vehicle, and there was no way we could escape. I had no choice but to unload the truck. Afterward, of course, he refused to pay! I sued the jerk, but at the first court appearance, he asked for a remand. Another court date was set for a couple of months later.

After about two weeks, I got a call from a detective at the Missisauga Police's Homicide Division. He asked if I knew Mr. X. I told him about my experience with him and the pending litigation, and then asked why he called me. He told me that Mr. X was *murdered* a couple of days before—stabbed to death in his office. Recovering from the surprise, I told him that, though I would have liked to, I did not kill him, but that I was sure he had it coming. The detective said I was "not a suspect—yet!"

I never found out if they caught his murderer, not that I cared. I did get a judgment against his estate, and his widow eventually paid me—in installments. I asked her if she knew who did it. She said "it was probably one of his fellow (visible minority). They were always fighting!"

Once before we had a customer block us in his driveway, while refusing to pay. I was determined to not getting caught again, and gave standing instructions to my drivers to get out of the customers driveway, and call me if there were any problems with payment. This caution paid off a couple of times. Once, a customer's wife got quite hostile with the driver while the crew was unloading. She called the police, claiming that the driver had threatened her. The driver called me, and I told him to put the truck on a public street and await the police. The cops came and determined that there was no "threatening" going on, but by now the woman was very hostile and refused to pay. Her husband had blocked our truck on the street, and I got the policeman on the 'phone and asked him to tell the customer that it was illegal to block a vehicle on a public street. He did, and the customer changed her tune and promised to pay up. Just to ensure he would, we had him prepay it! There are some nasty customers out there, but they don't make the news. In fact, some of the nastiest ones have been women. It seems that their worst side comes out through the stress of moving their household.

Ime Rotondi was one such woman. I went to see her at her home in Mississauga, and she told me a sad story about how her mother was throwing her out of the home, which she shared with her two children. She told me she was involved in a messy divorce and her husband owed her a lot of money, but he was fighting her in court, and she owed three lawyers money and they had all refused to do more work until she paid them something.

Our warehouse was full, and as she had no credit, and could not get a self-store unit on her own, I arranged to put her goods into Storwell Self-storage on Royal Windsor Drive and pay them on her behalf. She was to pack her stuff and be ready. Of course, she wasn't, and we ended up packing all her goods. Then, when the time to pay for the move came, she didn't have the money, but assured us she would get money from her husband soon, and pay up everything.

She never did. She did pay some of it, sporadically, but eventually I told her if she did not find some money soon, I would have to dispose of her goods at auction, as I was paying Storwell on her behalf, and she still owed from the move into there.

She went to a law firm and got them to apply for a Motion to have me release her goods! To fight the motion with a lawyer would have cost me about $ 2000.00, about what she owed, so I went by myself. Big mistake—the Motion was in the Senior Court and they required a written argument. The woman judge refused to take my verbal submission, and she granted her the Motion, telling me I could come back and sue for the money. That was akin to squeezing blood from a stone, so I gave up.

Her brother in law called me and told me the real story: She had bought the home with her mother, but did not contribute anything, so the mother had to sell the home as the bank was foreclosing. She took everything out of the house, even the appliances belonging to her mother, and her mother had to move in with her other daughter and son in law.

I had a bit of a last laugh though: she didn't pay this law firm either. Even they could not squeeze that stone—she was on welfare!

I received a call from a lady in Burlington, asking to come right away to pick up a few items and take it to our warehouse. Well, the "few items" was a houseful of furniture—nice and expensive furniture, and all the dining room and kitchen items to pack. I brought in reinforcements, and we spent the next two days packing and loading their belongings. It was a large, expensive house, but it was a "foreclosure", the bank had taken the house, and their representatives were there, observing us working. The husband and wife was a young, very good-looking couple that had gotten into financial trouble. They were both children of well to do physicians in Burlington, and I think they had not received any lessons in the "school of hard knocks". They seemed to blame the bank for their predicament. Later, the man's mother came by the warehouse to pay their bill and she spent some time telling me about how terrible the government was, how badly the government and the banks had treated her children. I thought, "no wonder they got into trouble, the mother had probably run interference for them all their lives."

They stayed in the warehouse for six years, and each and every month I had to call them to get paid. Usually, the parents paid the bill—eventually. They were staying with the man's parents. I was relieved when they finally got their own place and we moved their goods there.

I learned, through costly mistakes, to protect myself from some kind of claims. In the beginning, our crew often helped the customers to pack up items such as wall pictures, which the customers were to do themselves with the cartons we were *lending* them. However, after a few claims, we had to discontinue this, realizing that if we helped the customer and something broke, we were automatically liable. The fact that we were being helpful got us little sympathy. One customer had a large painting in the basement that they were supposed to pack themselves, but when our guys came, it was still hanging in the basement. The customer asked the men to take it the way it was, since it was not worth much. They did, and managed to punch a small hole in it. The customer claimed, and collected $ 30,000.00 from the insurance and us—some "cheap" painting!

Another customer had an oversized sofa that would not fit down the stairs to the basement family room. The customer told the men to just "push it through" as he cared little about the old sofa. They did, and made a hole in the drywall. When he later made a claim, I said that he had told them to do it, whereupon he replied that they were "professional movers and should have known better"!

Then there was the older gentleman who asked one of the men to help him disconnect his old washing machine. The coupling had rusted and he got a large plumber wrench and handed it to my man. The worker gave it a turn and it came loose but the water spurted out in great force. I ended up paying the customer for a plumber and for cleaning up the water from the basement. The story was the same: "your man should have known better." After this, I had an "exception form" made up, and made the customer sign a waiver if they insisted that we do something that was not part of a normal move. Live and learn but pay for the lessons!

Some people behave so strangely you wonder on which planet they live. We moved an old couple for the second time and as with the last time, they were very happy. They gave the men a tip, and filled out a glowing performance report. The job went over the estimate by about two hours, due to delays with their closing.

Several months after, I got a call from some guy at CTV, saying he worked for a *consumer show* that was doing a story on the moving business. He said he had a complaint from this same customer of ours, saying we had overcharged him. The man on the 'phone was quite arrogant, saying we had cheated a *war veteran*! I was astounded, pulled the file and saw the positive report and no indication of any complaint or discontent by the customer. I faxed the whole file to the CTV man, and also mentioned that we had done quite a bit of business with CTV/Baton, and he could check with his bosses to see what kind of movers we were (we had also moved the Chairman, Doug Bassett). I told him that I would sue him if he said anything disparaging about us. I never heard any more from him, and I still do not know what possessed my customer to call CTV to complain. I can only surmise that someone had put the old man up to it, or done it for him. Sometimes things are not what they seem and for every crooked mover there is a dishonest customer—or at least, a confused one.

One hot July we moved a couple into a very nice home. The couple asked the men to set up the picnic table and chairs in the back yard first, which they promptly did. The couple got out some food and a bottle of wine, and was having a nice dinner outside. After some time, the guys got very thirsty, so they asked the people if they could turn on the water so they could have a drink of water from the water hose. The couple refused, and the men unloaded the truck without a drop of water while the customers dined in the back yard! Most people would treat animals better than that.

Dishonest employees—The "Fifth Column".

Among the stresses of a mover's life are irate customers, claims, equipment breakdown, revenue shortfalls, accidents and *problem workers*, the latter is often the more serious and most persistent problem. They are few who do not smoke pot, and you are grateful if they are not into stronger stuff, like crack cocaine. Then there are the dishonest ones. The worst thing that can happen to a mover is having an employee steal from customers. I used to tell new employees that I could accept honest mistakes and judgment errors, but two things would get them fired immediately: theft and impertinence with customers. I thought that was a reasonable demand, but for some of them, it was excessive.

I shall only relate a few of the worst cases here. One driver was a crack cocaine addict. He got hold of a fuel credit card. With accomplices in a couple of gas stations, they put the card through for fuel and took the money from the till. Before I got suspicious and audited the fuel bills, he had gotten away with about nine thousand dollars. When I went to the police, they did nothing, but he did get picked up for having done the same thing at another, large employer earlier. He then had the temerity to 'phone me and ask me to post bail. He told the investigating detective (from jail) that he thought I was a great employer and he was so very, very sorry!

Another time I hired this fellow, Glen. He was a good talker, and was a qualified tractor-trailer driver. This guy stole from almost every customer, things like CD's, CD players, TV's and anything he could fence quickly. When I got suspicious and confronted him about all these "missing" claims on his watch, he got profane and I fired him on the spot. Mistake! He went to the Labour Board and I ended up paying the man for two weeks in lieu of notice. At the arbitration hearing, his wife commented that now, with the money he got from me, he could get his teeth fixed! I asked her if he did not get enough money for the goods he stole and fenced. Talk about putting salt in the wound. Yet, this cost was minor compared to the several $ 2500.00 deductibles I paid the insurance company for settling each customer's claims. He cost me about $ 15,000.00. About six months later, I got a call from his landlady. He had skipped, and left the house he rented in an awful mess, with a lot of damages. She was trying to track him down. I wished her luck.

These people steal from employers almost with impunity, knowing well the police will do little to apprehend them. Once I had evidence that one of my employees, Danny Murphy, had stolen a microwave, a TV, and a carpet. It was a strange combination, but it turned out that his mother was coming to visit him from "down home" and he wanted his place to look nice. He needed the microwave to cook for her. I gave the information to the police. A detective phoned the young man and told him that if he would bring the goods back, he would speak to me about not charging him. Then he called me to ask if I would drop the charges. Case solved by a 'phone call. It is the only one, of several "cases" that they ever "solved" for me. There is little glory in catching petty thieves, employees or otherwise.

A tractor-trailer driver took a shipment of military personnel to Montreal. When he got near Kingston, he apparently got a call from his mother saying his father was in the hospital, so he just turned around, came back, left the loaded trailer at his apartment building and disappeared without a word. I found the trailer and pressed into service a very "green"driver, knowing the fine I would get if I did not deliver the shipment in time. Well, the oil warning light came on during the drive along the 401. Instead of stopping, he kept going and blew the engine to smithereens just outside Montreal. I had to rent a tractor to make the delivery, pay the return train-trip for the driver, tow the tractor from Montreal to Mississauga ($ 1000.00) and install a new engine at a cost of $ 13,000.00!

Toward the end of my moving "career," I tried to hire a "broker", i.e. an "owner operator" with his own tractor. The first attempt was another failure. I advanced several hundred dollars to this fellow who had his own truck but needed repairs for which he had no money. He signed the usual contract but that did not stop him from disappearing without paying the money owing.

I tried again, hiring another man with a tractor. This time the man had a lien on his tractor, so before I advanced him the money, I transferred his ownership to my company to protect myself. No matter, he also disappeared with the truck though it had no plates on it. Last I heard he had driven it to his hometown of Edmonton, but it was not worthwhile for me to go after him there for the few hundred dollars he owed. Sooner or later he would get caught without plates, or with invalid ones. Or have an accident, with no insurance.

I have seen some "low life" in my time, and thought of myself as a "man of the world". I also had the rather egalitarian belief that all people have potential and can be motivated. That had been my experience in my industrial management past—my life before "moving". However, I eventually realized that there are some people who, for whatever reason, cannot be redeemed. They take kindness as foolishness, trust as weakness.

A trailer was broken into at the yard and the thieves spent the whole night sorting through the customer's goods, walking over furniture and causing as much damage as the value of what they stole. The insurance company paid $ 35,000.00; I paid the $ 5000.00 deductible. After this, I put in a digital camera system, and this did stop tampering with trucks and trailers parked outside. Yet, no camera can stop dishonest employees determined to steal. We had an expensive grand piano stored in our warehouse, crated and labeled. It was later, ostensibly, put into a storage container. When the customer wanted the piano shipped, the container was empty. Someone, clearly a supervisory employee, had collaborated stealing the piano, probably using our truck. Since the period elapsed was over two years, we could only narrow it down to three or four former employees. The police offered little hope of recovering the piano, as usual citing lack of resources and more pressing problems. I must admit I understood their predicament—and mine.

Even though we had a monitored electronic security system, our office was broken into by "smash and grab" thieves three times. The first time I lost a computer and had to fix the broken windows. After the second time, and a second computer, I put bars on the windows. Even so, they tried again, but did not get in. The police, to their credit, were there within ten minutes of the call from the security firm, and the total elapsed time from the alarm going off until the police arrived was only twenty minutes, but it was too late to catch them, they were gone. No one was ever caught.

One day I came to work to find a truck missing. I checked the security camera, and could see the truck being started up and driven away during the night. In the semi-darkness, I could not see the driver, he got into the cab without being caught on camera, and managed to get in on the passenger side of the cab, alongside the neighbouring truck which blocked the camera view. I reported the theft to the police, and after about two weeks, they called to tell me the truck had been spotted in an empty yard Brampton, and was now in the police pound.

I picked up the truck after paying the towing and storage charges. Nothing was missing, and this puzzled me. One of my recently hired helpers was missing, but I did not connect the two, until I heard from another employee that this person, Eddie, had taken the truck, mistakenly thinking it was loaded with furniture (the truck next to it was) which he intended to sell. When he found it to be empty, he just abandoned it. I had no proof, of course, and Eddie probably went on to other such endeavors with another employer.

Of course, I was not the only one who had "problem employees". This problem is endemic in the moving business. Whenever I fired someone for a serious infraction, they would end up with a neighbouring moving company—often the same day. In the eighteen years I was in the business, I never had one other moving company call to check references. Helper-labourers were generally referred to as "swampers", a term originating in the logging business. One mover told me, when I first started in business: "this is not the *grassroots*, it's the soil below it!"

And other employees

Casual labourers, with the exception of students, are almost always school drop-outs. Very few had anything more than grade ten or eleven, most have some form of learning problem, and/or emotional problems. I remember moving a "shop" teacher who spotted one of his former woodworking shop students among the moving crew. He said he was very happy to see that I had hired *Mike* and that Mike was a productive employee. He told me that Mike would get into a rage if corrected or admonished in any way, and he had not thought Mike would ever be able to work for anyone. Shortly thereafter, Mike did fly into an unprovoked rage and left our employment. A year or so after that, I heard he had committed suicide.

Summertime was employee hell. All the movers were busy stealing each other's workers. Even other Atlas agents would call my employees, especially drivers, directly, trying to entice them to their company, offering more money. Of course, the guys would get laid off as soon as the busy season was over, but for the kind of people we got, with their short planning horizon, this often worked. One day, they would not show up for work, and sure as hell, we would find them working with the competition. Once I hired two drivers from "down east"—they were friends and lived together. The next day, they did not show up. No calls, just no show. Later, I spoke to one of them. He said that the same day, after accepting my job offer, he got another offer for fifty cents more an hour, so he went there. Calling me? Wouldn't think of it. How do you explain to your customer that you cannot move them because your workers did not show up for work? You cannot. You scramble like wild to try to get someone from an agency, or rearrange the vehicles you have and somehow manage. It's pure hell!

In eighteen years of moving, I had only one or two workers who ever gave me notice of leaving. Some would just walk off the job if they got too tired. There was little commitment to work. They knew that they could always pick up a casual labour job anywhere.

Half the men did not have a bank account, and many did not have any identification documents, so my bank had to call me to verify if they were who they said they were when they tried to cash their pay cheques there. Most of them would go to a cheque cashing service such a *Moneymart*, paying a fifteen dollar fee for the service.

Herman Green was from Jamaica and worked for me for a couple of years. He was here on a temporary work permit, waiting for his landed immigrant status. He had been sponsored by his wife—a marriage of convenience. She had a child already, and he had one with her, but had left her and she lived on welfare with the two children. They were still friends, and I suspect they still had some kind of a relationship. Problem was, she was his sponsor, and now, living on welfare, she could not continue to sponsor him, and he was at risk of deportation. He came to me to ask if I could hire her, at least long enough for him to get his landing papers. He was a good driver and a fair worker, so I agreed to help him. I hired her as a general office clerk. She was a real flossy, spending most of her time filing her nails, talking to boyfriends on the 'phone or smoking cigarettes in the men's lounge. I was relieved when Herman told me that he had received his landing papers, and she quit. Trouble was; Herman also quit.

The exceptions ...

I did have *some* successes with employees. One employee, Les Smith, worked for me over several years, interrupted by intermittent jail terms. I went to court for him three times, trying to keep him out of jail, but his temper and drinking kept getting the better of him. After his last jail term, I hired him back. He was a very hard worker, and totally honest with me. When I sold the company, he stayed behind to finish up some work, telling me just to pay him whatever I thought was fair. The last day he told me that this had been his best job and I had been his best boss, in fact, he said I was more like his father. He was visibly upset. I managed to find him a similar job, and he called to thank me. It is the only time, as far as I can remember, that any of my workers ever thanked me for anything I did for them. He also told me that he had stopped smoking "pot" and as a result his short-term *memory* was getting much better. Tell that to the advocates of marijuana smoking.

Some guys were different. Although from the same environment and lacking education, they were more settled, even gentle in their behaviour. I realized there was a common thread: while these young men were also from single-parent families, they had a caring and strong mother.

Brian B was a "gentle giant" of a man from Alberta. He lived with a girlfriend in an apartment-hotel in Mississauga, where they rented a furnished suite by the week. He did not drink to excess and did not smoke pot. He was gentle and pleasant, and worked like a bull. Once he and I were moving a piano, and we had no ramp with us. *Brian*, standing in the rear of the truck, lifted one end of the piano by the piano-skid straps onto the end of the truck, and I was able to lift up my end so he could pull it into the truck. He was a human crane. Later, his mother became ill back home in Edmonton, and he returned to be with her.

Dan was another young man. He also had a nice girl friend and a concerned mother. She would call him at work sometimes, and I could hear him speaking very kindly to her. Unfortunately for me, but good for him, he got a better job elsewhere.

Shane was with me for several years. He had a temper, but was honest, hard working and conscientious. His girl friend was also stable, and held down a fairly good job. He was quite fond of his mother. Eventually, he left for a better paying job, but kept in contact with me for several years.

One day he called me and asked if I could hire his mother. I happened to need a receptionist and hired her for that position. She did not like "desk-work" much, but she took on the job of packing for our customers, and did this for us for several years. After I hired her, *Shane* came by to see me. "Thank you for hiring my mom" he said.

There is often a person that makes a difference in a young life. Sometimes it is a mother, but it can also be a teacher. No matter how disadvantaged they may be, if there is someone who cares and gives them encouragement, these young people, in spite of having been "short changed" in early life, can make something of themselves. Yet, others in the same situation, but without that emotional support in the crucial, formative years, will fail. Those failures drift in and out of dead-end jobs, such as casual labour, often getting involved in a culture of drugs and alcohol abuse.

I remember another young man who was trying very hard to "go straight," telling me about his childhood. Growing up, he and his mother moved back and forth between their hometown in New Brunswick and Toronto several times. He said that more than once a year he would have a "new daddy". I really hoped he would make it, but I heard later that he was in jail.

This young man told me a story that perhaps illustrates the social stratification these young, lower income people are up against. He was living in *Talka Village*, a townhouse complex with a poor reputation, abutting the upper middle class Clarkson and Lorne Park, and for that geographic reason, the high school students there went to Lorne Park High School, where they were a bit like "fish out of water". One year, he said, they formed a football team of village boys and played against the "Lorne Park boys". He didn't say if they won any games, but he lost *his* "game"—he quit in grade eleven. Lack of parental and community support and feeling like "outsiders" does not do much to encourage these young people to stay in school, or learn anything when they do attend school.

And the not so exceptional …

Jerome was a special case. He was hard working but wild, impetuous yet gentle, temperamental, but with a soft heart. He also had the "standard" drinking problem. One day after a long day of work with a new driver, the two of them decided to go for a beer after work. Later that evening, the driver wanted to go home, so Jerome told him he would lock up the truck and bring the keys to the office. Instead, he took the truck and drove it home. There, he picked up his live-in girlfriend and drove my truck to the pub. At closing time, now totally inebriated, he drove the truck home again, and decided to park it in the visitor's parking at his apartment building! He managed to hit two cars, one on each side of the parking space. Someone called the police, and he and his girlfriend ran away, leaving the truck in the middle of the parking lot.

About three o'clock in the morning, I got a call from the police, telling me to come and take away the truck. When I arrived, half the apartment building's denizens were up watching the goings on. There was my truck, in the parking lot, with our name, and the appropriate slogan "call us for a moving experience"! What wonderful advertising. I removed this slogan from the trucks shortly thereafter.

After a short jail term, Jerome came back to work. I had him sign a statement that if he ever touched another truck he was subject to instant dismissal. He stayed with me for seven years and never did anything like that again. His temper was a problem, though, and many times he would scream abuse at me in defiance of an order, but he would eventually do as he was told. My philosophy was that "sticks and stones could break bones", but a little yelling did not bother me, as long as the job was done, and the yelling was not done in the presence of a customer.

Dave was from Newfoundland. He was an excellent driver, strong as a bull, and good with customers. He always drove with a friend, insisting that they must work together. As he was a contract (percentage) driver, I went along with it, since he was paying the helper. Then he had a fight with his buddy, who quit. That's when I found out why he had to have his "friend" with him. He could not read or write. Not a sentence, not even street signs, but he was intelligent and covered up very well. What I cannot fathom, however, is how he was able to obtain a Class A Tractor-trailer drivers license!

Dave moved a woman who had just divorced her husband. She drove a Mercedes and had more money than brains. She became infatuated with Dave and moved him into her nice home with her two children. Soon Dave was driving to work in her Mercedes. Then she decided to take him on a vacation to the "islands", and bought him expensive clothes and a fancy suit. However, after the vacation, Dave had had enough. He told the "boys" that she was bossing him around, correcting his speech and criticizing his drinking, so he left her. She had the temerity to come to my office complaining that he owed her money. I mentioned something about "sleeping in the bed you make," which went over like a "lead balloon."

But, at least Dave could drive, which was not always the case with "drivers." Once, I hired a temporary driver who just graduated from *Punjab Driver School* somewhere in the GTA. He got into the truck with his two helpers and almost scared them witless! He was afraid of driving on the highway, so he drove along the city streets. He had not checked the fuel tank, and ran out of fuel. He managed to get some fuel from a nearby station, and after getting the truck going, drove to the station to fill up. Then he took down their awning—the station building's overhang. Finally, after I had calmed down the station owner, he was on his way. When they arrived at the customers home three hours late, the customer told them to "get lost!" Four hours pay for three men, an insurance claim from the gas station owner and no "job"!

Later, I called *the Punjab Driving School* and complained about the "qualified driver" they sent me. "Don't worry", the man said, "we have many more drivers; I will send you another one". "Please don't!" I said." No—I didn't say *please*.

I hired a *new immigrant* with a tractor-trailer license. He could speak just a few broken words of English, but he drove our straight truck quite well when we tested him. We had to take a tractor for service, so I asked him to "bobtail" behind me so I could drive him back after dropping it off at the "shop". Driving along the QEW, I changed lane to exit, and glanced in the rear view mirror, just to see my man turn right in front of a car, then swerve, spinning around and coming to a stop backwards against the median rail! He managed to get hit by two cars, but failed to hit any himself. He was fine, but badly shaken up. When the police came, they could not understand him; the investigating officer gave up and told me to talk to him "if you can understand him!" Consequently, I spent the afternoon at the police *collision center* filling out forms for my driver. I felt sorry for the man, but there is something wrong with our licensing system when tractor-trailer driving licenses are issued to people who cannot read and write, or who don't speak, write or read enough English to give an accident report.

I hired another fine specimen, this time with experience and good references, from someone at my church!

When he was asked to "lie over" a long weekend in Halifax for a load back, he refused and came home empty, without permission. I got a call from him late at night outside Montreal. He swore that the "damn truck" had broken down. After speaking with him a while and asking some diagnostic questions, I realized that he had not switched over to the other side fuel tank when one ran empty … (expletive deleted).

Another fellow driving for me in the U.S. collected cash from the customers, kept part of it and sent the bills back short-paid. By the time I caught on to him, he had taken about $ 10,000.00. When I confronted him with it, he quit and went back to Montreal where he came from, saying he would pay me back. The Police would do nothing. They said, correctly, that the man had permission to collect money, and any shortfall was a civil matter—I could sue him for the money! Well, that was years ago, and he still owes the money. I'll collect any year now.

One of the strangest *ménages a' trois* I have ever encountered was two young men working for me, both good workers, living in *Talka Village*, with a woman who was the mother of one and the lover of the other. One day the "step-father" beat up his girl friend, the other guy's mother, and she charged him with assault. He spent a couple of months in jail and the woman visited him in jail regularly. When he got out, he moved back in with her. The two fellows—lover and son—continued to work for me.

Many employees, while basically decent, have problems they cannot overcome or control. Alcohol and drug abuse are two major problems in this business.

One day we were loading a shipment from the warehouse, and one of the helpers disappeared. I called in a replacement, and the loading continued. After completion, the driver went into the truck and drove ahead. We heard a loud yell from underneath the truck, and found our missing man behind the front wheel of the truck, writhing in pain. The front wheel had run over his leg. Later, after getting him to the hospital, we pieced together the story of what happened. He had drifted away and entered a nearby pub. After spending his paycheck on booze, he came back to the warehouse, unseen by anyone, and fell asleep underneath the truck! He was lucky to be alive. His leg was not even broken.

For a couple of years, I had a whole dysfunctional "family" working for me—a father and his two sons. All three were alcoholics, but when they worked, they worked well. The only problem was that they would almost never make it in Mondays. Eventually, they drifted away but one: *Dennis* was a "working machine"—he would work all kinds of hours and as long as he worked, he did not get into too much trouble. However, once he got into a fight in a pub and some fellow broke his jaw. They wired up his jaw so that he could not open his mouth but a little, and he went around drinking liquids from a straw. He still continued working! One day he told me his jaw was now loose and he could eat again. Trouble was, the wiring had come out, but it was not healed and that night he ended up in the hospital again with internal bleeding!

I never thought Dennis would amount to much, but he surprised me. He quit and started on his own, running a couple of trucks from a trailer-office. He ran it for several years.

His father, Johnny, was a horse of another colour. One day, long after he left us, he called me at home on a Sunday morning. He was very upset and related his story to me: he had been drinking heavily at home and got melancholy, calling 911 and telling them that he had a can of gasoline and was going to blow himself to smithereens. Not long after, the police busted down his door and dragged him off to jail, where they dumped him into a cell stark naked. I think he was mostly upset about being left naked in a cell; he said he was thoroughly humiliated. I had told him, at one time, that should he be ready for help, I would try to help him get off the drinking merry-go-round. Well, he was ready, he said. I called the Salvation Army, who referred me to the Addiction Research Institute on University Ave. They said they would take him only after he had been detoxified and gave me the address of a detoxification center. I picked up Johnny and we drove downtown. Passing a pub, he said "lets go and have just one last drink before I quit" (!). I checked him into the center and felt quite relieved and pleased with myself, happy for having done a "good deed."

Later that evening I got a call from his wife. "Johnny called me," she said, "he wants me to pick him up, he says he is not staying there with all those drunks—he is not like them." I told her not to get him, that all she was doing was *enabling* him to continue his drinking ways. But, get him she did, and last I heard Johnny was still drinking.

You'd better be able to handle failure and disappointment if you want to play the "Good Samaritan" with alcoholics, or they will drive you nuts.

We used students during the summer, and some of them were quite good workers. *Don* was one of these; he was also "clean cut" and well spoken, and I was quite impressed with his work. One day he was on a job with two other workers who were smoking pot and drinking on the job. The customer later told me about it, and I asked Don, who never touched the stuff, why he had not told me about their transgressions. His answer was that he was not a "rat" and would not tell on his fellow workers, no matter what.

Two years later I got a call from the Metro Toronto Police's Personnel Department, asking about Don. Apparently, he had applied to the police academy, and they were doing a thorough background check on him. I told them he was a very good worker, and when asked if there was anything at all negative with his work, I related the story of the dope-smoking fellow workers on whom he would not "tattle". I remember the police Staff Sergeant's comments: "we have enough of those guys already, we don't need to hire any more," meaning they considered that anyone covering up for fellow workers misdeeds is not desirable police material. Don did not get the job. I don't know if my comment caused his rejection, there might have been other negatives, but I felt a bit bad that I had mentioned it. Little mistakes can have large consequences. However, I was very impressed with the thoroughness of the police screening. It is comforting to know the extent the police go to in order to screen out any potential misfits.

I have always believed that there is something good in everyone, but this belief was sorely tried and did, probably, become a bit jaundiced over time. The "there for the Grace of God go I" was more like "good God, where are these people going?" I could envision these young men, now still physically strong and healthy, in another thirty or forty years, when their backs have given in, and their minds, long saturated in pot and alcohol, can no longer sustain them. These young people, with all the advantages this country can offer, were slowly killing themselves by physical and mental abuse and sloth. Many of these men were fairly intelligent, but they had no ambition, little moral fortitude, and lived their lives day by day. Long range planning for them was getting by until the next pay cheque. Young, strapping men thought nothing of going to the welfare office to get money to tide them over until payday. I had to keep cash on hand, to give them pay-advances, or they would often not come to work because they did not have bus fare. Yet they could afford to buy six-dollar packs of cigarettes. I remember one young man who got angry with me and walked off the job (as most were wont to do—I really never got notice from anyone leaving). I got a call from the government Employment Office, asking why he left. I told them, and asked if they were going to give him unemployment insurance pay. The man said they would suspend him for a time, but he would just go to the welfare office for interim financing anyhow. He was right. A couple of days later the welfare office called to confirm that he was not working any longer. He was there to apply for "social assistance." He lived with his girl friend, who had a couple of children (one was his), and was also on welfare!

Office personnel

While my worst experiences were with the labourers, I also had some problems hiring office help. Once, I was trying to hire a receptionist through a provincial government program (sponsored by the NDP government under Bob Rae). This program paid part of the people's wages for three months, if you hired someone from their welfare rolls. They arranged for three applicants to see me, all single welfare mothers. I had set up interviews at nine, eleven and two o'clock. The morning passed and no one showed up. In the afternoon, I called the first candidate. She said, "Shit, I forgot!" The next one told me that she had checked the map and found that it was too far to travel (I checked the bus schedules later and found the travel time to be approximately twenty minutes). The third one said she was sick and would call me when she got better. Of course, she never did.

I finally did hire someone from the program. She was an immigrant, married with three children, had no working experience and could not type—one of the requirements for the job. I hired her anyhow and paid for a typing course at a local high school. She learned fast, and she stayed with us for over three years. She was invited to attend a press conference with Rae and his gang, showcasing their "training"programme. She was one of the "stars". Truth is, the program was a sham and a failure, and was cancelled soon after the NDP lost office.

My experience with office staff has been this: hire a foreigner and train them if you must. They have a better work ethic than our native kind. Especially people from the Asian countries—the Philippines, China and India. That has been my experience anyhow.

I had a woman employee working for me as my accountant for a few years. Her life was a mess: she had several disastrous marriages in her past, and went through several relationships while working for me. She would pick up her beaus in bars. She was grossly overweight and had had a triple bypass after a heart attack, yet she stuffed herself with every kind of unhealthy food from French fries to chocolate. Her desk was covered with bags of potato chips and other junk foods. She would stay late at night and I wondered what she was doing. One evening I dropped back in to the office and I found out: she was gambling on the Internet.

She was intelligent and capable, yet unable to escape her vices.

I did have some outstanding employees over the years, particularly in the office. I was a demanding task-maker and expected much of the office help. Only when I had to deal with some other moving company's receptionist did I realize how well my employees did their job in comparison. To those "unsung" stars, a belated Kudos!

Long-distance hauling

Operating in the U.S. had special considerations. You could take a Canadian shipment to a U.S. destination, and you could load from the U.S. directly to Canada, but you could not stop and pick up and then deliver within the U.S. That is called *inter-stating,* and you would run afoul of the U.S. immigration rules. This was not policed as closely then as it is now, and Mayflower would often ask us to "interstate" if they were short of U.S. drivers or equipment. I had a French-Canadian driver working for me, one of the best long distance drivers I ever had, but he had a very strong French-Canadian accent. One day, the Mayflower dispatcher had him pick up an American family in New York, relocating to a place in Wyoming. What my driver did not know was that this was an American *customs official* that was transferred! At the end of the journey, the wife asked him, casually, where he was from. He answered, truthfully, "Montreal, Quebec". The man said "but you live in the U.S. of course." My man said no, he did not, whereupon the customs official promptly arrested him! I had to pay his US $500 fine, pay an American driver to deliver the shipment, send another man to pick up the trailer in Wyoming and have my driver "bob-tail" (driving an empty tractor) back to Toronto from the Saskatchewan border to where he was escorted by the U.S. immigration service. The poor guy was so upset by the experience that he quit, went back to Montreal and gave up long distance driving.

Keith was also running cross-country for us. He hated to crawl underneath the trailer in order to check the air brakes. He was caught with slack brake adjustment at the Manitoba border's weigh scales and given a warning, but never reported it. Then he was checked again at the Oakville QEW scales, and the jig was up. The trailer was impounded and the whole thing cost me about $ 3000.00, including fines, towing and storage charges. I did not fire him, because he was a fairly good driver otherwise, and good drivers in the moving business are scarcer than hen's teeth. Then he did it again, and, the trailer was impounded a second time. It was loaded with people's furniture on the way to Montreal, and I had to get another trailer there and transfer the load. The fine was doubled—for a second offence, and this time I did fire him. Later, we had a "facility audit" by the Ministry of Transport, and again his number came up: he had fudged the logs and driven over the time limit. Another fine. Same guy.

I hired a man with his own truck, as a "broker". However, his tractor broke down and needed a major engine overhaul, costing about $ 12,000.00, and, of course, he didn't have the money. I agreed to purchase the tractor from him and let him pay it back from his earnings as a broker-driver. He made a couple of trips thereafter, and all seemed fine. Then he disappeared, with the tractor. The police could not find it, but after a few months I got a call from a repair shop in Gravehurst, Ontario. The man said he had a tractor there, and had noticed my firm's name underneath a poorly done repainting job. The man's motivation for calling me, I later found out, was that the driver could not pay the repair bill, about three thousand dollars. He hoped to get it from me, as he had a "mechanics lien" on the truck. I would have to pay him to get my truck back. I also found out that the driver had managed to transfer the ownership papers to himself, by forging the original ownership document. The police would not get involved, as they felt it was a civil matter, so I went to Court to get a Court Order to transfer the ownership back to my firm. Then, finally, I drove to Gravenhurst, paid the shop, and had the truck taken back to our yard.

I ran the truck a couple of trips to Eastern Canada; then it blew a piston right through the block and caught fire. The intrepid driver put out the flames with the fire extinguisher. I wish he had not, because the insurance would pay only if the truck had burned. Now it was just a mechanical problem, albeit a $

13,000.00 one, because the tractor needed another rebuilt engine! I sold it for scrap for $ 2,000.00.

In the Big League (van line agent)

Operating as a van line agent was a new experience but not altogether a good one. In addition to having to satisfy customers, you had to follow the van lines rules and regulations, and you depended on the van line operation for much of your revenue. Paperwork multiplied, and you were working with two different systems—one for Canadian and one for U.S. activity.

Van lines manage employee relocations for the Federal Government, the RCMP and the Canadian Military. The military, through their agency the DND (Department of National Defense) allocates moves on a rotation basis, between and amongst van line agents, and the volume is a considerable amount of the total van line revenue, at about twenty-five percent. In order to participate, however, an agent must have an acceptable warehouse operation, which was inspected by the DND with diligence and gusto each year, three or four members showing up to do this. Some of the rules and regulations were common sense, but others were plainly idiotic. For example, when packing books, we had to wrap each book in newsprint paper. We could not work beyond a certain time without explicit permission from the local military base. They would send inspectors around to check to see that all rules were followed, and breaking any rule would result in various fines and penalties proscribed in their thick rulebook. This system has been modified and made more sensible the last few years. I guess the military is now so depleted of staff that they cannot spare several people to supervise movers.

RAE R. SIMPSON
6 GLADE CARSE WAY
NORTH YORK, ONTARIO M2R 3H1

PHONE (416) 398-2541
FAX (416) 398-5195

29 Jan 96

Sig Roseth
A & S Roseth Moving and Storage
2350 Royal Windsor Drive, Unit 20
Mississauga ON L5J 1K5

Dear Mr. Roseth:

In the course of my final military move at the end of September 1995, a move which your company performed, I had the opportunity to speak to you on one occasion regarding the unpacking services and potential damage claims. I liked your attitude at the time, and now that it is all completely over, I wanted to say thanks for a job well done.

The people who packed me were Dave, Karen, and Pat. The movers were Russ, Paul, James, and Ian. Without exception, they were all extremely pleasant and, from what I could see and by evidence of the satisfactory move, they were careful, effective, and efficient. It was two long days, moving day in particular, but no one ever tried to hurry things any more than could be done carefully and safely. All the time, they were responsive to our wishes which, as I'm sure any mover knows, can be frustrating as the day wears on.

It was the best move of my service career. I've said so to CFB Toronto (Base Traffic) - copy of the letter enclosed for your information. Would you please pass my thanks to your crews.

Yours truly

Rae R. Simpson

Mayflower Transit, Inc.
P.O. Box 107
Indianapolis, Indiana 46206-0107
317-875-1000 • ICC No. MC-2934

April 1, 1993

Mr. Sig Roseth, President
A & S Roseth Moving and Storage
2359 Royal Windsor Drive, Unit 20
Mississauga, Ontario Canada L5J 1K5

Dear Sig:

Congratulations on being named the #1 Agent - Canada. Enclosed is a trophy commemorating your agency's receipt of this honor. I would like to extend appreciation on behalf of Mayflower for your achievement and offer best wishes for continued success throughout 1993.

Sincerely,

Patrick F. Carr

Patrick F. Carr
President and Chief Operating Officer

Enclosure

Competition has been brutal for van lines; they have faced the same rationalization and consolidations that truckers faced before them. Originally conceived as a coordinating body for individual agents (usually small, family-run operations), there is now a steady attrition of smaller agents who cannot compete with the larger ones within the van-line structure. Each van line has a major entity within its organization that, because of their size and strength, has a major influence on the operation. I predict that internal and external competitive pressures will change the van-line from a rather loosely organized agency system to a tightly controlled, monopolistic franchise organization. In fact, it is all ready happening. For example, *AMJ Campbell Van lines Inc.*, which is a van line within the Atlas Van Line family, commands a 25% share of the van line revenues and is now totally a franchise operation. That is not necessarily bad. From a consumer's point of view, rationalization and consolidation should result in less waste and duplication, more central control on quality, and lower rates. That is, if they do not get so large that they exercise monopoly power over moving operations. In Canada, there are now just four van lines operating nationally: Atlas, United, Allied and North American. The same investors own the last two. Mayflower, that venerable old name, has left Canada, and in the U.S., after struggling for years, it was taken over by United Van Lines.

We joined Mayflower Van Lines in 1988, just before deregulation began to rock the industry. Mayflower was originally agency-owned and also owned a school bus company. The school bus operation, in contrast to the van line business, was quite profitable, and came to the attention of Harry DeGroote of Laidlaw Transport. They were then just getting into the school-bussing business. Laidlaw bought the school bus operation, but did not want the van line, so it was purchased by a group of employees in very leveraged buyout in 1977. It had a nice head office facility in Indianapolis, Indiana, where they also operated a truck driver school and a movers training facility. However, the company was struggling financially, and in 1993 it leased its money-losing Canadian operation to Allied Van Lines on an eight-year lease agreement. Allied intended to run Mayflower as a separate operation, but Allied itself ran into financial problems and was eventually taken over by FTC Plc, parent company of Pickford Transport, a large transport and removal carrier operating primarily in Britain and Australia. Allied-Pickford, as the new entity was called, told us Mayflower agents that they would not support the Mayflower name, forcing us to move to the Allied "flag." Most of the agents left Allied and joined one of the other remaining van line operations—mostly Atlas. We moved over to Allied in Canada, but continued to operate with Mayflower in the U.S. until the U.S. operation was sold to United Van Lines and moved, "lock, stock and barrel" to Fenton, Missouri, United's headquarters. At that time we, belatedly, moved to Atlas, but as the "new kid on the block" we struggled to integrate, and did not succeed in obtaining intra-organizational business in the U.S., and very little in Canada. This was not any fault of Atlas, but the reality of being new and unknown in the organization. The hole left in our U.S. operation was serious, and we never did recover our US revenue level.

Allied was a bad experience. The Brits did not fully realize the problems facing the industry following deregulation, and they did not understand the sensitivities of individual agent entrepreneurs. After a time trying to manage with their own people from Britain, they put in charge a hubristic, supercilious American from Chicago, named James Beatty IV. He proceeded to further alienate most agents, and the clamour for his blood must have finally been heard in London. That, combined with some really foolish management decisions caused his demise, and eventually, Pickfords. They sold it to some American investors who had already bought North American Van Lines from its railway owners. The remaining Pickford/MacCosham (APL Delstar) group then went bankrupt.

We became an agent for Atlas Van Lines just before Allied's debacle, and found an organization reminiscent of the Mayflower family, but more dynamic. They have seen the future, and are actively trying to change and adapt to new realities. I predict there will be just two van lines standing when the "battle" is over—Atlas and United. It could take ten years, but much less if there is a major contraction in the economy—the Canadian market is not large enough for all the current operators.

There is still a huge overcapacity nine months of the year, and corporate transfer/relocation behaviour is changing in that important market segment. Many firms now, when relocating employees, give them an allowance and let them chose their own moving company, rather than signing a contract with a moving company giving them exclusive access to their relocating employees. It saves hassle and administrative costs for the organization. However, some firms still prefer to take this responsibility from the employees, especially in a tight employment market, for hard to replace and highly valued employees. There is also more reluctance to relocate today, where the spouse might have a career that he or she is reluctant to leave. A growing practice is for firms to "outsource" this function to professional relocation companies who make all arrangements for the employee, such as choosing a mover, selling and buying a home and other incidental services needed when relocating to another city. This, of course, adversely affects all the van line organizations. They lose control over the process, and face a more skilled and tough negotiator. Competitive pressures are increased; putting further downward pressure on prices, making the van line agents fight for every move. Third party relocation companies, often in conjunction with Real Estate companies (such as Royal LePage), now control a large share of corporate relocations (especially the banks), and the railways are recapturing much of the long distance market.

The demands for investment in technology and systems by the large buyers, such as the Government (DND) and "third party" agencies increase mover's costs without concomitant economic returns. For example, the agents are required to purchase scanners and digital cameras, all designed to protect the client employees, but adding cost to the mover and the van line that must implement and maintain these systems mandated by the customer. While rates are squeezed down, costs go up.

Running a truck to Vancouver over the road, and then coming back half empty after a lengthy layover is neither profitable nor efficient, nor environmentally friendly. In fact, environmental factors militate against over-the-road transportation and point toward the railways as the more environmentally friendly way, as well as the most cost efficient. The van line's agency system will likely prevail as a coordinating entity for long distance rail transportation of household goods, and for pick-up to and deliveries from the railway yards. There is no "high-tech" way of transferring furniture from one house to another without "manpower". Local, independent movers—the galley slaves of our modern day—will still be around. Even with technology requiring more and more educated people and less physical labour, there will always be available a supply of men with "strong backs and weak minds", or what is worse, with good minds, wasted.

A few success stories

If I have given the impression that we had only bad customers, this is wrong. We had many happy customers, in fact, they were the routine, so you tended to forget about them, and remember the problems. That's only human, I guess.

We moved over five hundred people a year in the GTA, plus many others long distance, and overseas, so by the law of averages, we were bound to get some problem cases, but most went well. We often got very nice letters from our customers. Like the young girl who wrote a long letter thanking us—her mother had hired some "fly-by-night" operator instead of us, because he was "cheaper". However, he did not show up, and she called us in panic. Her mother was sitting on the stoop, crying. We, the jilted mover, pulled out all stops to get her moved. Another lady, whose house caught fire from faulty wiring, wrote to thank us for "rescuing" her things.

We left self-addressed envelopes with our customers and got many nice evaluations back. I would give copies to the crew involved and post it on bulletin boards, and use these replies as a basis for picking an "Employee of the Month" and give them a prize. Problem was, the same few employees won each month, the rest were, pardon the pun, "unmoved."

It was very gratifying when we had customers call us after many years to move them again, or when we were recommended by happy clients. Our referral rate was twelve percent of our bookings, which is not bad, and the commendatory performance reports made up for the more deprecating responses. Unfortunately, there is no possible way to ensure totally consistent standards. There are just too many variables. The same crew that got a laudatory report one day would get a complaint another day. Different day, different customer, same crew! Expectations vary greatly from customer to customer, but I also think the guys at times had "bad hair days." They were not machines and could not be "fine-tuned." At other times, they went beyond duty, soothing the customer's apprehension and putting them at ease.

An older lady, Mrs. Moore, moved with us seven times, once a year for seven years. She called us the first time after the death of her husband, saying she could not stay in the condo with all the memories. Each year she called us to move her again. She could not seem to find a place she was happy with. The last time she moved right back to the same building, and she was, finally, happy. She called me to tell me that she would not be moving again, for she could see her husband's grave from the window, and it felt just like home again.

Two months later, Mrs. Moore passed away, and was buried in the same graveyard. Finally, she is back with her husband.

The difference in people's attitude is perhaps best illustrated by the following story. In the early years, we gave a silk rose to the woman of the house after the move was completed (the guys did not like to do it, and many roses ended up in the garbage, or were just not handed out, so we discontinued the practice after a few years). One older lady had lost her husband and was moving from the house in which she had lived for forty years. When, after the move, the crew presented her with a silk rose, she burst into tears, thanking them profusely. Later, she called the office to thank us for the kindness!

Another customer, after receiving the silk rose, commented "could you not afford a better quality rose?"

Years later, we still got calls from people looking for the "Silk Rose Movers".

Some people were exceptionally considerate. We moved a family to the Gravenhurst area, in the country. Late in the evening, after unloading, the truck would not start, and we could not get a mechanic until morning. The customer drove the boys to a motel and paid for the room and their breakfast. He did not even ask for re-imbursement!

A & S ROSETH

MOVING AND STORAGE

We strive to provide good, consistent service, and to help us maintain quality service, would you please take a few minutes to complete this survey and return it in the enclosed postage paid envelope, after you have had time to assess the move. Please circle your choice.

Your Name: Margaret Marland Phone: 905-822-8416, Date: April 23, 2001
Move from: ____________________

Were the movers courteous and helpful?	(YES)	NO		
Did they handle your goods with care?	(YES)	NO	Very careful handling.	
After loading, did the driver check the residence with you to ensure that everything was loaded?	(YES)	NO		
After unloading, did the driver check the van with you to ensure that everything was unloaded?	(YES)	NO		

How would you rate:				
Our Packing Service?	(VERY GOOD)	GOOD	AVERAGE	POOR
The Sales Consultant	VERY GOOD	(GOOD)	AVERAGE	POOR
The Administration(office)	VERY GOOD	(GOOD)	AVERAGE	POOR
What is your overall impression of us?	VERY GOOD	(GOOD)	AVERAGE	POOR

How did you hear about us: Yellow Pages Mailing Referral (Repeat) Other_____

SUGGESTED IMPROVEMENTS OR COMMENTS: Rick & Galen were exceptional! Very careful and courteous. They were a pleasure to work with and Roseth Co. is fortunate to have two such reliable men.

CREW NAMES: RICK / GALEN / ________

PACKING CREW: ________ / ________ / ________

M. Marland.

THANK YOU FOR USING OUR SERVICES. IT WAS A PLEASURE TO SERVE YOU

Corporate customers

I was lucky to obtain a corporate customer that gave us a substantial amount of business over the years: *Oracle Corporation* (Canada) Ltd. We moved their executives all over the world, and within Canada, including three of their Presidents. We also moved all of their newly hired employees, within and without Canada. Oracle had a particular situation, which was a bit of a two-edged sword for them. They kept losing their experienced employees to their customers. The good part was that they had their former employees with the customers; the bad part was that they were constantly hiring and training new employees. Of course, this was very good for us—we got to relocate them. It was a very service-sensitive business, especially since most of the time we had no direct control of the move, we had to rely on fellow agents across the country and internationally. Most of the time it went very well, and we developed good relationships with specific agents, whom we would assign to the job. Just one time did we run into trouble.

Our agent in Winnipeg, Manitoba had closed his branch office there, and we arranged with a newcomer to look after an executive transfer for Oracle, from Winnipeg to Edmonton, Alberta. The customer had a very expensive car, I believe a Karmann-Ghia, that he was very concerned about. We arranged for the agent to haul the car in the trailer, together with the furniture, in order to assure maximum safety for the car. Well, the agent did not have enough room in the trailer, and to save costs, arranged to have his workers drive it along with the tractor-trailer load. The guys took it for a joy ride right out of the Pryor movie "Moving". They put something like a thousand kilometers on it, and arrived the day after the furniture. In addition, the movers managed to damage much of the expensive furniture.

Atlas' insurers ended up paying over thirty thousand dollars in damages to the customer, and I had to "pedal hard" to keep the business.

Oracle, however, was also affected by the hi-tech "melt-down" in 2001. Suddenly, they did not need to hire many new employees; the "old" ones were not enticed away. It made a big hole in our business. We had a few other corporate clients, but nothing like Oracle.

Oracle Corporation Canada Inc.

110 Matheson Blvd. West
Suite 100
Mississauga, Ontario
Canada L5R 3P4

Phone 905.890.8100
Fax 905.890.1207

February 16, 1998

To Whom It May Concern:

I am pleased to provide the following reference on behalf of A & S Roseth Moving and Storage.

Oracle Corporation Canada Inc. has been using the Relocation Service of A & S Roseth for the past 2 years. With over 900 employees in Canada and over 35,000 employees worldwide there are certainly occasions that have required Oracle to move employees not only in Canada but internationally as well. To meet this need Oracle has relied on the professional and competitive services offered by A & S Roseth Moving and Storage.

Each move has been handled on an individual basis and the feedback from our employees has always been that of a positive experience.

My experience with A & S Roseth is that they are very "customer focused" and have always been eager to partner with Oracle in order to provide our employees with a full service approach which meets their very personal and individual relocation requirements.

Please do not hesitate to contact me for further information.

Sincerely yours,

Margaret Clark

Margaret Clark
Director, Human Resources

Some personal successes

I had some *personal* success that I was very happy about. In 1997, *Microsoft Canada* was running a contest, listed on their web page, called "Technology to the Rescue". It was a countrywide contest for independent, small businesses, to see how the various firms used computers to become more efficient and customer focused. You had to write an article delineating your experience with in-house computer systems and their applications. We had computerized quite early, and did all functions in house, such as accounting, scheduling, costing and pricing. We also had a web page with links to several support organizations and business associations. However, the most innovative thing I did was developing a web page for Oracle's relocating employees, where they could find information about their move and useful links to other related areas, such as the city to which they were moving. It must have made an impression, because I won the top prize, got about ten thousand dollars worth of computer equipment and furniture, and great publicity, including having my story posted on Microsoft Canada's web page for the next six months.

Except for winning the prize as number one Canadian quality agent for Mayflower in 1991, this was the acme of my moving experience.

Small Business Winners

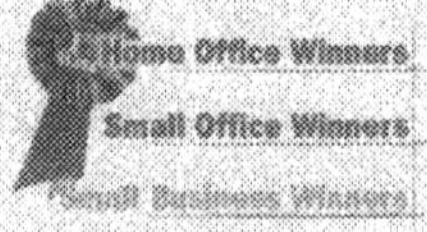

SmallBiz Home

Grand Prize Winner

Sigmund Roseth
A&S Roseth Inc
Mississauga, ON
email: sroseth@netcom.ca

Three years after starting his moving and storage business, Sigmund Roseth invested in his first 286 computer. Now ten years later, he has upgraded to four networked computers using Microsoft® Windows® 95. One of the computers acts as a server, and the others are accessed by operations, accounting, and dispatch to ensure everyone has access to the database, including customer records, sales activity, and booking information. Located in Mississauga, Ontario, **A and S Roseth** (http://www.yellowpages.ca/asroseth/index.htm/) is affiliated with Atlas Van Lines and currently has gross annual revenues of nearly $1.4 million. **A and S Roseth** has seen significant savings of time and money, particularly in the accounting area. Preparing payroll used to require one employee a full day each week. Now, once the data entry is done, the cheques can be prepared in less than 15 minutes, and the ability to track both payables and receivables has kept the company on an even keel financially.

Second Prize Winner

Grant Movold
Fabco Plastics Wholesale Ltd.
Maple, ON

… and personal problems

In the heyday of property speculation, in the late eighties, we moved people who were moving from house to house, gambling on property value appreciation. One ordinary fellow I moved had seven houses, all rented out, and mortgaged to the hilt. He would sell one to get some cash, and then reinvest it in another property. Some real estate people also played the game, buying a new property with a long closing time, counting on appreciation until closing, then moving in for a short time to avoid capital gains tax, and selling it again. One agent moved with us seven or eight times within five years. He had all black lacquer furniture, which he said made the house look better when selling. Some people would buy huge homes and just furnish a couple of rooms—all they could afford. It was a crazy time, fueled by the $ 500,000.00 capital gains exemption (later reduced to $ 100,000.00). I was cautious, but did buy a couple of houses over a five-year period, one I "flipped" (i.e. sold it without taking possession) and made $ 10,000.00 with very little effort. It seemed for a time that real estate speculation was a much better and easier way to make a living than moving people around and getting beaten up for doing it. However, I did not jump into the fray, figuring that what goes up will come down—crashing.

And it did. I remember moving one older couple who told me their sad tale: hoping to become mortgage free, they bought a smaller new home on a long closing, waiting to sell their old home until their new one was almost ready. Well, their timing was off, the market crashed, and they ended up in a smaller home with a larger mortgage! After the crash, one fellow told me he had eight properties falling in value and was expecting the bank to foreclose soon as he could not keep up mortgage payments. Another effect of the deflated housing bubble was that the renters seemed to evaporate into thin air—vacancy rates went up as rental rates came down.

I had bought an apartment in Brampton just before the bubble burst. I had planned to sell it again, as I had done successfully once before. I got caught, because the builder could not register the condo, as he did not have enough sales. I had to rent it out, and did so for seven years, eventually selling it for less than I had paid for it. I managed to rent it to mostly good tenants. Except one. I had advertised the unit for rent and this fellow, Mr. Brown, came to see it, driving a Mercedes, and well dressed. I checked with his last landlord who gave him an excellent recommendation (I later realized, he wanted this fellow out badly and managed to foist him on me). There is an old adage that you should not " judge a book by its cover", in this case, so true. He had a nightclub in Brampton mainly patronized by fellow Jamaicans, and he kept getting raided by police and charged with drug offences and other infractions. Eventually, he was closed by the city, and *my* trouble began. At first, he would call me to tell me his cheque would be late, then eventually he would not call and the cheque would not be late, it just wouldn't be. I gave him notice to vacate, but he did not, and I spent the next four months going to court three times trying to get rid of the guy, his girlfriend and child living for free in my condo. The last time in court was an "interesting" experience.

During break, Mr. Brown offered me $ 1000.00 cash—a third of what he now owed. When I told him to keep his money, that I just wanted him out of my property, he took it rather personal, and challenged me to "come outside". He said he would "diss" me, which went over my head, as I had never heard that word before. I declined the fisticuff outside the courthouse, and a lady in a wheel chair came over to me and asked if I knew what "dissing" me meant. I told her no, I hadn't a clue. She told me it was gang slang for killing me, and that the guy was wearing gang colours. I had thought it was designer jeans and jacket! She told me she was a former social worker who had worked with gang members in Toronto for several years. I asked her if she would testify to that in court, to which she readily agreed.

When my case came up, I approached the bench and told the judge that my life had been threatened by my tenant, and asked to have the lady testify for the court record, so in case I was found dead later, the police would have an easier time of catching my killer. The judge seemed a bit stumped, but allowed the testimony. After that, we had a break—I think the judge needed time to scratch his head—and while outside the courtroom, the lady told me I just bought a priceless insurance policy—there was no way the guy would send any goons after me now—he would probably have someone watch over me like black angels in the air.

When we returned to the courtroom, the judge asked him why another landlord was also suing him the same day (the other landlord had been up first, and Mr. Brown was given two weeks to pay him). Incredibly, Mr. Brown said, with a straight face, that he had another apartment rented from that landlord, where his other girl friend and his other child lived. He wasn't paying that rent either!

That was the last straw. The judge ordered him to vacate within two weeks or I could have the Sheriff do it for him. He also ordered him to pay the arrears, and Mr. Brown actually counted out $ 1000.00 in twenty dollar bills right there on the table in front of the judge—assuring him that he would indeed pay the outstanding rent in two weeks. He did, and here is the clincher: he asked me to move him to his new apartment! I did it, collecting the cash in advance. I have never been happier to move anyone in my whole career as a mover!

I felt sorry for his new landlord, but whoever he was, he did not check references with me, so I figured he had it coming.

… and in the family

I hired my son as a salesman in 2000. This was the second time I tried to have him work for the family firm. Ten years earlier, I had tried it—he lasted a year, but after I caught him and my salesman doing moves in secret with company vehicles and pocketing the cash, I fired him.

This time, I thought he would have matured, and I badly wanted to be able to pass the company on to family. He worked quite well as a salesman for a year or so. Then I made the mistake of making him General Manager, putting him in charge of the whole operation. I should have known better, but I was blinded by my desire to have a corporate heir.

My son did not see himself as owner. His reference group was the labourers, with whom he associated both at work and privately, including smoking marijuana. He didn't take to the pressure of managing very kindly, and became quite resentful toward me, to the extent that we "had words" in front of the men and the office staff. He would be quite sarcastic and critical in front of them.

He became enamoured with the receptionsit, a young girl I had hired from Tim Horton's where she served coffee. She was young and inexperienced, but intelligent and a quick learner. In her personal life, however, she was a *slow* learner. She had a child when she came to work for us, and got involved with one of the men with whom she had another child. The man then went to jail for two years, for beating up another woman, in a drunken stupor.

After having his child, she returned to work after a short maternity leave, and was living with her parents in their town house. It must have been stressful for her.

I told my son, who was married with two children, to not get involved emotionally with her, pointing out the serious consequences for his own life. He assured me they were just friends.

I detected a strange spike in labour costs, and did an audit, but could not pinpoint the cause. The time cards were approved by my son, and the girl processed them for payment. The only possible answer was that the hours were overstated intentionally, but I could not bring myself to believe that the two of them would collude in ripping off the company. I did not have a full-time accountant at this time, so it was difficult for me to do a proper audit, and I hesitated to bring in an outside audit firm.

While my son was away on holidays, the girl asked me for a week off. She told me she had received a free holiday in Florida from her grandparents. I had no real choice; I let her go, and hired a temp to help out for the week.

While she was gone, I discovered major problems in her paperwork. I found six or seven accounts that had never been billed (she did the preparation for the accounting), and began checking her work. I found plenty. Nothing I could point to as intentional or fraudulent, but an incredible amount of errors and careless mistakes; yet, well covered up.

I was talking to my daughter-in-law and she told me my son had gone to Florida by himself! Click! I put one and one together, and it came out two.

When the girl returned, I confronted her with my suspicion. She denied being there with my son, and so did he. However, when I began to question her about the errors and problems I had found with her work, she quit abruptly, without notice. My son left his wife and two children and moved in with the girl!

We purchased materials through an Atlas central volume buying arrangement, and one day we were ordering supplies when the supplier told the girl doing the ordering that Atlas had cut off our credit! I was surprised, and immediately called Atlas head office to find out what the problem was. They told us that they had information that I was closing up and laying off everyone. I told them that I was not, but if and when I was, they would be the first to know. I insisted they tell me how they got this erroneous information, and was told that my son had called one of the vice presidents, looking for a job with Atlas, and he told them that he had left and the company was going bust. Considering whom he was, they panicked and pulled our credit. It was quickly reversed, but it was embarrassing, to say the least. What saddened me the most was the total lack of loyalty displayed by my son. His mother, no doubt, had contributed to his resentment over the years, but he was now a fully-grown, mature man, and should have known better. I had employees who came from terribly dysfunctional and abusive homes, but even so, they would be protective of their parents. Such callous indifference and outright recreant behaviour on the part of a son toward his father is something rare.

… beginning of the end

I lost interest in my company and started to look for a buyer. I could not see struggling with the business with no one to take over.

I sold one unit of the warehouse, for less than I should have, but I needed the money. I paid off the bank, and was broke again. But, I had gotten the bank off my back and some breathing room. I set about cutting costs, taking almost no salary for the next two years, and I stopped the bleeding. But, I had lost interest in the business. When I found a lifeline, I grabbed it.

… the end, and a beginning

A time to get, and a time to lose.
A time to keep, and a time to cast away …

—… Ecclesiastes 3:v 6

By the end of 2002 I had enough. There was no family member to take over when I retired, and I despaired of finding someone dependable to help with the operational management. I faced the need to make a large investment in equipment, with no guarantee of profitability, and I was tired. I sold the truck running trans-Canada, keeping just one running in the U.S., with a driver who had worked for me for about ten years. However, he was sixty-six and had high blood pressure, so I knew it was only a matter of time before he must retire. Then, in the summer of 2002, the tractor he was driving caught fire and burned up on the highway. I received $ 17,000.00 from the insurance company for it; just a fraction of what it was going to cost me to replace it. Then I got my insurance renewal—with a seventy-five percent increase! My other trucks were getting old and needed replacing, and I too, at sixty, was getting worn. I needed, if not replacing, at least a rest from the inexorable grind of the moving business.

Small, entrepreneurial firms often grow until they reach an impasse: they require outside capital to make the leap to a medium size business that can afford to hire and pay professional managers. In mature, highly competitive industries like moving and storage, the profit margins are too narrow to entice venture capital, and so the manager entrepreneur is faced with the ever expanding task of stretching his reach over a larger and larger area of management tasks, ending up doing some of everything and none adequately. That's what happened to me, and the story is legion.

Doctors Thomas H. Holmes and Richard Rah (1967) developed what is called The Social Readjustment Rating Scale, or Stress Scale for short, listing life events of the previous year that would seriously affect a person's mental and physical health within two years of the event(s). The scale listed forty-three events on a declining value scale, beginning with 100, equaling the death of a spouse. Divorce rated 73; marital separation 65; retirement 45;change in financial state 38; taking on a mortgage 31; major change in living conditions (e.g. new home) 25. A score of between 150 and 300 gives a 50% probability of a major health breakdown. I reckoned that with all my combined stresses, I should be dead.

I first tried to sell the firm as a "going concern" but failed in the end. Potential buyers could not afford to pay market rent for the warehouse and office, and I needed that income to live on. Following some serious "soul searching", I decided to sell the assets separately: the warehousing operation and the equipment—trucks and all physical assets, then rent or sell the real estate. I barely got enough money for the assets to pay my bills, but when I sold the building, I did better. The real estate saved me; I got some income from it, though not nearly enough to compensate for eighteen years of (paraphrasing Churchill) "blood, tears and sweat." However, the company did provide a living for eighteen years, though at what emotional price, I will perhaps never know. I think if I had put in the same effort and investment in another business, the returns would have been greater and the emotional toll much less. No small business is a "cake walk", and I didn't expect a "rose garden", just enough time to smell the roses once in a while, between the bouts of perspiration.

But, there is little profit in bemoaning our missteps, especially if our intentions were noble. We are in the present because of the past, and some have chosen better than others, or were luckier, managing to grab the "golden ring". If we did the best we could, it must suffice, even though it didn't take us to where we wanted to be.

It was a relief to wake up in the morning without worrying about what problems lie ahead this day, whether the jobs would go well, with no truck breaking down, all workers showing up for work and getting paid for the work without hassle; with no daily worry about collecting money or paying bills. I still got nervous when the telephone rang at home. It used to mean trouble much of the time, as I used to forward the business line to my home whenever there were jobs in progress.

I was amazed to find how little I missed the daily strife and enjoyed the peace and quiet. I sensed only relief and liberty, a release from physical and emotional bondage.

> *Only the day dawns to which we are awake. There is more day to dawn. The sun is but a morning star.*
>
> —Thoreau: Walden, ibid p.351

Epilogue

... If I am not for myself, who is for me?
But if I am only for myself, what am I?
And if not now, when?

—... Rabbi Hillel (Hillel Hazaken), 1BC

I would like to leave a legacy, and to believe that I will leave this world just a *little* better off going out than coming in. Perhaps that is a lot to ask, but if not asked, I will have no answer. If not now, then, when?

"It's not over until the fat lady sings." I failed to reach the stars, or even the moon, but at least I did not suffer the fate of Icarus. I could have had more success, especially in my personal life. Yet, it could have been worse. Much worse.

It has been a series of two steps ahead, one—sometimes two—steps back. I did what I was capable of, given the circumstances. I had no extended family to encourage and support me, no community and social connections, no one that cared whom I could ask for advice. That is a paradox with driven people: they strive to overcome their insecurity by attempting to achieve independence and control over their lives, yet in needing to dominate and control their environment, they lose the very support they need. I had no one to advise me, but would probably not have heeded such advice anyhow, if it differed from my own inclinations. I relied on my own judgment, but lacked the self-confidence and emotional maturity to make the really though choices, to take the road less traveled. Like a stream, I followed the path of least resistance. I recognized opportunities, and took them, but often without enough critical evaluation. I was not always astute enough to choose well among the alternatives—to reject the ones that might lead to perdition—thus, like a fish jumping at the bait, I often got hooked. In my defense, at first I was hampered by language, unfamiliarity with the new environment, and got a slow start in education. I was exhausted by the concurrent demands of work, studies and family, and stymied by the lack of emotional and economic support. That's my excuse anyhow, and I am sticking with it.

But, there is still time to make a difference.

Others apart sat on a hill retired,
In thoughts more elevate, and reasoned high,
Of providence, foreknowledge, will, and fate,
Fixed fate, free will, foreknowledge absolute;
And found no end, in wandering mazes lost.

—Milton, Paradise Lost, Book ll

Sometimes I do see life as a maze, where I struggled with good intentions—intentions of arriving at that fixed but obscure duality: *Success* and *Happiness.* But, not knowing where each turn was leading, I sometimes got lost, and that obtuse "end" that I was so ardently seeking, now seems to have been a mirage—a constantly changing target. In this, I am joined by much of humanity. Dissatisfaction with the status quo propels us forward, some with more force and velocity than others—and more "success". Society benefits from our achievements and our goal oriented drives. As *Adam Smith*[1] postulated—"the polity benefits from individual selfishness, based on the aggregation of individual attributes into collectivities." Yet, too often we are like Sisyphus, pushing against gravity—never happy, never satisfied, always seeking that elusive goal: the mountaintop, our *Shangri-La.* Sometimes, in striving for a goal, the frustrations and disappointments outweigh the benefit, especially if our focus is self centered, self-serving and materialistic—the personal cost is too high. In chasing a butterfly, we often fail; if we sit still, it might alight upon us. In our wake are the flotsam and jetsam of our failures. And when we achieve the material goal we have been seeking, it disappoints us, or becomes routine and trite. *Abraham Maslow*[2] said, a satisfied need is not a motivator any longer, and we are off chasing another tail. Success, of course, is a relative thing, and ultimately, we are our own toughest judges. The poet was right:

---

1. Adam Smith: *An Inquiry Into the Nature and Causes of the Wealth of Nations* (Methuen & Co. Ltd.,London).
2. Abraham H. Maslow: *A Theory of Human Motivation,* Psychological Review, vol.50, pp.370-96.

Life is a journey, not a destination.
There is no way to happiness; happiness is the way ...

As we grow older, and sometimes wiser, our focus changes, and we become more interested in achieving *meaning* in our lives, having tired of our toys, and exhausted chasing rainbows. But, *meaning* is often as much a mirage as *success,* because we look outward and outside for it, when we should be looking within. We fail to live the eudemonic lifestyles of our ideals.

I have heard people wistfully say, "If I could live life again, things would be different". Would it? And what if? Would it be better? More successful? Or would we just make different errors and fail in other endeavours? And what about the happy times and our achievements—would they be also gone? Is anyone ever totally happy with their life—never wishing that they had done something better or different? I think not. It is a waste of time to carry the baggage of regrets, bemoaning yesteryears. But, we should learn from our errors and missteps, using the past to guide us today and in the future. Today is a fact; tomorrow is only a wish.

No individual will be judged by some fixed result, but by the direction in which he is moving. The bad man is the man who no matter how good he has been is beginning to deteriorate, to grow less good. The good man is the man who no matter how morally unworthy he has been is moving to become better. Such a conception makes one severe in judging himself and humane in judging others. It excludes that arrogance which always accompanies judgment based on degree of approximation to fixed ends. Growth itself is the only moral end ...

—John Dewy, Reconstruction in Philosophy (1920).
From Lectures at the University of Japan, Tokyo, 1919.

There is a natural dichotomy in most people's lives—between the ideal and reality—and this has the potential for much internal conflict that one needs to resolve in order to live a reasonably satisfactory life. In my case, as a young man, I had an idealistic and overly positive outlook on life and the future. I have always had the feeling that "things will get better in the future". Optimism is not a bad thing, it is necessary for a successful life, but it needs to be paired with a dose of realism, or it can lead us astray in a world full of dangers and pitfalls. I had, in particular, two serious misconceptions: First, was that if I just did the right thing and tried my best, success would ensue. Along with that belief, I also expected that if I pleased my boss or superior, they would instantly like me and recognize my intrinsic worth (and conversely, if I behaved improperly, I would be punished, as would others who misbehaved). The truth is, that life can be rather cruel, that people don't always see the person you think you are, and the world can be very unfair. I came to the bitter realization, that no one but me had my interest at heart, and no one but me could look after me. On the line from naiveté to cynicism, I fairly soon moved towards the latter. It was a bitter pill to swallow. The conflict between good and bad, or good and evil, is part of life, and it is hard not to be overwhelmed by the horrors we see around us, and maintain a positive outlook. It is hard to realize that nature is totally indifferent to our plight. It is not for us or against us, it just is. It doesn't care if our loved ones die, if we are ill or lonely. I suppose we should be happy that nature is not actively working against us, but sometimes we wish it would give us a push in the right direction. But, nature has no feeling, no empathy. Only other humans can have that, and they, we, are fickle. To reconcile this conflict, to solve that conundrum, is the Sisyphean task with which we strive, but never fully complete.

The second mistaken ideal was my attitude towards women. I think I tried to idealize a wife, expecting her to be a cross between my own mother and a saint. When the cold fact hit me, that a woman and a wife is a person with her own problems, insecurities, faults and needs, I became disillusioned and even resentful. Too high expectation of others can lead to conflict and disappointments unless reconciled with reality. That is true of all relationships—male or female.

I still don't know where the true balance is, between idealism and optimism on one hand, and pessimism and cynicism on the other extreme. Somewhere along this continuum there is an optimal balance, where critical thinking and evaluation keeps us anchored in our beliefs and comfortable in our own skins. I have learned a bit in sixty-some years, but I am not nearly ready to graduate.

In, selectively, describing my life, I hope I have not sounded too sententious, or dwelled too much on the negative. The struggles and stresses of life are, I believe, more instructive and interesting, both for the story's subject, and for the reader.The daily news serves up a cornucopia of disasters and mayhem with only a smattering of happy stories. It is not the easy and routine, but the unusual and difficult that makes news and captures our interest. Our victories we can suffer alone, our miseries need company.

In spite of the many conflicts and frustrations, I learned from the struggles—from successes as well as mistakes, and I think I am a better person for it—or perhaps, in spite of it. Life is didactic, and the lessons we learn can make us a fuller human being.

> *- Sorrow is better than laughter: for by the sadness of the countenance the heart is made better …*
>
> —Ecclesiastes 7, v. 3

> *- Shall a man go and hang himself because he belongs to a race of pygmies, and not be the biggest pygmy that he can? Let everyone mind his own business, and endeavour to be what he was made.*
>
> —Thoreau: Walden, ibid p. 345

Some immigrants have spectacularly overcome obstacles; aided by luck, ability and serendipity. I had some luck, and some success, but more often it was a Sisyphean struggle. I have ventured to share some salient parts of it, hoping that as you read it, you found a few nuggets of insight, shared a few laughs and enjoyed the ironies of my life. If I have accomplished that, I have achieved my goal.

END

978-0-595-42554-
0-595-42554-2

www.ingramcontent.com/pod-product-compliance
Ingram Content Group UK Ltd.
Pitfield, Milton Keynes, MK11 3LW, UK
UKHW040603210726
13854UKWH00008B/1842

9 780595 42554